W9-BUR-794

THE TASTE OF TOMORROW

THE
TASTE OF
TOMORROW

DISPATCHES
FROM THE
FUTURE OF
FOOD

Josh Schonwald

HARPER

An Imprint of HarperCollins*Publishers*
www.harpercollins.com

HarperCollins books may be purchased for educational, business, or sales promotional use. For information, please write: Special Markets Department, HarperCollins Publishers, 10 East 53rd Street, New York, NY 10022.

FIRST EDITION

Designed by Richard Oriolo

Library of Congress Cataloging-in-Publication Data

Schonwald, Josh.
The taste of tomorrow : dispatches from the future of food / Josh Schonwald.—1st ed.
p. cm.
ISBN: 978-0-06-180421-2
1. Food. 2. Food industry and trade. 3. Natural foods. 4. Genetically modified foods. 5. Food—Biotechnology. I. Title.
TX353.S343   2012
641.3—dc23   2011029004

12 13 14 15 16   OV/RRD   10 9 8 7 6 5 4 3 2 1

To Kristi

CONTENTS

PROLOGUE: GASTROPUB 2035

IMAGINE THAT YOU ARE EXTREMELY HUNGRY. You want a burger and a beer, and you will be sating your appetite in Colorado Springs, Colorado. Also, please consider that the date of this beer and burger quest is not now, or next year, but July 25, 2035.

You choose to go to Moby's, a pub on Tejon Street.

You sit down in a booth. You check out the menu on your 10G iPhone.

Moby's has a "Real Beef Burger" special tonight—a quarter pound of grass-fed, free-range, antibiotic-free Hereford; char-grilled, topped with coarsely ground Balinese long pepper, slathered with white cheddar and homemade papaya ketchup, with a side of cassava fries and choice of soup or salad. Sounds fine. It's sixty dollars—it's by far the most expensive thing on the menu.

The waitress, detecting your price point discomfort, notes that "it's *real* meat." She suggests another burger—that's almost as good—and is only ten dollars. "We have cow meat, bison, chicken, and pork—all fresh out of the bioreactor. We have an excellent meat-grower."

You tip an eyebrow.

"If you want something more *traditional*," she responds, "you should try the blackened rabbit."

Then she waves toward the kitchen, and smiles. "We have our own rabbitry."

We're not in some foodie-hipster hotspot; we're in a regular-guyish brew pub, a bulwark of comfort food, in the Air Force Academy's hometown. Still you, the time traveler—a well-read, adventurous, food-inquisitive time traveler—need a translator to decode the appetizers.

The salad of the day: "A bed of Afghan greens, topped with elderflowers, cloudberries, puntarelle, and a Sinaloan sea vegetable." The soup: "a simple yet classic Egusi." The appetizer special: Zanzibari pizza.

You order the soup—it's unbearably spicy. Inedible. You gasp. You then ask for this "Zanzibari pizza"—it tastes nothing like pizza. It has Indian spices, and thin slices of rabbit meat, in a bed of naan. It's amazingly good.

Moby's, like any restaurant in 2035 (and many in 2012), provides copious information on all of its food—ingredients, health issues, production methods, chemicals used and not used, place of origin. All the Moby's servers wear big buttons that say, "Try me! Ask about your food source!" Amused, you start quizzing your twenty-something server. The salad: "It's the chef's favorite—a mix of crucifers and blue lettuces native to an area in Afghanistan's Swat Valley." The sixty-dollar beef burger? Seventeen percent fat, 612 calories, slaughtered two days ago at the Gunnison Ranch, sixty-five miles away.

The house-grown meat? "Heart-friendly! It's loaded with omega-3s and enhanced with an extra dose of albumin."

The server's knowledge is not terribly alien—you've heard know-it-all waitstaff—but what piques your interest is when you start grilling her about the unusually long "Catch of the Day" list.

Colorado Springs is landlocked; it's more than 1,000 miles from the nearest salt water, the Gulf of Mexico. The state isn't exactly teeming with freshwater lakes. Yet several fish are listed as "today's catch." Puzzlingly, the place of origin for all of Moby's seafood—African pompano, Atlantic salmon, Dublin Bay prawns, Arctic char, Chilean sea bass—is "Colorado Springs, Colorado."

The server chuckles when you ask, skeptically, how it's possible that African pompano, a saltwater fish, can be from Colorado Springs. She points across the street to a steel-and-glass tower that looks like a corporate headquarters. "That's Deep Sea Farms—the largest aqua-farm in Springs."

The strangest aspect of your Moby's meal has nothing to do with Moby's, its food, or its food vendors. It's the other patrons. The high-volume fellow to your right, evidently a Las Vegas–based water broker and rabid believer in the virtues of quercetin, boasts about how he bred some blue bananas for his mom. The man's companion is underwhelmed. "Anyone can do that," she says.

And the couple sitting next to you—a pair of nonagenarians, judging from their conversation—eat two burgers (real and house-grown), a rabbit quesadilla, fried emu nuggets, and then put away what looks like a chocolate cake with two scoops of ice cream. The elderly man drinks at least three coffee stouts, and several single-malt scotches. When he orders a shot of tequila, he turns to you with bloodshot eyes. "A toast . . . to honor the downfall of the last Islamic theocracy."

At the end of the gluttonous display, the ninety-something pulls out a pillbox from his breast pocket and produces a thin wafer. He puts it on his tongue, smiles at his companion, and looks at his watch. "I'll be perfectly sober in ten minutes. Thank God for nano-encapsulation."

PART
ONE

BEGINNINGS

1.

The Next Salmon and the
Bagged Salad Moment

BEFORE I LONGED FOR A CHICKEN NUGGET made from a stem cell, or a cherry tomato spiked with lemon basil genes, before I dreamed of the blue-green lettuce of Afghanistan or the spicy soups of northern Nigeria, before I tried emu burgers, ostrich hot dogs, beefalo steaks, or algae-sugar cookies, before I knew the Trickle-Down Theory of Food Innovation, or the location of the Last Culinary Frontier, before I cared about the optimal breeding temperatures for marine finfish, or the technology needed to achieve the food pill, before I gave any thought to what food circa 2035 might look or taste or smell like, there was a chicken dinner.

What was significant about this meal in Miami, Florida, in December 2005, was not the actual quality of the chicken—neither unusually good nor bad—but rather the conversation that surrounded it. Toward the end of the meal, somewhere between a final nibble on a dry thigh and a stab at the soggy green beans, one of my dining companions, a short, brown-haired naval reservist named Ivy Kupec who served as a PR person for the University of Miami, uttered the following four words: "There's this new fish."

The simple combination of words intrigued me. A *new* fish? Could there be such a thing?

As it turned out, this new fish was not new in the Darwinian sense, nor was it the ivory-billed woodpecker of fish—recently discovered in, say, an isolated reef off the coast of Papua New Guinea. It was not even endangered—it was even better than that. "It tastes like a cross between Chilean sea bass and swordfish," said Kupec. Swordfish was one of my personal favorites. "It's really, really good as a steak. You can even grill it. Like a burger." The name of this new fish was cobia, and the strangest thing about all this talk was the fact that the new fish had a maker. "Dr. Benetti," said Kupec. "He thinks cobia is going to be really big someday, like salmon."

IT WASN'T EASY to make an appointment with Dr. Daniel Benetti. During the time that I pursued Benetti, I received messages that he was in Brazil one week, Washington, D.C., the next, then at a conference in Hawaii. A month later, I heard he was on his way to Saudi Arabia.

This globe-trotting is, I later learned, not unusual for Benetti's ilk: aquaculturists, or more commonly, fish farmers. Benetti is among a subgroup of fish farmers—marine finfish specialists, or "mariculturists"—who are perhaps even more prone to globe-trotting. In fact, one of Benetti's consiglieri made it sound as if a marine fish farmer's life is something like that of a surfer.

"Hawaii, Australia, the Mediterranean. The travel is rough," he said wearily, also noting that most aquaculture researchers had been divorced.

After reading about Benetti and talking with a few of his peers, I still didn't know what to expect. Perhaps he was a sun-scarred old mariner—he had, after all, pursued fish for the past twenty-five years, had traveled from the southernmost seas of the Atlantic to the northern extremes of the Pacific. Perhaps he was some lab-rat scientist who mates fish like an aquatic Frankenstein. When I finally did meet Benetti in person—between his trips to Brazil and Hawaii—he looked like a Spanish soap opera star and sounded like one, with his thick Latin accent. He's tall, handsome, silver-haired, fiftyish. He wears polo shirts and drives an Audi, and seemed more like the type of guy you'd meet at a South Florida tennis club than in a lab.

Benetti got his start in fish farming working for, of all places, the Brazilian Navy. He proved himself a sort of aquaculture prodigy—by the age of twenty-four, he managed the first spawning of a marine fish in Latin America, a mullet. He emerged as one of the world's foremost experts in taming the tigers of the aquatic world, the hard-to-domesticate marine fish.

I was extremely eager to see the cobia, but Benetti insisted that before we went to his lab, I watch a short PowerPoint presentation that he had on a DVD. I soon learned that aquaculturists are, in some respects, like people in the natural gas, oil, tobacco, or direct marketing industries. They've been portrayed negatively in the media, consistently. They've taken a beating for creating the ichthyological equivalent of industrial-sized "hog lots"; they've been blamed for creating mutant fish, for displacing fishermen, for ruining coastlines. And so, they've become political and defensive.

We went into Benetti's office. He inserted the must-see DVD into his Mac, clicked a mouse, and then started narrating in his thick Brazilian accent. "We're breaking the ocean," he said, then noted a litany of depressing but vaguely familiar statistics. Seventy-five percent of the world's fisheries are at risk for a serious population decline. Some stocks, like Atlantic cod and snapper, had already been fished out. Tuna is on the fast track to extinction. And meanwhile, compounding the problem, people are eating twice as much seafood as they did in the 1960s.

"This is a way to save fisheries," he said, gesturing to his computer. The must-see DVD featured what looked, on first glance, like three space ships—one was a gigantic geodesic dome, two smaller ones were shaped like diamonds. They were cages; housing thousands of fish, moored to the ocean floor with thick steel. Benetti called the dome the "Aquapod"; it was as tall as a six-story building. He pointed to a human figure, in scuba gear, swimming outside the dome. "That's a farmhand," he said, smiling broadly.

The Star Trek–like display was Benetti's response to environmental concerns, a kind of Aquaculture 2.0. You put the fish farm miles offshore, and ninety feet underwater, and it's barely visible from the surface, he explained, pointing to an innocuous buoy. By farming in deeper water in the ocean, you get higher water volume and swifter currents, which disperse fish poop and other farm waste. The fish are stocked at lower densities, in their native waters. Not only are the fish happier, he said, "but it leaves virtually no environmental footprint. There is no other means of food production that can produce a higher yield with a lower impact."

It sounded like free-range fish farming; Benetti called it "open-ocean aquaculture" and said it was beginning to happen at an experimental level off the coast of Puerto Rico. This is where Benetti hoped his cobia would grow.

After about forty-five minutes of fish politics talk—mostly lobbying for something called the National Offshore Aquaculture Act, which would open up federal waters for underwater fish farms—we headed across the roaring highway that bisects Virginia Key and separates Benetti's office from his lab. The two sides of the island are very different: one is tourist-friendly, housing Miami's aquarium and a marina. The other side holds perhaps the strangest collection of facilities in Miami: the city's main dump, a ramshackle bar named Jimbo's, an abandoned stadium, and a National Oceanic and Atmospheric Administration building. Much of this north side of Virginia Key is federal property, tucked behind barbed wire fencing.

On a dirt road directly behind the NOAA building, I spotted a structure that looked like little more than a Quonset hut. This was the "hatchery." It was sweltering inside, nearly 100 degrees, even with two powerful fans roaring. The hut had four small tanks that looked like kiddie pools. Above each tank, just below the hut's ceiling, was an elaborate maze of white PVC pipes. Plastic tubes came off this PVC scaffolding, feeding oxygen and carbon dioxide and other fish larvae essentials into each of the tanks. One tank had days-old larvae, each smaller than a grain of rice, another held three- or four-inch fish that Benetti said were "nearly ready for growout." One pool at the back of the hut, apparently fishless, held a bubbling, greenish stew that was said to "soothe" the larvae. The whole place, hissing with the sound of generators, cluttered with beakers, lamps, and cone-shaped incubators, felt like an ICU.

A few of Benetti's farmhands milled about. I watched one, a longhair named Ian, as he dipped a tool into the greenish stew. Benetti waved me on. We exited the back of the Quonset hut and headed outside toward two larger pools, just yards from Biscayne Bay. The pools looked like the backyard pools you might find in a lower-middle-class suburb.

Benetti was smiling. He led me to the edge of one of the pools, then pointed at about a dozen thirty-pound creatures. With their dorsal fins and flat faces, they looked eerily like sharks. "This is it," he said, as we watched five of the fish instantly devour several pounds of chilled sardines. "Look at the power of the fish. Look at the speed," he said reverently. "They are as close to a perfect species as I've ever seen."

Gazing over what he called his brood stock, Benetti described the freakish biology of the cobia, *Rachycentron canadum*. It grows ten times faster than most fish. It has no known relative, but could be a cousin of the remora—the famed shark-sucker. It behaves bizarrely well in captivity—almost like a pet. It has a high spawning rate and a low juvenile mortality rate. "It's one of the sturdiest fish I've seen," he said, as if he were describing a prizefighter. And, he added, "It does a great job converting fish meal to body fat."

Perhaps detecting that a layman would quickly grow weary of this approach—a nerdy recitation of aquaculture data—Benetti smartly shifted his tack. There was, he said, another reason for cobia's promise. "Have you tasted it?" he asked, shaking his head. "Oh my." The riff began.

Cobia doesn't taste "fishy," Benetti said. It's white and firm. It can be grilled, sautéed, or served as sashimi or bouillabaisse. It's more flavorful than Chilean sea bass, and makes better sushi than the famed hamachi. In his native Brazil, a fisherman who catches a cobia "never gives it way." Then, after praising the culinary properties of cobia and telling me where in South Florida I might be able to find a cobia sashimi, he made the declaration:

"Cobia will be the next salmon."

Even as a newcomer to the fish farming industry, I instantly understood the outrageousness of this prediction. Claiming an obscure sport fish will become the next salmon is like saying a six-year-old will become the next Michael Jordan.

At the time of Benetti's claim, the global cobia output was *far* less than 1 percent of salmon production.

"It's inevitable," he said, noting that he's not the only aquaculturist to believe cobia is the next salmon. "In five years, cobia will be everywhere. Costco, Sam's Club, the Outback Steakhouse, frozen food entrées. Everywhere. It's not ninety-nine percent," he said. "It's ninety-nine-point-nine-nine-nine percent."

In just a few weeks, Benetti told me, his team would begin a potentially revolutionary experiment. In effect, Benetti planned to trick the brood stock into believing it was breeding season. They'd change the temperature and light to simulate spawning season. "If we are successful," Benetti said, "cobia could be bred all year."

As we walked back toward the Quonset hut, Benetti, seemingly sensing a skeptic, turned to me. "If you were starting a fish farm, and you could raise a ten-pound fish in one year, or another fish that takes two years to grow one pound, what would you do?"

Initially I was simply fascinated by cobia—and intrigued by the world of marine aquaculture. Reading trades like *Fish Farming International* and *Growfish*, I found that there were more Benettis trolling the seas, capturing and breeding new species, racing to find the next salmon. And I learned about the stakes: the discovery of a hot new species that could be farmed at industrial scale could spawn a billion-dollar industry.

I wrote a story about cobia for *Miami New Times*, waited expectantly for cobia to appear in my local Safeway (never saw it), and then largely forgot about the "next salmon"—for a year. But then, the following winter, I saw the first sign that Benetti's prophecy might be true. A group of entrepreneurs—with support from the state of Virginia—were investing more than $30 million in a fish farm, and the farmers weren't raising salmon, catfish, or trout—they were farming cobia.

Maybe Benetti was right. Maybe cobia would be the next hot fish. Maybe the McCobia sandwich and cobia nuggets weren't so far-fetched. The experience with cobia raised some important questions. If cobia is the Next Salmon, then is there . . . a next cow? A next tomato? A next chicken? A heretofore unheard-of but spectacularly delicious fruit? And are there more Benetti-like figures in other parts of the food world? Is some fellow hunting the mountains of Madagascar for a delicious new species of swine? Is there a meat lover breeding a superspecies of Holstein that puts Argentina's grass-fed best to shame?

The Bagged Salad Moment

One summer evening, nine years before Dan Benetti declared his cobia revolution, and a day after the 1996 Democratic National Convention ended in Chicago, a young Democratic National Committee staffer took the train north to Kenosha, Wisconsin, to have what he fully expected to be a typically mediocre, uneventful dinner.

The twenty-six-year-old website developer was going to visit his mom. He was a non-foodie, with young bachelor ways; if he didn't pick up kung pao chicken from a Chinese takeout place, he typically made pasta, black beans and rice, or fried eggs, aiming for under ten minutes of food prep time. His mother, a social worker, had an equally cavalier attitude about meals. Most of her dinners involved the microwave, stops at fast-food restaurants, or store-bought rotisserie chicken. Rarely did they include homemade food or more than twenty minutes of thought and preparation; but they almost always included a salad.

On this particular night, there was one highly unusual item on the table. For as long as the son could remember, Mom-made salad meant little more than iceberg lettuce, some carrots, maybe some cucumbers. This salad, however, didn't even look like lettuce; it was an unruly mix—there were different sizes of leaves (small, jagged things; frizzy ones), different colors (light greens, dark greens, reddish greens). It looked like a bunch of weeds.

Puzzled by the exotic display, the young man raised a mild objection. His mother parried the complaint, saying, "Leafy greens are more nutritious." So the young man warily sprinkled some olive oil on the greens, added some pepper and salt, and began what would be the most transformative meal of his life.

Stunned by the superiority of the salad—its varying textures and hard-to-describe flavor (kind of peppery, also buttery, sometimes bitter, a tinge of sweet)—he wondered about its provenance. Was it from a garden? A restaurant? Maybe from Mangia, the upscale Italian place?

His mother showed him a plastic bag. The salad was purchased from a local grocery store. It was called a "spring mix."

He did not eat iceberg lettuce for another fourteen years.

What happened in Kenosha in 1996 was not, apparently, uncommon. For much of the twentieth century, iceberg accounted for more than 90 percent of the lettuce consumed in the United States. But in the 1990s, the produce section changed—radically. Consumption of previously obscure "tender leaf" greens (green leaf, red oak, arugula) exploded; by 2000, bagged salad was a $2 billion industry. By 2003, even McDonald's was selling $150 million in spring mix. Some have called this era the "fresh-cut" or "bagged salad revolution." The lettuce hierarchy was so altered in the '00s that in 2010 the *New York Times* ran a story on iceberg titled "The Charms of the Loser Lettuces."

I'm telling you about the Bagged Salad Revolution because it explains two of the most important things about this book.

1. THE NEXT BIG THINGS IN FOOD—AND THE PEOPLE BEHIND THEM

Bagged salad was a game changer: it changed the American salad-eating experience, ended a half century of iceberg's totalitarian-like grip on the salad bowl, and brought arugula, frisée, red oak, green leaf, and mizuna to places like Kenosha, Buffalo, and

Lubbock. In the same way, farmed cobia in Dan Benetti's telling could transform the seafood section—joining household names like shrimp, tilapia, and salmon. That's the spirit. Not just a new variant of chipotle chicken burrito, but a whole new ethnic food. Not a new cut of meat, a new species. Not some slightly faster, better microwave, but a radically improved, market-changing, paradigm-shifting appliance. This book is fundamentally a search for people who think they have the Next Big Thing in food.

2. SCHONWALD'S TASTING MENU TO NEXT BIG THINGS IN FOOD

Bagged salad also reveals the inherent subjectivity of this search. If you hadn't already guessed, I'm the hick who didn't have a spring mix until I was twenty-six. I fell in love with the flavor, the texture, the convenience, the staggering superiority to iceberg. I've had a bagged salad mix in my fridge pretty much consistently since that fateful dinner in '96, and I would rate bagged salad right below the Internet and birth control on my list of best twentieth-century inventions.

When I started researching the future of food, I quickly learned that it is a very big topic, especially during the current food revolution. As such, I had to think of this endeavor as a "tasting menu." Tough choices had to be made. As you'll see, I've devoted months to investigating salad, seafood, and meat, but nary a moment to cheese or dairy products. This unequal treatment is due to a couple of things: a gagging reflex that is provoked by cultured dairy products, and my obsession with finding the salad of the future. So full disclosure: this is a look at the food frontier, a search for the next big things in food, through the eyes of a human with some food preferences and prejudices. There will be some food reviews ahead. I can only say that—aside from a mildly deviant interest in greens, beef, and wild mushrooms, an extreme aversion to sour cream, and a penchant for hot and spicy (up to 30,000 on the Scoville scale)—I'm pretty mainstream.

3. FRANKENFOOD CAN SAVE LIVES AND PROTECT THE PLANET

The third important thing to know about this investigation: It's pro–agricultural biotechnology. (I don't call it Frankenfood anymore.) At the outset, I didn't expect to side with Monsanto over Alice Waters. My original aim was simple—to give Americans a sneak peek at the dinner table of 2035 (yes, 2035; I settled on the twenty-five-year watermark after learning how long game-changing food ideas take to gestate). This book was supposed to be neutral, friendly, glib, Switzerland-like—steering clear of thorny issues that could alienate 80 percent of the foodie population. And for about six months, it was. I looked for tasty food you might find in Whole Foods in 2035, not, say, what's needed to feed the Sudan. But over the course of this journey, my approach and views did change.

And although I began this project with a vague distrust of highly technologized food solutions, by 2011 I had come to believe that many of the ideas of the foodie mainstream are dangerously myopic, potentially destructive, and possibly the source of widespread blindness in Southeast Asia.

But don't get me wrong; save for some enthusing over green technologies that could feed the world and protect the planet, and a short plea at trip's end ("the perfect sustainable meal"), this is not a food politics book.

What you're about to embark on is, more than anything, a tour of the food innovation process. You'll learn why some foods take twenty years to reach the mainstream, while others explode virtually overnight. We'll visit the country's most influential food R&D lab, a Pentagon research facility that has quietly changed the face of the American supermarket, and a California microfarm that has been the launchpad for produce trends.

And you'll meet the food pioneers—the entrepreneurs, scientists, farmers, chefs—who are trying to change what we eat, how we produce food, how we think about food. The Harvard-trained pediatrician with a new and seemingly unnatural approach that he thinks will change the way we raise fish; the mayor who believes a currently obscure Italian vegetable will change the American salad; the celebrity chef who is trying to convince the world that he's found The Last Culinary Frontier; the lawyer-turned-nanotechnologist who believes he can solve human nutritional needs without using food.

This is a journey, and as with any journey there will be some deviations, some bumps in the road, encounters with false prophets, and moments of episodic delusion (see "The Weed Period"). But in the end, we basically stick to the original itinerary:

I look for the meat of the future. I search for the Next Pad Thai—aka the soon-to-be-big ethnic food. I keep track of the Next Salmon. And I search for another bagged salad moment. That's why this search begins in Salinas.

PART
TWO

SALAD DAYS

2.

Into the World's Salad Bowl

A THICK FOG ROLLS IN EACH MORNING from the Pacific, blanketing the valley. At around 10 a.m., like clockwork, the fog starts to burn off, yielding cloudless, sunny afternoons. For nine months the temperature, among the most consistent in North America, is a near-perfect consistency—averaging around 60. The soil is rich and loamy, packed with nutrients, enriched by a vast underwater aquifer. The land is pancake flat.

Salinas, California, heaven on earth for leafy green vegetables, was the most obvious place to begin searching for the salad of 2035.

The town of 140,000, about two hours south of San Francisco, home of the California Rodeo and the National Steinbeck Museum, is as central to the American salad-eating experience as Detroit is to the automobile and Hollywood is to filmmaking. Salinas is the primary city of a valley nicknamed the "World's Salad Bowl." For most of the past sixty years, the ninety-mile-long Salinas Valley has single-handedly accounted for more than 90 percent of the lettuce eaten in the United States. These days, more than 4 billion pounds of greens are grown in the Valley. Salinas is also the nerve center of the industry; it's the home base of companies like Fresh Express and Dole and Mann Packing, the Apples and Microsofts of the salad world. In other words, Salinas is not only where our leafy greens are grown; it's where the decisions about our salads are made.

I certainly knew that Salinas = Salad (just take a peek at the fine print on a bagged salad mix). But when I first set out to find the salad of the future, I fixated on Salinas not because of production stats or corporate headquarters but because of two people: Todd Koons and Ed Ryder.

Koons was the obvious target for any Next Great Green research; he is probably the closest living thing to a salad celebrity. Koons has been called the "Johnny Appleseed of Salad" and the "Soothsayer of Salad." Koons has appeared as "Salad Guru" on Martha Stewart's television show.

His story was legendary. He grew up in Oregon, the son of hippies with a love of food and dinner parties. One night, when Koons was in his teens, the family hosted a special guest, a Berkeley restaurateur named Alice Waters. Koons was given the task of preparing that evening's salad. At the end of the dinner, Waters, impressed, invited Koons to contact her if he was interested in a job. He took her up on the offer. At the age of eighteen, Koons started working at Chez Panisse. He made salads and managed the pantry. He also dated Waters for several years.

And then he revolutionized the American salad.

Koons was more than a maestro at choreographing a salad

mix; he was an entrepreneur. After his Chez Panisse stint, and his breakup with Waters, he headed to Salinas, where he set out to do something many believed impossible. He wanted to turn the mesclun salad served at Chez Panisse into a mass-market product. Traditionally, low-growing greens like arugula and baby spinach were harvested by hand. They were fragile. They grew at different rates. It was thought to be a time-consuming, costly, and unavoidably artisanal process.

But in the late 1980s, Koons figured out how to bring art lettuce to the masses. Though far from an engineer, Koons was one of the first to develop a baby-greens harvester that could do the work of hand laborers yet still preserve the delicate baby greens. Koons also helped invent a mobile washing system and a machine that filled and sealed bags of prewashed salad. By the early 1990s, his company, Todd Koons Organics, had become so successful (multimillion-dollar business, shipping nationally) that several of the major Salinas growers started copying him. By 1995, Koons was out of business. It was, in part, farmer's bad luck (heavy rains flooded his fields). But it was also because the larger growers, due to their size and scale, easily underpriced him. Still, Todd Koons was, many believed, the heroic individual who revolutionized how average Americans eat their greens.

Koons didn't stop with bagged spring greens. He started another company in the late 1990s, called Epic Roots, and started to mass-produce another relatively obscure green, mâche, which he billed as having mainstream potential, "the next spinach." Mâche hasn't lived up to the promise yet, but Koons was undeterred. He was a specialist in "start-up vegetables" who wanted to change the American salad. Koons was as fixated on finding the next great mass-produced green as thousands of Silicon Valley programmers were on finding the next killer app.

If Koons was the Johnny Appleseed of salad, then Ed Ryder was the Thomas Edison of lettuce. Or perhaps more aptly the Luther

Burbank of lactuca. Burbank, regarded as a god among plant breeders, developed more than eight hundred plant varieties during an almost six-decade career. He's probably best known for the potato that bears his name (the Burbank), but the range of Burbank's contributions is staggering—Shasta daisy, the Fire poppy, the July Elberta peach, the Santa Rosa plum, the Flaming Gold nectarine, the Wickson plum, the Freestone peach, the white blackberry, to name just a few.

Ed Ryder wasn't a generalist like Burbank, but within his realm, the lactuca kingdom, he was a breeder of unrivaled success. Unlike Koons, Ryder was little known outside of the Valley and agriculturalist circles. Mentions of Ryder's work were limited to plant science journals, trade magazines, such as *Western Farm*, and the United States Department of Agriculture's house newsletter.

Ryder was perhaps best known for his early work. One day in the early 1970s, he made a routine visit to a farm north of town to inspect several varieties of newly bred iceberg lettuce. The farmer, who was hosting Ryder's experiment, was upset. He pointed to row after row of wilted heads, pocked with brown edges and covered with slime. But after showing Ryder how disease was ravaging his fields, he led him to one anomalous row. It looked perfectly healthy. Ryder was stunned. He carefully inspected each of the row's fifty heads—the outer leaves, the interior—they were spotless. This row of iceberg was apparently immune to what's known as "tipburn disorder." In the months that followed, Ryder discovered that his new line of iceberg had far more than just tipburn resistance. It grew fast, had a crisp texture, an attractive shape, and a distinctive grayish-green color that made it unmistakable. Ed Ryder had developed a superstrain of iceberg lettuce.

The breed Ryder introduced to the world as "Salinas" in 1975 came to nearly monopolize the salad world like nothing before; at its zenith, more than 95 percent (yes, that's 95) of the lettuce consumed in this country was Ed Ryder–bred Salinas iceberg.

But he wasn't a one-lettuce wonder. You can safely assume that if you've eaten iceberg lettuce in America, it can be traced to Ryder. Variations of his work—there have been spin-offs—account for more than $300 million a year in the Salinas Valley alone.

Ryder has created many varieties of lettuce over his career. He's invented lettuces for particular conditions (a cool coastal climate, a hot desert), lettuces that are resistant to diseases and pests. And according to stories around the USDA, Ryder was prone to playfulness. At one point in the early 1990s, his lab came up with a midget head of lettuce, specifically for single people who eat alone.

A native of the Bronx (not a traditional hotbed of plant-breeding prowess) who went to Cornell, Ryder was clearly an old-timer. He'd been in Salinas since 1957, and he was technically retired. But if one watched the USDA website, he seemed furiously productive. During recent years, seven new varieties of lettuce were introduced, naming Ryder as breeder.

What made Ryder such an intriguing character was not just that he was a lettuce breeder of unparalleled achievements, who had invented some of the world's blockbuster greens—it was that he was nearing eighty and still productive. Reading about Ryder, I started envisioning a movie. The elderly Luther Burbank–like figure facing mortality, creaking away slowly in his greenhouse, trying to breed his pièce de résistance, a vastly improved variety that would restore iceberg's dominance. Meanwhile, across town, Koons, equally obsessed, was stealthily assembling a new mix, working on a Cyclops-like harvest machine.

Why the preoccupation with these two—Ryder and Koons? They both had a titanic impact on salad in America. They also had a seductive symmetry: Ryder represented the Age of Iceberg, the Ancien Régime, while Koons was, in my subjective view, the harbinger of the Enlightenment, the democratization of greens. They were peers in the scope of their impact on what we eat. But in a way they were most interesting because of their difference. Ryder is a scientist, a breeder. Koons is a restaurant guy turned produce marketer, a self-taught inventor. They are examples of the different ways that our salad can change, how innovation can come from different sources.

Why Iceberg Ruled and Why Egypt Matters

Arranging a short talk with Koons, now the owner of a small produce company with offices in Salinas and Sausalito, was like scheduling an interview with a celebrity, say Lady Gaga, or maybe Brad Pitt. Koons was maddeningly hard to reach. He would ignore emails and phone calls for months. And then, just when all hope was lost, he would, almost torturously, return a call, saying he really wanted to talk. His messages always had an element of intrigue. One time he called saying he was on his way to Asia. Another time he called saying he was "busy at the Obama inauguration but can talk later this week." Once he even said he was planning a trip to Cincinnati in the coming weeks and would like to come up to Chicago to see me (yes, fly up specifically to see me!), but the trip never materialized.

Fortunately, reaching Ed Ryder was a different story. Part of the reason Ryder was easy to reach was because he was *really* retired. He was living near Salinas, gardening (for fun), working out with a personal trainer three days a week, and writing a novel, *The Departments*, which centered around a fractious debate about the future of plant breeding. When I mentioned his seeming flurry of late-in-life productivity, Ryder laughed and explained how crop invention works. It's an iterative process. Ryder wasn't currently breeding, he was getting credited as breeder for foundational work he'd done years ago—sometimes more than a decade—that others have continued. "If you create the first generation, you'll still get credit," he told me, adding, "I really am retired."

Hearing that Ryder had given up new lettuce development—there would be no flavor-enhanced iceberg sequels—was upsetting initially. But it didn't take long—two phone calls, to be precise—for Ryder to get me dreaming excitedly about the possibilities of salad, circa 2035.

During our first call, Ryder, who has a calm, NPR-esque voice with a faint whiff of his native Bronx, offered a quick survey course on twentieth century lettuce history, touching on such topics as vacuum packing and the transition from trains to trucking, with particular attention to the key moments in iceberg lettuce development. The "iceberg" developed in 1894 by W. Atlee Burpee—patriarch of the Burpee seed company—is misnamed, Ryder explained. "That's not really an iceberg! It's actually a patatia, a lighter, looser variety. It was just called iceberg." He gave a short primer on the morphological and taste differences of the four most popular families of lettuce—crisphead (of which iceberg is a variety), romaine (also called "cos"), butterhead (like Boston and Bibb), and looseleaf (the baby greens, the red oaks, the green leafs). Ryder's favorite-tasting lettuce wasn't one of his creations; it was Little Gem, one of the Latin lettuces, which is like a cross between a butterhead and a romaine. Seemingly reveling in the opportunity to unload lactuca trivia on a newbie, Ryder told me several surprising facts. China, though not known for its salads, is the world's largest consumer of lettuce. The Chinese eat cooked stem lettuces, a type of lettuce popular almost exclusively in Asia. (It won't be popular here, he added. "Too bitter.") Ryder also reported, with exhaustive enthusiasm, numerous nonfood applications of lettuce—it could be used as an industrial lubricant, as a medicine, as an ingredient in the manufacture of plastic, and as a cigarette. (Yes. I learned that a ninety-something New Jersey man has devoted much of his life to getting people to smoke lettuce instead of tobacco.)

Ryder wasn't comfortable making bold pronouncements about

the salad of the future. "I am much better at talking about the past," he demurred. He did, however, predict that the salad of the future would almost surely be shaped in some manner by genetic engineering.

Asked if there would ever be a lettuce as dominant as Salinas I (his legendary contribution), Ryder laughed, then stated curtly, "No. It could never happen again." He had many reasons why this feat—nearly total market dominance—would never be replicated. It's a different era. Consumers want more variety. The precut, bagged salad industry and packaging breakthroughs have changed everything.

More than anything, iceberg lettuce nearly monopolized the American salad experience because of its extraordinary durability. Iceberg, vacuum packed, stored in refrigerated cars, could endure the three-week Salinas to New York trip and still look good, because of its unique biology: Head lettuce retains much more water and iceberg has strong cell walls. Looseleaf lettuces, such as red oak or baby arugula, are by contrast fragile and so decompose rapidly. They could never survive the trek. Talking about the superior virtues of Salinas I, Ryder grew wistful. "Buyers used to say that it had that special shine. They used to pay more for it." It pained Ryder to hear the way some people trash iceberg today. "They say they won't eat it. They say it doesn't have any flavor. It does have flavor. It has a wonderful flavor." (This was an awkward moment for me after fourteen years of iceberg abstinence.)

RYDER HADN'T JUST spent the past fifty years breeding fabulously successful types of lettuce. He had also quietly gone about assembling a massive library. Called the Salinas Germplasm Collection, it has more than fourteen thousand types of lettuce seed. (Only two places in the world are believed to have more.) Ryder was explaining the global scope of the Salinas collection—it has seeds from North America, Europe, and Asia—when he went off on a tangent.

"Lettuce is from Egypt or Iraq." He paused, as if he knew this particular factoid would fascinate me. "That's the center of origin."

Drawings found in tombs in Egypt and the Fertile Crescent depict what look like stem lettuces. "The ancient Egyptians ate lettuce; they used it like we eat celery."

The comment struck me as highly curious, as curious as the "there's this *new* fish" comment. Until that moment, I did not know that lettuce could be "from" a place—let alone Egypt or Iraq, places that conjured up visions of desert and camels and Shiite and Sunni, not leafy greens.*

Ryder added that plant breeders and ethnobotanists still embark on what are called "germplasm hunting" expeditions and that only a fraction of the world's lettuce has been cultivated—and that the thousands of seeds in Salinas represent a fraction of the lactuca world.

I asked Ryder if he thought any of these wild, yet-to-be-cultivated lettuces could play a role in the salad of 2035.

"Yes, absolutely."

ABOUT TEN DAYS later, a bulky mail package arrived—it was fifty-plus photocopied pages, co-written by Ed. The title was somniferous (the lactuca chapter of *Genetic Resources, Chromosome Engineering, and Crop Improvement*, volume 3) and much of the text was in dense, nearly inscrutable plant geneticist–ese. But amid the taxonomic classifications and regeneration protocols were pages devoted to exactly what Ed had told me about—the Asian and African lactucas.

It turned out there was actually far more lettuce from Asia and Africa than anywhere else. Fifty-one varieties of lettuces from Asia, compared to only twelve from North America. Ed's chapter

---

*Most crops do have an established "center of origin," and many of these ancestral homes are surprisingly exotic; for example, apples are traced to Kazakhstan.

was loaded with exotic lactuca curiosities—descriptions of wild lettuces with unusual forms from places like eastern Turkey, Afghanistan, and Kurdistan, and photos from Egyptian tombs depicting Cleopatra-like figures holding lettuce stalks. While the European and American lettuces were largely domesticated, most of the Asians and Africans were still at large, uncultivated, lurking in the wild.

In this age of GPS and Google Earth, at a time when a typical Whole Foods stocks four kinds of kale, it was surprising— thrilling, life-affirming—to think that there are still lettuces to find, that lettuce hunters still exist. After thumbing through *Genetic Resources, Chromosome Engineering, and Crop Improvement,* volume 3, I started thinking about the universe of possibilities. I fixated, in particular, on one of the more peculiar Asian lactucas. It was just hard to imagine a blue lettuce from Central Asia. Questions emerged: Was it actually possible that we could be eating *Afghan* salad mixes in 2035? And what did the native lettuce of Iraq taste like?

THE BEST PLACE to see the lettuce of Egypt or Iraq, this side of a full-blown plant expedition, appeared to be the Salinas Germplasm Collection. And to get inside the collection, I needed to get approval from the collection's owner, the United States Department of Agriculture.

It was during a brief phone call, a simple ironing out of details with the USDA, that I received a highly curious and fateful suggestion.

"You should probably talk with the mayor."

"Are you kidding?"

"He's a radicchio grower."

The source of the mayoral referral was Ryan Hayes, the USDA's chief lettuce breeder in Salinas, the "new Ed." Hayes was being helpful; he had offered the names of other scientists, other breeders to speak with during my Salinas Valley visit, before he dropped this unexpected recommendation.

Talk with the mayor? Was it possible that the Salad Kingdom had some kind of Chicago-style patronage system? It also occurred to me that maybe Salinas was like Los Angeles—everyone in L.A. seemed to be kicking around a screenplay idea, and likewise maybe Salinasans had visions of the next great greens?

That was light speculation. The notion that the mayor of Salinas could have something meaningful to say about the salad greens of 2035 was, if anything, amusing. The purpose of my first Salinas trip was clear: Ed Ryder, Ryan Hayes, the invention of new lettuces, the seed bank, the chance to see—and perhaps taste—a variety in development, a green that few have tried.

The Western Hemisphere's Largest Lettuce Lab

The Station, shorthand for the U.S. Agricultural Research Station–Salinas, is a sprawling complex of greenhouses and trailers on the southeast side of the city, near a golf course. Here you are unmistakably in the World's Salad Bowl. You can see some of the Valley's signature topography. To the east, the Gabilan Mountains, patched with scrub oak and bluegrass; to the west the jagged hills of the Santa Lucia range. And to the south, just behind the parking lot—the fields. The Station is essentially the beachfront of a sea of salad greens—lettuce, broccoli, cauliflower, spinach—that extends virtually uninterrupted for ninety miles.

The Station has twelve greenhouses. Each one I visited was rigged with powerful lamps, a lattice of irrigation systems, and thousands of plants in various stages of growth. In addition to the greenhouses, there are growth chambers, where you can simulate various conditions (temperature, light, humidity), and test fields:

one begins right behind the Station, and another fifty-acre plot is a short ride south.

"It's the most important lettuce research facility in the Western Hemisphere, that's for sure," Ryan Hayes told me as we walked past row after row of lactuca labeled with names like Calcia, La Brillante, Holborn, Pavane, Eruption. Hayes focuses exclusively on lettuce. All told, he said, the Station has thirteen other scientists on the lactuca beat.

It quickly became clear that the Station functioned as a kind of Centers for Disease Control for lettuce. Hayes told me that four scientists on site were pathologists, devoted to understanding lactuca disease. In his office, Hayes had scrawled on a whiteboard in black Sharpie his big projects—all were disease related. One disease, downy mildew, sounded particularly vexing; it keeps developing different strains (twenty-plus and counting), eluding breeders. Verticillium—"vert" in breeder-ese—was the worst. Some diseases just cause partial losses, but vert causes an iceberg head to collapse like a deflated ball. If it hits your field, it causes total losses, and not just for a year—the fungus can stick around for a decade. "It's a big concern around here," said Hayes, sighing.

The first serious inkling that the Western Hemisphere's—and possibly the world's—largest lettuce lab might not be the last stop on my salad quest came in Hayes' greenhouse. After passing dozens of plants that looked familiar—romaine or iceberg lookalikes—we stood in front of the first of two oddballs: a spindly thing with jagged leaves that looked to me like a very unhappy arugula. Hayes didn't recall what exactly this plant was—it was labeled with the Station's own cuneiform, a numbered, lettered code. A few plants away, there was another odd exotic with a code. Hayes knew this one: it was a *Lactuca virosa*.

I started getting excited; we were in the realm of the wild relatives, the yet-to-be cultivated.

When I asked him what the two greens taste like, he chuckled.

He had never *eaten* them. Scanning the motley mix of mutants and wild varieties, he said, "We're looking at them as sources of disease resistance." Hayes told me that he had only eaten a wild green—as part of breeder duties—once.

My dreams of eating an Afghan salad mix were further deflated a few minutes later in the seed bank. The world's third-largest collection of lettuce germplasm is stored in an eleven-by-eleven walk-in freezer—not much larger than a restaurant's. After I viewed the facility and passed a growth chamber, a young man who was sorting seeds into packets handed me a thick binder. It was the master catalog to the collection. Here you could shop the lactuca universe. They had everything from the "iceberg" that Atlee Burpee created in 1894 to the Ed Ryder–Salinas variety that dominated the Valley. There were dozens of heirloom varieties, seeds of the blue-green lettuces of Central Asia, the oilseed lettuces of Egypt. They had an almost kaleidoscopic spectrum of lactuca—every shade of green, green-yellow, red, purple, spotted lettuces.

I asked Hayes how he uses this treasure trove of lactuca germplasm, tantalizingly close to his greenhouse. "Wild varieties," he said, "are a good source for disease resistance."

The troubling reality was becoming clear: Breeders here weren't dreaming of domesticating an Afghan lactuca or adding a feathery, sweet-tasting green to our spring mix; they were dreaming of protecting iceberg from vert, corky root, and aphids.

In other words, the whole massive ten thousand–variety, fourteen-scientist, twelve-greenhouse research station was about protecting the status quo, supporting the incumbent greens, not toppling them.

Hayes later estimated that even in this era of ten kinds of lettuce at a mediocre Whole Foods, roughly 90 percent of his work is focused on iceberg and romaine.

It's a simple matter of priorities, explained Jim McCreight, the Station's director. The mission of the Station is to support industry—the $1 billion–plus, world-leading California leafy green industry. Inoculating iceberg against verticillium wilt could save growers millions annually. Curbing the effect of big vein—more millions. The economic impact of introducing Afghan greens to American foodies—uncertain.

But what about Ryder's earlier work—his clever, original, playful ideas—the miniature head of iceberg lettuce for single people? Or the iceberg-romaine hybrid introduced in the 1970s? What was the economic logic there?

The short, sad, incredibly simplified answer is that things have changed.

To be sure, the Station has always been primarily focused on the unsexy, behind-the-scenes task of breeding in invisible traits that prevent a field of lettuce from turning into inedible mush. But back when Ryder came to Salinas in the 1950s, the Station bred for disease, pest resistance, increased yield, *and* cool new specialty crops. Lactuca breeders had more time for whimsy. They had time to play with a mutant dwarf variety of iceberg and release it to the world as "ice cube." (That's what Ed and Bill Waycott did in the early '70s.)

According to the geneticists at the Western Hemisphere's largest lettuce lab, the search for The Next Great Green has become more squarely in the domain of the private sector. Circa 2010, it was the Koons types and the big private seed companies who would likely introduce a radically innovative green to the world.

The full-blown private shift started happening in earnest in the 1990s—but its origins can be traced way back to Luther Burbank.

The legendary breeder was not a government worker content with contributing plants to the public commons. He was a businessman who complained frequently that he was getting shafted. "A man can patent a mousetrap or copyright a song," he wrote, "but if he gives the world a new fruit he will be fortunate if he is rewarded so much as having his name connected with the result."

It was not until sixty years later, and a long legal evolution, that Burbank got his wishes. A series of rulings, culminating in 1991's revision of the International Convention for the Protection of New Varieties of Plants, meant farmers who bought seed could use it once and no longer propagate it. What's more, other breeders could not modify the seed without negotiating a payment to the creator. The new guidelines, paired with the emergence of biotechnology, made breeding appealing to companies such as DuPont and Monsanto that dominated the agrochemical market.

In the United States, private sector R&D investment in agriculture increased from $2 billion in 1970 to $4.2 billion in 1996.

Meanwhile, publicly funded breeding stagnated, or stopped altogether. In the United States, government funding for breeding was virtually the same in 2011 as it was in the 1970s. The United Kingdom sold its public breeding institute to Unilever, which in turn sold it to Monsanto. As large, profit-driven companies got involved, the Station's role has changed. It had fewer resources, and less time to experiment with new specialty crops, such as dwarf iceberg heads for single diners. There were, after all, plenty of diseases to focus on. You could easily spend a whole career fighting off downy mildew alone.

After the tour of the Station, still smarting about my naïveté, I had lunch with Ed Ryder (he had a spring mix). There was a tinge of melancholy in his voice when we talked about the changes in the world of breeding. Technology was changing—shifting plant breeding away from fields and greenhouses and more and more into the world of biomarkers and electron microscopes. And public breeders, who viewed their work as contributing to social good—who saw their plants as part of a global commons to be used by all—were an increasingly endangered species.

The Mayor and the "Thinking Man's Vegetable"

Salinas mayor Dennis Donohue is strikingly friendly in the way most politicians are—you almost instantly feel permission to call him "big guy," and to invite him to join your fantasy football league. This is partly because of his look—he's fiftyish, biggish, and barrel-chested (looks like a former high school football player), and dresses in a regular-guy uniform: oxfords, khakis, vaguely disheveled.

At first the mayor seemed primarily concerned with (a) validating my smartness in coming, first, to Salinas, California, to find the salad of the future and with (b) reinforcing the "Salinas Valley is the World's Salad Bowl" moniker. Apparently there had been some talk—specifically, from the mayor of Yuma, Arizona (the nearest city to the main winter lettuce-growing region). Donohue scoffed at this Yuma business. "Now, would you say that Silicon Valley isn't the capital of the high-tech world because more chips are made in India?" he said. "It's not as simple as looking at the crop numbers. The crops grown there are controlled by companies based here." Research, innovation, financial, marketing—that's all centered here. "This is the intellectual center of the produce industry."

Having made it clear that I had to come to the right place to see the salad of the future, and after offering a short chronicle of the Steve Jobs–like figures of the Valley, I asked the mayor for some specific input: What is a potential paradigm-shifting green?

"Well," he said, tipping his eyebrows thoughtfully, "radicchio is a kind of sleepy item, not very well known . . . but I do remain convinced that we will knock iceberg off the top of the charts someday. Probably not in my lifetime . . . but I believe it could happen."

This is an outrageous, Don King–like statement, because iceberg, while not as universally dominant as it was in the 1980s, is still among the biggest single crops in the Valley—its total value was estimated at $460 million in 2009. Radicchio, by contrast, was a measly $13.5 million.

Donohue, who does double duty as mayor and president of Royal Rose, LLC, a radicchio grower, then started rapidly riffing on radicchio, saying that it's misunderstood by Americans, that Americans haven't tasted its range, that people don't know how to use it. "People tell me they don't like radicchio. I tell them, No you don't, you just don't know how to manage the flavor."

I asked Donohue how radicchio, then number twenty-two on the Valley's list of "Ten Million Dollar Crops," could possibly become a top-five crop—an iceberg or romaine or spring mix rival.

That's when he brought up "the perfect storm."

It happened in the early 1990s. Romaine lettuce was a sleepy green, hovering somewhere in the pack of Valley crops. "Then," Donohue explained, "Little Caesars comes out with the Caesar! Caesar! campaign. Buy a pizza, get a free Caesar's salad. For eight weeks, romaine sales doubled. Prior to Caesar! Caesar!, Donohue said, the Caesar was a higher-end item, a "special-event salad," the type of thing you might get at a metropolitan hotel. "This brought the Caesar right into the heart of middle America." Right around the time of the Caesars campaign, Donohue said, casual dining restaurants (translation: places lke Chili's and T.G.I. Friday's) started doing things like blackened chicken Caesar, and pre-cut salad makers started featuring bagged Caesars in grocery stores. "It was, in my view, the perfect storm."

As Donohue began to expound on the rise of romaine, and its expansion into the heartland, a City Hall staffer interrupted. It was an anxious week in Salinas—a gang war had erupted (two men were shot the night before I arrived)—and the mayor had another meeting. He looked at me apologetically. He wasn't done with the salad of 2035 conversation. "When can you meet again?"

TWO DAYS LATER we met again, this time at an Italian restaurant near City Hall. The mayor almost reflexively started unloading the "Salinas is the epicenter of fresh" talk. He drew a map on a napkin to explain the unique climatic confluence that makes this "the best fresh valley in the world." Donohue, who started his pre-produce career at companies like Microsoft and Atari, compared the talent in Salinas to the Silicon Valley. ("You don't think anyone else can be cutting edge when you work up there . . . but nothing moves as fast as produce.") He started telling me that Salinas Valley should be marketed as an appellation just like Napa or Sonoma. "It could be the first fresh appellation . . ."

Then our pizza came.

"Have you tried radicchio pizza?" he asked as I chewed on a slice of pepperoni.

"No."

"Radicchio risotto? Grilled radicchio?"

I shook my head.

Through this brief interrogation, Mayor Donohue had established that I hadn't really tried radicchio—I was like the millions of Americans who *thought* they knew radicchio but had only had radicchio in the bag. After getting me to achieve this self-awareness, the evangelism began.

"Have you been to Italy?" he said, which then led to his description of this parallel universe—a region called "the Veneto"— where salad green culture centers on radicchio, not lettuce, and where festivals are held to honor the radicchio harvest.

I must have shot him a suspicious look, unable to suppress some skepticism about the idea of festivals devoted to the bitter red stuff in bagged salad mixes.

Clearly familiar with naysayers, the mayor was ready—his

finger extended out—as if poised to make a point in a council meeting. First, he told me about varieties of radicchio (Chioggia, Treviso, Tardivo, Castelfranco) with varying tastes and qualities. "Lucio," he said, referring to Lucio Gomiero, his boss, a cofounder of Royal Rose, "won't even eat the radicchio we sell to processors" (i.e., bagged salad mixes). Then Donohue claimed that no vegetable grown in the Valley has more "applications" than radicchio. "And if someone says otherwise, I say, 'Prove me wrong. Show me twenty different things to do with jicama or lettuce.'

"Spinach? It's closest. You can serve it warm or chilled. You can sauté it. You can go salad. But," he added, with a sly grin, "it's not quite like radicchio."

To prove his point, the mayor had actually come up with a proof, something he called "the Greek syllogism."

"If A is lettuce, and B is your favorite dressing, say, Caesar, add them together. You still have B. It'll be the flavor of the Caesar.

"Same is true for spinach. It eats fairly pleasantly, but a little blandly. You're still gonna get a B." But with radicchio, Donohue said, "depending on your B, you can get C. If you marry radicchio with blue cheese, you get one taste. Pair it with citrus, you get another. You just can't do that with spinach."

We talked a little about what many consider the deal-breaker for radicchio—bitterness. The mayor said this was a plus, not a problem. "You just have to manage it. That's why I call radicchio 'the thinking man's vegetable.'" He portended a future where thinking men and women would smartly pair radicchio with fine wine ("You're not going to do that with broccoli, are you?").

He then described scenarios that he called "power moments" (say, Mario Batali or Emeril or President Obama starts enthusing about radicchio) and predicted that most likely the power moment will be driven by a "power application." "It could be pizza," he said, pointing to my pizza. "Radicchio interacts beautifully with cheese. It has a great mouthfeel.

"But we believe the power application is grilling. Grilled Treviso—an heirloom varietal of radicchio—paired with romaine hearts. Once Americans tasted grilled Treviso," he said, throwing up his hands. "That's the breakthrough."

At the end of his riff, Donohue concluded that the success of this "grilled Treviso" could have much bigger implications. "This could go to the category level," he said, raising an eyebrow.

I asked what a category is.

"Broccoli is not a category. It's just broccoli. Artichokes? Not a category. Lettuce is a category. There's red leaf, green leaf, romaine."

There are nineteen varieties of chicories, Donohue said. "We believe six are commercially viable."

In other words, grilled Treviso radicchio could drive the category and unleash a chicory revolution. "We could be the fresh chicory leader," Donohue said, smiling.

I didn't know what to make of this mayoral encounter. Was he a master salesman, a gifted bullshitter, a typical politician? He was, lest we forget, claiming that radicchio—the bitter red stuff in the salad mix—would essentially achieve a version of vegetable jujitsu, moving from bag mix bit player to center-of-the-plate star. Preposterous? On the other hand, he was right—I had never really had radicchio, had no idea that radicchio had varieties, let alone heirloom varieties of varying quality. And perhaps more important, I hadn't heard anyone else in Salinas talk so brazenly about a plan to revolutionize the American salad. Revolutionaries come in different forms. Was it possible that a breakthrough salad idea was coming, not from Ed, or anyone at the Station, but from a politician who used to work for Atari?

3.

The Radicchio King, the Produce Oligarchy, and the Greatest Engineering Feat in Salad History

ONE OF THE LEGENDARY STORIES IN THE Salinas Valley, a legend akin to the Silicon Valley tale of Steve Wozniak and Steve Jobs founding Apple Computer in the Jobs family garage, centers on a Sicilian immigrant named Stefano D'Arrigo. It was after the end of World War I when D'Arrigo started planting a "new vegetable." The vegetable was not literally "new," since it had been eaten as far back as Roman times, but it was virtually unknown in the United States.

D'Arrigo imported the seeds from Italy, and early reaction to his new vegetable was highly negative. For one, it gave off a noxious sulfurous smell when cooked that some compared to human flatulence.

The Sicilian kept growing the stinky vegetable, and he found a small niche: fellow Italians in the Northeast, especially in New York and Boston. D'Arrigo was one of the first Salinas growers to take advantage of rail transportation.

But a few years later, Stefano and his brother decided they wanted to move beyond the Italian market. They believed more Americans— German-Americans, Polish-Americans, African-Americans—would love broccoli.

The broccoli campaign was not an overnight success. Radio ads the D'Arrigo brothers had airing across the country were widely ridiculed, perhaps most famously by E. B. White. "It's broccoli, dear, I say it's spinach," White wrote, "and I say the hell with it!" But slowly the sulfur-smelling cruciform caught on. During the 1940s and 1950s, broccoli, benefiting from the awareness that it was a healthful choice, became a popular frozen vegetable and a fixture of American family dinners.

By the late 1980s, broccoli had become such an institution in the United States that when then-president George H. W. Bush declared his dislike for it—he actually banned it from the White House and Air Force One—it wasn't broccoli that was ridiculed. Rather, the president's brocco-phobia was deemed deviant and inspired widespread amusement. Today, the D'Arrigo brothers' "new vegetable" is perenially one of the country's most-consumed and valued vegetables—in the Salinas Valley it's a $200 million crop.

Why is broccoli so important to the future of salad? Take a look at the crop reports and you can see how long it took for broccoli to assimilate: years of lollygagging in vegetable nowhere-land, followed by the consumption spike in the 1950s. If broccoli could leap from obscurity, then it at least suggested the *possibility* that the American salad could be radicchio-ized. A precedent existed.

The Rise of Broccoli

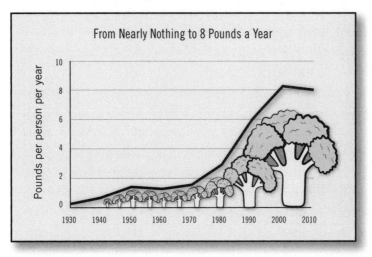

From Nearly Nothing to 8 Pounds a Year

Source: the U.S. Department of Agriculture's Economic Research Service.

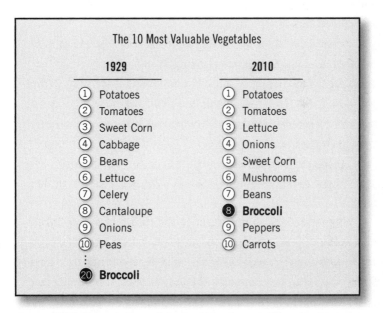

The 10 Most Valuable Vegetables

1929	2010
① Potatoes	① Potatoes
② Tomatoes	② Tomatoes
③ Sweet Corn	③ Lettuce
④ Cabbage	④ Onions
⑤ Beans	⑤ Sweet Corn
⑥ Lettuce	⑥ Mushrooms
⑦ Celery	⑦ Beans
⑧ Cantaloupe	⑧ **Broccoli**
⑨ Onions	⑨ Peppers
⑩ Peas	⑩ Carrots
⋮	
⑳ **Broccoli**	

Source: USDA's Economic Research Service. List ranks vegetables and melons in the United States by production value.

Donohue had succeeded in undermining my assumptions about radicchio—but it was the tale of Stefano D'Arrigo that prompted me to start reading everything I could find about the red stuff in the bagged salad mix.

EVEN THOUGH *RADICCHIO* sounds about as Italian as a word could be, it turns out that it was a Belgian who gave it its distinctive trait. A botanical relative of escarole and endive, *Cichorium intybus* has been around since ancient times. The ancient Egyptians bred it, Pliny the Elder praised its medicinal qualities, medieval monks used it to spice up their largely vegetarian diets, but it was Francesco Van den Borre, a Belgian agronomist, who applied the same techniques used to whiten Belgian endive, a cousin, to give radicchio its rich red wine leaves and white roots. The Italians call the process *imbianchimento*. It sounds like prisoner torture, and involves trimming the radicchio's outer leaves, storing it in a dark shed, and bathing its roots in 60 degree water for several days.

I'd assumed Donohue's description of radicchio-mad Italians was an exaggeration, but it turned out to be, for the most part, true.

After the Belgian did his work, the Italians continued their breeding and created dozens of variations. There are at least four popular types of radicchio around today—each with a different look and flavor. There is Chioggia—the red-cabbage look-alike that Americans know; Treviso, which has a torpedo shape, much like Belgian endive; Tardivo, which is said to resemble "exotic feathers"; and Castelfranco, which from photos looks beautiful, like butter lettuce with red speckles. Each of the radicchio varieties had its own taste, and it appeared that Chioggia, the only one I'd ever tried, was indeed the entry-level variety and the most bitter.

There are radicchio festivals in Italy, radicchio Facebook pages, and a cookbook with over seven hundred radicchio recipes. There are even radicchio appellations—like wine regions in France. In Italy there's something called *Indicazione Geografica Protetta*. You can only sell Treviso as "Treviso" if it's from Treviso *and* supervised by the radicchio consortium of Treviso.

The undisputed Radicchio King in the Salinas Valley, and hence the United States, is in fact Lucio Gomiero, Donohue's boss, the CEO of Royal Rose.

Gomiero is from Padua, which is in the center of the radicchio heartland, but he is a highly unusual choice for Radicchio King. Radicchio growing, after all, was a hundreds-year-old tradition in the Veneto. There were families with rich radicchio-growing histories, and chefs renowned for their radicchio recipes. Lucio, however, is the son of a construction company owner, who went to the University of Venice to become an architect.

Lucio's entrance into the radicchio business was an accident. With his architecture degree, Lucio was working for his dad's business when he became friendly with Carlo Boscolo. Carlo's family grew radicchio. One day in 1986, Carlo asked Lucio if he'd ever thought of moving to America. Carlo's family had been getting lots of faxes from Americans who wanted radicchio. But Carlo thought it was silly to ship radicchio across the Atlantic. Why not just grow it there? There must be some radicchio-friendly growing regions in the States. Lucio wasn't interested in following in his father's footsteps. He'd studied a little agriculture in college and had caught the winemaking bug. He liked Carlo's idea.

American growers had not had great success with radicchio on an industrial scale. It's a notoriously tempestuous plant, sometimes called the "wild child," in part because of its tendency to bolt. But Lucio and Carlo had one huge advantage. Having grown radicchio for generations, Carlo's family had access to hundreds of seeds suited for different climatic needs.

At this point, the Lucio/Carlo story turns into the type of thing you might hear at, say, a Republican convention. The two guys from the Veneto come to America and set up their radicchio farming operation in Georgia. This is not Atlanta; this is two hundred miles south, near Valdosta, in Okefenokee Swamp country. "We had never seen a pickup truck," Lucio told a reporter, "or an alligator."

Why Georgia? Why *south* Georgia?

Before departing, Lucio and Carlo had consulted their natural ally for such global entrepreneurial ideas, the Italian Trade Commission. They tried several ITC offices in the United States, without success. The only office to respond to their faxes was in Georgia.

The climate for radicchio wasn't horrible in Georgia, but at some point during their Georgia stay Lucio and Carlo heard about this place called the World's Salad Bowl. They took a trip to California, quickly recognized that it could be a radicchio Valhalla, graced with a climate that was even better for radicchio than the Veneto and an existing transportation and distribution infrastructure that could get radicchio anywhere in the United States.

They wanted to move to the Salinas Valley. They asked an agricultural extension agent about getting twenty acres to start out. The agent laughed at them. The Salinas Valley is the farming equivalent of midtown Manhattan; it has some of the priciest farmland in the world. (In Georgia, you could buy an acre for $500; in Salinas, you might spend $2,000 to rent an acre for three months.)

After the laughing subsided, they got some land, and in 1987 Lucio and Carlo began their Salinas operation, with no machinery, no workers, and one acre. By 1992, that single acre had grown to more than 3,000. The two Italians were spectacular beneficiaries of the bagged salad revolution. Because of its distinctive color, American salad makers wanted radicchio in their mixes.

Within just five years of their Salinas arrival, Lucio and Carlo had become the world's largest radicchio growers, even supplying McDonald's with radicchio (the fast food giant also wanted color in its salads). By early 2000 a feature on radicchio in the now-defunct *Gourmet* magazine presented Lucio as doing quite well in Salinas—driving through his fields in a radicchio-red Mercedes, experimenting with puntarelle, a southern Italian chicory, and owning a new vineyard back home in Italy.

Perhaps the most alluring thing about Lucio, though, was one sentence—one word, actually—in a story by *Los Angeles Times* restaurant critic Russ Parsons.

"'They could just as easily use flowers,' says Gomiero, mournfully."

Mournfully. Lucio had succeeded in growing the difficult plant, he'd built a worldwide network of farms that ensured year-round radicchio, he was producing 10 million pounds of radicchio a year, but that wasn't enough. More than half of Gomiero's harvest wound up chopped into pieces in bagged salad mixes. Observed Parsons: "You can't help but feel that his happiness will only be complete when Americans learn to love radicchio the way he does."

The Radicchio King and I

Megafarm monoculture agribusiness is a highly mobile operation. Shortly after Thanksgiving, hundreds of people and semis split town, heading down Highway 101 bound for the Imperial Valley and Yuma County, the winter home of industrial salad and the source of the mayor of Yuma's bragging rights. Another mass migration occurs in late February, when the industry shifts to the San Joaquin Valley; tiny Huron, California (population 800), the center of it all, explodes to 10,000 for six weeks. All told, for about three months, including January (my first visit), Salinas feels bleak, semi-desolate, like a mill town without the mill.

But in July the Valley is at full power—streets clogged with eighteen-wheelers and inexpensive motels filled with methylooking men. In July you can see fields of lettuce growing within Salinas city limits. You can also experience the reason why your store-bought salad is most likely from here: the relentlessly monotonous weather. The fog, which Steinbeck compared to "gray flannel," greets you every morning. Afternoons—always the same. Sunny, low 70s, the wind starts gusting around five o'clock.

Royal Rose LLC, the world's largest radicchio grower, is on Growers Street, the epicenter of the epicenter of the leafy greens industry. Several industrial-scale grower-shippers—Fresh Express, River Ranch, Mann Packing, Tanimura & Antle (T&A)—have sprawling plants out here. Green Giant has a towering sign with its trademark giant. T&A has an imposing headquarters that looks like an antebellum plantation.

The industry-leading radicchio grower, though, was in an unassuming warehouse, marked with a blink-and-you'll-miss-it sign. Inside, it was far from kingly. In fact, the only things that distinguished the headquarters of Royal Rose from, say, a state legislative race campaign headquarters were a few boxes of radicchio in the hallway and a sign calling the conference room "The Radicchio Café." There are only six full-time employees at Royal Rose because the grower, like many in the Valley, relies heavily on outsourcing. They don't employ field hands, seed planters, packers, or soil scientists; they just hire companies that do.

Lucio, the Radicchio King, was also a bit of a surprise. It wasn't his looks—he's tallish, in his fifties, fadingly handsome, with brown hair, a slight gut, dressed California casual, in jeans and oxford—as much as his temperament. Before the trip, based on the story (immigrant, "tireless missionary," parlays one acre into a radicchio empire) and the fact that he employs the high-octane Donohue, I expected a work-ass-off Type A who wasn't going to waste any time unveiling the radicchio manifest destiny strategy.

My profiling was way off. When we first met in the Radicchio Café (aka the conference room) we spent at least twenty minutes talking in great detail not about the types and flavors of radicchio, but about the types and flavors of Chinese tea (to my lasting benefit and gratitude, Lucio introduced me to pu-erh tea). When Shoko Matsuda, the Japan sales manager, entered the room, it prompted ten minutes on the Italian restaurants of Tokyo.

Lucio was far from monomaniacal about radicchio. In fact, if he had any dominant character trait, it seemed to be all-around perfectionism. Asked for a suggestion on restaurants in Salinas, he scoffed, "None." Asked if he ever went to the Republic of Tea, a popular chain that sells many tea varieties, he said, "No," and glared at me as if I'd farted. When the conversation strayed to Asian food in the Bay Area—an area renowned for its range of Chinese restaurants—he conceded that he liked one, near the airport.

A slow, precise talker, whether the subject was Chinese tea or refrigerated trucking, he was exhaustive on the subject of *Cichorium intybus*, the chicories. After giving his own botanical narrative (Lucio began not with the Belgian, or even Pliny, but with the "blue flower" common to all chicories), he shifted to some poster-sized photos of his radicchio (Chioggia, Treviso, and Tardivo) and its two cousins, frisée and puntarelle, that hung from the walls of the café. He would look at each, then calmly discuss its idiosyncrasies, its town of origin, its culinary potential, its challenge. ("Ah, puntarelle," he said, gazing at a chicory, popular in southern Italy, that looks somewhat like spinach. "It is very difficult. If you try to farm in the wrong time, you will not succeed.")

THE NEXT MORNING, July 21, the day of my initiation into the deeper mysteries of radicchio, we went in Lucio's van (the radicchio-red Mercedes of the *Gourmet* story? "Totaled years ago.") to the fields, about ten minutes south of Growers Street. After passing field after field of lettuce and broccoli, we arrived at one of the reddish fields filled with the red cabbage look-alike, Chioggia. Lucio inspected the heads, deemed them suitably ripe, then pulled a knife from his pocket. "You have to cut it like this," he said as he dug his knife into a spot on the base. "Because if you cut it too short, you get loose leaves, and if leaves are not attached to the core, they will wilt in a few days." A properly cut, trimmed radicchio, Lucio said, should roll like a ball.

After loading up on Chioggia, we drove a bit farther and I spotted the unfamiliar cousin, Treviso, which on first sight looks strangely phallic. Lucio surveyed the plants—a little young (a week away from perfect maturity), he said—then he explained why Treviso was The One that could stir the passion of the *Americani*. Treviso, far less than 5 percent of the total crop, has a thicker leaf than Chioggia. "It not just the flavor, it's the texture," he said, pointing to its white rib. "It has a meatiness, it can hold the grill and benefits from the smokiness."

It appeared we were set for dinner—the van's backseat was full of radicchio—but then Lucio spotted some romaine fields, and we pulled over again. (This made sense; romaine was, after all, part of what Donohue called "the power pairing.") As he grabbed a romaine heart, Lucio explained the idea. Romaine, they had found, also works well on the grill, and it has a similar elongated shape to Treviso. "We cut it longwise, apply olive oil, put it on the grill, then cut it crosswise, and serve it as a warm salad. . . . And that, we hope, will be the next thing for America."

A few minutes later, while cruising down one of the dozens of dirt roads that crisscross the Valley floor, Lucio stopped and parked in front of what looked like a field of beans. They were sugar snap peas. "Mann Packing is pushing it," Lucio said, eating some straight from the field and handing some to me. I'd had sugar snap peas before—in a microwave-friendly bag, in Chicago, probably from Mann. But these fresh peas were especially wonderful. It was a rush eating freshly picked peas, probably illegally, treating the World's Largest Fresh Valley, the belly of the modern agro-industrial complex, like my backyard garden. Salad greens as far as the eye can see. Lucio wasn't, in general, lavish with affection for Salinas, but he did point out that grocery greens here are incredibly fresh. You'll find stuff in the local Safeway that was picked the day before.

This idea that store-bought salad greens are fresher in Salinas than in Chicago or New York won't surprise anyone familiar with the concept of "food miles." The Salinas Valley is, after all, the antithesis of locavorism for East Coasters (it's a roughly seven-day trip). But though megafarms don't exactly conjure up the locavore ideal, the Salinas Valley is, transport-wise, local for millions of Californians. It's only sixty miles from the Bay Area. (Hearing that a Salinas Safeway might have day-old greens was pleasingly just— in the spirit of Maine Safeways deserving fresher lobster and Iowa Safeways having fresher corn.)

A few fields later, still buzzing from the snap pea, I learned something upsetting in precisely the opposite way. Lucio, ever eagle-eyed, was watching one of his harvest crews, mainly Mexican women, cut and grade heads of Chioggia. He furrowed his brow, muttered something about the way one man was trimming the heads, and we headed toward the group's foreman.

The foreman approached us carrying hairnets. I thought this was a joke. No. Ever since a 2006 outbreak of E. coli, attributed to bagged spinach in the Valley, hairnets have been standard. The prevailing theory, Lucio explained, is that the farm needs to be treated like a kitchen to avoid contaminants.

Standing in front of one of the hairnet-wearing graders who was placing heads in bins, Lucio pointed to one bin and said, "Those are the best; they're export quality." He turned to me. "They go to Japan." I knew that Japan was an important market for Royal

Rose—Mayor Donohue once emailed me from Tokyo, and they have Shoko, a Japanese speaker, on their sales team. But still it was strange—okay, flabbergasting—to think that the best American radicchio was being shipped 5,000 miles away. (Everyone in the food world knows the Japanese are obsessive about food. When the subject of Japan comes up among food people, you'll frequently hear about the twenty-five-dollar Japanese plum, presented like it's Swarovski crystal.) Lucio shrugged. "They will pay for quality." He added respectfully, "They are perfectionists."

Lucio often sounded snobby when talking about American salad-eating habits—he cringed at the mention of dressings, like Caesar and Russian. He couldn't understand why Americans can't accept seasonality ("Why can't you wait for something wonderful?"). He also couldn't understand why Americans were so price-conscious (even middle-class Italians will pay for something like white truffles, he told me).

On the other hand, he would boast of his ability to cope with these vulgarians. He and Carlo were the first radicchio growers to have achieved year-round production because "you have to in America." And after driving by a field of romaine and hearing his feelings about Caesar, he revealed that he had commissioned some Culinary Institute of America students to develop a perfect dressing; in other words, a Caesar for radicchio. Lucio could separate his personal preferences from business needs. Still, it was a bit shocking to learn that he had conceded something seemingly sacred to his identity.

As we drove back to town, Lucio decided to take a look at a field test. Field tests are a way for growers to compare variables—fertilizers, seeds, tipburn resistance, herbicides, fungicide performance. Cruising down one of the ruler-straight roads, looking for the flags that marked the test rows, Lucio explained that the field test in question pitted an heirloom variety against a hybrid.

It sounded routine until Lucio revealed that the control was the hybrid. Hybrids are the de facto seed in American industrial agriculture (they grow faster, have a more reliable yield and consistent shape, they're less prone to disease). But this was Lucio, a man who talks about the "character" of his radicchio, and who describes Tardivo radicchio as the "product of love." The whole two-guys-from-Italy story centers on the open-pollinated *heirloom* seeds. Earlier he'd told me that in the Veneto, a good heirloom seed is treated like "a family treasure. They won't give them up."

Everything I'd heard suggested that the key to Lucio and Carlo's success was their superior seeds—their heirloom seeds. Looking out at the field, Lucio admitted plainly that the hybrid Chioggia he was selling today was inferior, that the heirloom radicchio he sold a few years ago tasted better. Lucio wanted to improve the taste.

But taste wasn't the only factor. Heirlooms often have different-shaped heads, grow at different rates, and sometimes you have to harvest a field two or three times. Hybrids have predictable shapes and double the yield. Processors—the big grower/shippers in the bagged salad industry—made up the vast majority of Lucio's business. Processors don't care nearly as much about quality (radicchio makes up between 3 and 10 percent of most mixes) as they do about price. Throw in competition from other radicchio growers, such as an upstart in Guatemala, and Royal Rose had to constantly cut costs to compete. The price of radicchio has plummeted; it fetched eight dollars a pound when Lucio started; now it's less than three. "We had to trade flavor for yield," Lucio said.

The little flags represented Lucio's plan to change his seeds. In part it was cost-driven. The maker of the hybrid seeds, a Dutch company, had increased the price of their seeds by almost 20 percent. The company had a world monopoly on commercial hybrid radicchio seeds. Fuming at the monopoly—"I can't pass these costs to my customers"—Lucio sounded like an Iowa farmer railing against Monsanto.

But Lucio seemed even more troubled—disturbed, really—by the "character" of the hybrid radicchio. The taste was not right: radicchio should have a bitter taste at first, but it should have a sweet finish—the hybrid lacks that. A good radicchio head should make a sound when you squeeze it. It should crack. This hybrid lacks that. Radicchio should have a particular color. When this hybrid is exposed to the air for a few hours, it turns purplish and loses its crimson color. These qualities are unnoticeable to most. "If it is a salad bag with three percent radicchio, nobody will know," Lucio said. "But if we try to bring radicchio to America in the way I was dreaming when I came here, like we eat in Italy, then we need quality."

The plan, Lucio said, pointing to the flags, is to create "our own hybrid." Lucio and Carlo (who is based in Italy) had 120 lines of heirlooms. They had commissioned geneticists at the University of Venice (the Ed Ryders of radicchio) to create a Chioggia variety that improves yield yet doesn't lose the character of the heirloom. Lucio turned to me with a fiery, messianic look. "We have a goal. I know we can achieve this."

Hearing that Lucio was using hybrid seeds from a Dutch agribusiness concern was unsettling, like discovering that a hardcore, free-trade coffee shop is serving Guatemalan Antiguan from Sam's Club. Yet Lucio was unashamed of the business realities of his work. He proudly told stories about his efforts to find the right microclimates in Chile and Okinawa, and his experiments with cold-storage warehouses near Merced. One of his proudest achievements involved adopting his seedbed width to tractor-wheel bases. Lucio boasted that he'd increased his per-acre yield by 50 percent by planting eighty-inch seedbeds instead of forty-inch beds. "And right now," Lucio said, beaming, with the same glee as if describing the flavor of a bumper crop of puntarelle, "almost fifty percent of everything grown in the valley has an eighty-inch bed."

Other Italians came to California to grow radicchio, but most failed—not because they couldn't farm, Lucio said, but because they lacked business acumen. Lucio warned about the perils of being too big in the Valley. About a decade ago, one of the Valley's big growers had offered Lucio and Carlo a partnership. After some soul-searching, the two decided to stay independent. ("We are like Switzerland," he said.) When they declined the partnership offer, the grower threatened to destroy them. After a few anxious years, the big grower gave up on radicchio, even selling his surplus to Lucio and Carlo. "We are committed to radicchio," Lucio said with a princely bravado. "We are a chicory company."

DRIVING AROUND SALINAS, it was hard to imagine how Lucio, Italian sophisticate, gentleman vintner, could possibly be happy here. Salinas seemed like a cross between a Mexican border town and a Chicago suburb, a blur of down-in-the-mouth Mexican restaurants, bail bond places, Bed Bath & Beyonds, and Home Depots. Any concerns for Lucio's well-being were instantly resolved when the mayor and I arrived at his house, up in the hills, about midway between Salinas and Monterey. Lucio's house isn't extravagant, but the location, in an area called Corral de Tierra, is comparable in niceness to the Tuscan hills, Maui, or heaven.

The Treviso was cut and prepped. Shoko was dipping some Chioggia in batter for a tempura. Lucio was sprinkling some radicchio on a pizza. A bowl of Chioggia stood ready for the risotto. There were bottles of white wine from Vignalta, Lucio's vineyard in the Veneto, on the table. Steaks were primed for the grill. Three Brits, produce buyers, also radicchio neophytes, were there as well. Shoko served us white wine. Lucio cued some Italian restaurant–style music (like "Volare"); we grazed around the house; the TV set to an Italian cable station; the Chinese teapots proudly displayed.

It was, no doubt, a wonderful show—the wine, the setting, the chatter (Donohue, hilarious, life-of-the-party type; Lucio, worldly raconteur)—but even in this wine-enhanced splendor, I sensed something was missing. No fire in the belly.

If felt, well, weary. Lucio had been pitching radicchio to the unconverted for years. He would do another variation of the radicchio and romaine show later that week, presenting the "power pairing" concept to Fresh Express. Radicchio at Lucio's, with an obscure journalist and a few Brit produce buyers, was, I suppose, the veggie version of a stump speech before a small crowd of World War II veterans at an American Legion—oh so routine. Even when asked about the Fresh Express pitch—could this be the big break?—Lucio seemed stunningly nonchalant. As for Donohue, he was admittedly distracted by his other job, saying much of his energy was devoted to passing a sales tax increase to pay for more police.

There were four preparations served that night—pizza, tempura, risotto, and the power application, a warm salad of grilled Treviso paired with romaine. There was also some talk about other applications and mayoral power. (When the mayor mentioned radicchio ice cream, Lucio winced. When one of the Brits asked if being mayor of Salinas aided the radicchio effort, Donohue said yes. He joked that he wanted to make radicchio the Official Vegetable of Salinas, but he couldn't, because Salinas, unlike, say, Chicago, had a "weak mayor" form of government. Laughter ensued.)

Here is a highly subjective, wine-impaired account of radicchio night:

- The tempura radicchio—very good, but so was the tempura okra, and so is tempura zucchini, and so are deep-fried white mushrooms, and for that matter, virtually anything deep-fried and battered.

- The radicchio pizza—excellent, the slight bitterness jived well with the cheese, and the white ribbed part of the radicchio seemed to give it a little extra girth, a good mouthfeel. It occurred to me then that radicchio could be among those rare veggies that could carry a pizza. (I'm typically among those troublemakers in group pizza orders who insist on meat.)

- Radicchio risotto—fine. Lucio had selected Arborio, the favored risotto in the Veneto, which I really liked, but the radicchio itself, I didn't really catch it. It seemed like a serviceable alternative to spinach or mushroom risotto, if you wanted to mix things up.

- The power app—the warm salad, grilled Treviso radicchio with romaine hearts. Very interesting. The grilling mollified the bitterness. The leaves of the radicchio were crisp, slightly caramelized, the heart softened. It was a great pairing with the lightly charred, slightly smoky romaine. It definitely intrigued me.

This grilled Treviso in particular merited a repeat, but was this like the bagged salad moment (Kenosha, August 1996) or the fatty tuna epiphany (Bethesda, Maryland, 2004) or the French roast coffee transformation (St. Paul, September 1991) or even the first encounter with moo shu pork (Zion, Illinois, circa 1976)? A moment of rapture, a certainty, a sense of a cataclysmic life-shifting food experience?

No.

As we drove back to the Valley that night, the mayor made the point that radicchio is not necessarily love at first bite. "It takes time to truly appreciate its versatility," he said, reminding me, "it's the thinking man's vegetable."

The Produce Oligarchy: The Genius of Bagged Salad Explained

The Produce Marketing Association Foodservice Expo isn't the granddaddy of produce shows—that would be the Fresh Summit—but it was big: 500 vendors, 1,500 produce hunters, hundreds of different produce products present, a special appearance by Ted Allen of *Queer Eye for the Straight Guy* fame. The big buyers were here (Sysco, U.S. Foodservice). The produce media was out in force: *The Packer, Supermarket News, Americafruit*, and my favorite produce opinionator, Jim "the Perishable Pundit" Prevor.

The main reason I was here: Growers Street was here. The "Foodservice" show, annually held at the Monterey Convention Center, a thirty-minute drive from Salinas, was one of the gatherings of Big Salad. Taylor Farms, Green Giant, River Ranch, Mann Packing, D'Arrigo Brothers Company, plus Fresh Express and Dole, the two agrigiants that single-handedly account for nearly 90 percent of the bagged salad sold in the United States. It was here—or at the other can't-miss events, the Fresh Summit or the United Fresh Produce show—that the Microsofts and Apples of salad unveil their newest products to the market-moving buyers. I also was curious to see a handful of produce wholesalers and importers at the show—companies like Cooseman's and Melissa's and Frieda's—with an industry-wide reputation as "innovators." It was Frieda Caplan who started hawking a small, hairy oddball fruit—known in Asia as the Chinese gooseberry—at produce shows in the 1960s. That was the debut of the previously unknown kiwifruit in North America. For years, fruit and vegetable people have been telling the kiwifruit story as a way of illustrating the potential that exists in the American marketplace for something new.

Coming to the PMA show was, originally, the mayor's suggestion. On the one hand, it was a straightforwardly helpful suggestion in the spirit of his offer to "open up the Valley." On the other hand, it could have some self-interest. "You'll see a lot of things tomorrow," he said, driving back from Lucio's, "but I don't think you'll see anything with the range of applications as radicchio."

Donohue was, I soon started learning, basically right.

The Monterey Conference Center floor was overflowing with fruits and veggies, but it was overwhelmingly status quo, Safeway stuff. Row after row of mesclun mixes, iceberg, romaine hearts, Vidalia onions, tomatoes, apples, oranges, potatoes, pecans, walnuts . . . You could get a prewashed bagged salad in a "new two-pound recyclable clamshell," you could get fruit salads "with 10 percent more mango."

One common tactic: new "applications" for old vegetables. A man in a white chef's hat handed me what looked like a bowl of spaghetti and said "guess what it is?" as I chewed. "Onions!" An apple vendor enthused about the virtues of precut, prepackaged apples. A grape entrepreneur offered his innovation—grapes packaged in a kid-friendly, cartoon-dressed bag. "It's an idea whose time will come." (Big Produce was clearly hungering for a bigger piece of the kids market—envisioning a future where fruits replace candy.) One avocado grower was pitching guacamole as the couch potato food of the future, linking guac to an ABC television show, with the tagline: "Girls Night Out! Stay in. Tune In. Dip in."

Most depressingly, the Valley agrigiants didn't seem to be fighting to find the iPods of the salad greens world. Fresh Express had updated its line of bagged mixes—River Ranch had some mixes. Dole, ditto. Tanimura & Antle had an especially nice-looking "artisan lettuce" line that included three mixes of red and green leaf varieties and Sweet Gem (a variant of Little Gem, Ed Ryder's favorite). As far as I could see, the lone curiosity from the big Salinas companies came from D'Arrigo Brothers, the same family that introduced broccoli to Americans eighty years ago. The D'Arrigos were pitching the "prickly pear," a kind of cactus fruit especially popular in Mexico, where they're often called "tuna."

There were some lesser-known items on the floor. One grower from San Diego had Lilliputian versions of familiar greens like arugula, fennel, and spinach. Melissa's, a Los Angeles wholesaler with a reputation for novelty, didn't have any salad greens, but they were rolling out a line of colored potatoes. Cooseman's, another company known for "new," was on to the microtrend, hawking miniaturized eggplants. A Salinas company specializing in colored vegetables—red corn, multicolored carrots, green cauliflowers—was claiming that "red corn" has 350 percent more antioxidants than yellow corn.

I got excited when I saw the booth for Epic Roots—that's Todd Koons' latest venture. Remember Koons—the hard-to-reach mesclun salad mix innovator? Adding to his Oz-like quality, Koons wasn't personally at the show ("out of the country," a salesperson said) but Epic Roots did have a new product launch for the Monterey show. Did Koons have a new Next Great Green from his global travels?

No. The "new product" was an "application"—mâche with pears.

The PMA Foodservice Expo was not the produce show of my dreams but there was one major breakthrough during the weekend.

For the past year, I'd held a view of bagged mesclun mix history that was Koons-centric—that Koons was the salad boy wonder who somehow figured out a mechanized way of mass-producing the low-growing spring greens and hence made them affordable to the commoner. But in Salinas I started learning that the history of my favorite food innovation was far more complicated. The bagged salad revolution hinged, I learned, not simply on the inherent taste superiority of a well-choreographed mix of tender, sometimes feathery, sometimes spicy baby greens, or even on the ingenious methods needed to harvest and wash these delicate low-growers. No, the bagged salad revolution was, more than anything, about the *packaging* of those greens. It was about the bag.

And this packaging breakthrough, strangely, involved the Whirl-pool Corporation.

It was Dr. Bob Whitaker who first clued me in to the rich history of the salad bag during a conversation in Monterey.

Whitaker, a biologist, and the Produce Marketing Association's in-house science expert, known simply as "Dr. Bob" among PMA people, was telling me about a wide range of issues, such as Web-based traceability (you'll soon be able to trace the origins of a bag of salad online) and the latest produce safety research. Talking about packaging technology (not a particular interest of mine), he used the term "modified atmosphere." I gave him a curious look. "Modified atmosphere took twenty years to develop. That was a game changer," he said, adding, "Bagged salad mixes would have never been possible without modified atmosphere."

The great challenge with pre-cut lettuce—explained to me in a post-harvest physiology primer—is that as soon as you cut lettuce in the field, it starts to respire. It's like a human getting cut. The lettuce uses extra oxygen to speed up metabolism and accelerate its immune system response. For growers, this just means that as soon as you harvest cut lettuce, the clock starts ticking. Refrigeration is one great way of staving off the wilt. For every ten-degree drop, the chemical reactions in a leaf are cut in half. If you keep it cold—refrigerate it in the field and ship it in a refrigerated truck—you can keep the lettuce fresh for a week or so. But that's not much for industrial-scale, shelf-life-sensitive agribusiness. It takes roughly four days to get greens from Salinas to Chicago. Iceberg could handle a two- to three-week trip; by contrast, looseleaf lettuce—no chance.

All of this started changing when a group of scientists at Whirlpool in the early 1960s began examining how various foods, including iceberg lettuce, behaved without oxygen. At the time, Whirlpool had subsidiaries in the food business, including a division focused on produce. Their theory: if you deprive lettuce of oxygen, which feeds the "respire" instinct, it could stay crisp much longer. They put some lettuce leaves under a glass jar, pumped out all the air, and replaced it with carbon dioxide and oxygen. The approach basically worked, except that it was far more nuanced— you couldn't take away too much oxygen, or other bad things would happen. Lettuce also has an anaerobic metabolism, so it could start to ferment. The trick, more or less, was to keep lettuce barely breathing, in a sleeplike state.

The first attempt in 1966 at a bagged salad product—iceberg, endive, and cabbage—was a miserable failure. "You had to perfect the package," Whitaker told me. "If the bag was too airtight, the lettuce would use up the oxygen and ferment. If the bag was too porous, the lettuce would wilt." Early bagged salad adventurers could get a nasty cocktail of surprises—pink lettuce, black slime, and stink.

It took almost twenty years, numerous failed attempts, and the efforts of many polymer chemists and post-harvest physiologists before they figured it all out. Fresh Express started introducing bagged salads to consumers in 1989. That packaged salad mix at your Safeway actually has five to ten distinct layers, each with its own function. It must be the perfect balance. The wrong label ink alone can throw off the balance. As the bag sits in the fridge, the gases are in constant flux—consumed, released, and replaced. Oxygen, nitrogen, and carbon dioxide molecules bond with polymers on one side of the plastic and are released on the other, diffusing from high concentrations to low. Perhaps the most extraordinary feat of all: each type of salad requires its own unique bag because it has, depending on its components (lettuce, radicchio, endive, frisée), its own peculiar atmospheric needs, as vegetables respire at different rates. The end result of all this engineering extended shelf life almost five times. It was *then* that Koons and others filled the void. With longer shelf life, we could finally get an alternative to iceberg.

IF ANYTHING CAPTURED the essence of the PMA show, it was a conversation with yet another bagged salad mix salesman.

Walking a produce show with the mayor of Salinas was, as you might imagine, an overwhelmingly good thing. He knew virtually every vendor, he was chock-full of produce industry lore, he introduced me to many of the Valley's leaders, and he's reliably hilarious. But there was a downside to the mayoral escort—the waiting, while the mayor joked, and answered questions about gang task forces and school funding. During one such wait, a salesman approached me. He glanced at my badge, extended a hand, and started his spiel. I interrupted, and told him my peculiar mission. "I'm not looking for another bagged salad, I'm looking for the *next* spring mix, the next bagged salad revolution."

He laughed. "Well, that's what everyone here wants to know. If you find out, come tell me."

He tried to be helpful, suggesting, "You should probably talk with Todd Koons."

A half hour and a few more bagged salad mix vendors later, I parted ways with the mayor. Genial as always, he offered more contacts in the Valley and urged me to go to Veneto if "you really want to learn about radicchio."

Driving back to the San Jose airport, periodically eating one of the kid-friendly prepackaged grapes that I was told would change kid snacking, I felt somewhat depressed.

After two trips to the World's Largest Fresh Valley, what did I have? There were good things: I had a growing curiosity in heirloom radicchio, an appreciation for how to properly cut Treviso, and a newfound fascination with the Fresh Express salad bag. But I really hadn't found what I wanted: a mind-blowingly good salad green.

4.

Alice Waters' Farmer
(The Weed Period)

ALICE WATERS' FARM IS NEAR THE END of a steep, winding road, on the west rim of the Valley of the Moon. The farmhouse is small and rustic, and its front porch was barren—save for a hoe, a boulder, a barrel, and a picnic table. I expected some cultural markers—a rainbow flag, a Greenpeace sticker, Slow Food Nation—but there was nothing.

There were also no people. After a few minutes of prowling around, I spotted a man on a tractor. With a mop of unruly white hair, blue jeans, flannel shirt, mud-caked boots, and a frosty, unsmiling demeanor, he didn't look like the type who brewed tea for his radicchio or talked about the soul of his chervil. He looked like, well, a regular farmer.

Yet Bob Cannard was, by all accounts, far from regular. And lurking behind his cottage, on the other side of the live oak tree, was one of the most diverse and coveted twenty-five-acre gardens of vegetables and fruit and herbs on planet Earth.

I had come to visit Cannard because of the following realization: Going to Salinas to find the salad of the future was like going to Walmart headquarters to find the future of fashion.

In short, it was profoundly ass-backward—for my peculiar needs. Sure, I saw the wonders of mass production, discovered the genius of packaging, the army of researchers fighting verticillium. But what I really wanted was something different, something more artful, a different kind of innovation.

A recognition of the inherent backwardassness of my initial strategy took months to fully realize, but it was all ultimately triggered by a visit on Saturday, August 29, 2009, to the farmers' market in the parking lot of the Evanston, Illinois, technology development incubator.

AFTER COMING BACK from Salinas, I wanted Treviso radicchio, but none of the grocery stores had it—not the high-end (Fox & Obel), not the big produce specialist (Stanley's), not the store that billed itself as "America's Most European Grocery Store," not even the Italian specialty stores. Aside from the guy at Stanley's, no one had even heard of Treviso or knew that other kinds of radicchio existed. There was an heirloom radicchio option in town: two produce wholesalers who supplied high-end restaurants had it. I wanted Treviso badly, but getting a wholesalers' "box" seemed ridiculous. I'd all but given up on finding a retail source, and was actually considering the wholesaler option when a neighbor told me about a once-a-week farmers' market about a mile from our new house.

The Evanston Farmers' Market was, one could tell instantly, a pretty good one—twenty-plus vendors, a diverse crowd, lively. They had the essentials: nine-grain bread, goat's milk mozzarella, wild mushrooms, grass-fed free-range Piedmontese beef. We were blitzing the options, pleased with our new farm-to-table resources. One vendor had a nice collection of at least four kinds of purple carrots.

I poked inside the Henry's Farm stall briefly—they had an Austrian heirloom lettuce called "Forellenschluss," four kinds of kale, several types of Asian greens. With the two-year-old in tow, we were in a bit of a rush, so I just quickly scooped up two bags of spring mix ($2.50). At home, on closer inspection, I saw this was not an ordinary spring mix—there were a few familiar types of lettuce like red oak and green leaf, some mizuna, tatsoi, arugula. There was a flower, a nasturtium, and lots of unidentifiable greens. Most important: it was one of the most explosively flavorful salad mixes I have ever had.

We came back the following Saturday and, with more time to inspect the Henry's Farm stock, the true magnitude of the find became apparent. There were at least ten different types of lettuce, three or four kinds of cucumbers (Indian, Armenian), at least eight varieties of beans, five different kinds of melons. I was pinching myself. Imagine if you're a book lover, and you find a great independent bookstore five minutes from your house. They had heirloom lettuces I'd never heard of (one was a revival from eighteenth-century France), Asian greens I'd never heard of (komatsu, Shanghai bok choy, Korean shiso).

I asked one of the smiling staffers if somewhere amid this awesomeness they had Treviso radicchio. He shrugged (predictably). Never heard of it. But he told me to "ask Henry" and pointed to a smallish, unshaven man wearing an Afghan-style hat. He was hunkered over a bin of blue potatoes. "Yes, we'll have it in about two weeks," he said, without even lifting his eyes. I was so surprised to hear an affirmative that I had to ask again. "That's *Treviso* radicchio, not Chioggia." "Yes," he said, looking at me. "And we should have Verona, as well."

Thus did Henry Brockman, owner of a ten-acre organic farm in Congerville, Illinois, became my radicchio source.

At last I could test Treviso in the fast-paced, modestly appointed, real-life heat of the Schonwald kitchen. It was late September and Henry said he would have Treviso, Verona, and Chioggia for about two weeks. It was ephemeral, but then again, this was in keeping with Lucio's values. ("Why can't people wait for something that's good?") For two glorious weeks I had a chance to play with radicchio—sautéed radicchio, radicchio risotto, radicchio pizza, radicchio tempura, radicchio on the grill, radicchio cooked at the end of a good day, and after a bad day.

My wife had a strong preference for the milder flavor of Treviso. And even though our heirloom radicchio experience was short-lived, we found our personal "power pairing"—grilled Treviso on burgers, paired with a Sierra Nevada Pale Ale. Kristi and I loved it. I forced radicchio on the knee-jerk skeptics. It worked; grilled radicchio was overwhelmingly popular.

But it was a statistically invalid sample, a mere anecdotal canvassing of friends, nonexperts, hoi polloi. To really understand if radicchio had mainstream appeal, I needed an expert, an impartial, independent produce industry insider.

So I visited Peter Testa, a prominent Chicago produce wholesaler whose family has been in the business since the 1920s. His company serves many of the top restaurants in town; he's a greengrocer to Grant Achatz and Rick Bayless. Testa is not only well respected, he's also famously blunt—for years his weekly market reports posted online included a disclaimer ("the following report may include remarks that may be offensive to some").

When I told Testa about the idea of a chicory revolution, and that radicchio would be the next great green, he shot me an are-you-f'ng-kidding look. Testa, who has been hearing about various next great greens for thirty years, shook his head. "Too bitter. Americans don't like bitter," he said, adding, "It's not like radicchio is new. We've seen it." I clarified, explaining that I meant the milder Treviso, not Chioggia, and also added that it would be grilled. He smiled. "What's Bobby Flay grilling? Radicchio Treviso? Not so much. He's smoking bacon and shit."

But another well-respected greens expert had a totally different reaction. Georgeanne Brennan, who has written more than twenty food books—including *The New American Vegetable Cookbook* and *Great Greens*, with a foreword by Todd Koons himself—is what you might call a leafy greens pundit. She evaluates greens for potential, then writes cookbooks explaining how to use them.

Brennan was extremely enthusiastic about radicchio and the idea of a chicory influx. "There are so many chicories you don't know, but should." As for the bitterness, she was nonplussed: "Americans have a notoriously sweet palate, but as their desire to eat healthier grows, and as they start becoming more adventurous with greens that will change." She predicted that radicchio and other Italian greens like minutina and herbatella could become components of an Italian bagged salad mix. "Most of what we have right now is French. We haven't even begun to explore Italian and Asian mixes."

Prior to her days as a food writer, Brennan was a produce entrepreneur herself—a seed importer. After living in the south of France in the early 1970s, she started Le Marché Seeds, one of the first importers of French seeds, such as mâche and arugula. We talked about the early adopters of her mesclun mix. "It started with a group of innovative farmers, and certain restaurants with innovative chefs. And then it gradually caught on, eventually making its way to the mainstream. There's definitely a trickle-down," she said of the process. "But the first place you'll see it will be with the real pioneers, the people who are always looking for something new."

Alice, Desert Revival, and Vegetable Dreams

If you accept the trickle-down theory of American salad evolution, and if you then attempt to trace that theory literally to its fountainhead, you will arguably come to the Cannard Farm, which is in a place that writer Jack London called the "Valley of the Moon."

The Valley of the Moon, also more boringly called the Sonoma Valley, is, of course, in northern California. Northern California is what you might call the Fertile Crescent of the American salad. "California," the food historian Jonathan Leonard wrote in the 1960s, "is the only place where truck drivers eat fresh salads without fear of being considered effete." The spring green mix, the "salad that changed America," was being served in Bay Area restaurants in the early 1970s. Arugula is believed to have made its American debut at a farm near Bolinas, which is about ten miles from Cannard. Two of the earliest inventions in the salad dressing realm—crab Louis and green goddess dressing—were the inspiration of San Francisco restaurants. California has the farmers' market perfect storm—climate (fifty-week growing season), an audience with the right attitude, scads of food pioneers (farmers, chefs, food intellectuals). Perhaps most crucial to its salad innovator reputation, northern California is home to Alice Waters.

In addition to pioneering California cuisine, and being one of the most visible leaders of the organic and local foods movements, Waters changed the American salad. It was Waters, at Chez Panisse in 1971, who introduced the mad mess of baby greens that is the ancestor of the bagged salad mixes of today. And the reason why this tiny plot, surrounded on all sides by vineyards, on a hilly ridge pocked with lava flow, is of particular interest is because it's the Alice Waters farm. For more than fifteen years she's been calling it "our farm."

Waters' farmer, Bob Cannard, is an organic legend in his own right. In the early 1970s, Cannard, a Pennsylvania native whose family moved west when he was a teen, left the Fresno State agriculture school because of ideological differences. Cannard was anti-pesticide, anti-herbicide, anti–chemical fertilizer, anti–large farm. A few years later he found a small plot in the rugged foothills of the Sonoma Mountains. It's hilly terrain, fine for vineyards, but considered poor farmland. Cannard put his unorthodox views to work. Instead of using chemical fertilizer, he fed his crops volcanic dust, along with seaweed and crushed oyster shells that he gathered on the Sonoma coast. He brewed massive vats of compost that he called "nutrient tea," and he was known to spread eggs and milk and jugs of molasses on his crops. Occasionally he'd even make lavender or rosemary tea to feed them an "energetic aroma." Instead of aiming to expand his twenty or so acres, Cannard stayed small. He practiced low-impact, extremely biodiverse microfarming. He talked about his farming practices in his job as an agriculture instructor at Santa Rosa Community College, and to pretty much anyone else who would listen.

In the 1980s, Waters, who was looking for a farm within a one-hour drive of Berkeley, interviewed several farmers, including Cannard. And thus one of the grand farm-to-table relationships was formed.

Cannard's farm supplies much of Chez Panisse's produce. In the Bay Area, where Waters is regarded with papal reverence, her farmer has, through association, became a minor celebrity himself. Over the years Cannard has supplied Wolfgang Puck and Judy Rodgers and many of the Bay Area's most celebrated chefs. When Odwalla, the juice and smoothie maker, needed a special organic carrot patch, they commissioned Cannard.

Cannard had just finished plowing a field when I arrived. He greeted me expressionlessly, and after leading me silently to his porch, grumbled "I'm a farmer" when I commented that he was working on a Saturday afternoon.

I had come here to ask one question: What are you growing? (Which, by proxy, would reveal what Alice and Wolfgang and Judy Rodgers and all the fastest cats in the salad world wanted.) But before we could talk about the contents of his garden, we had to talk about some other issues, such as volcanic dust fertilizer and the reclamation of the Negev.

What happened is that Cannard spooked me into sycophancy. Cannard is a powerful-looking man in his late fifties with a weathered face and intense blue eyes. He's ruggedly handsome, in the cowboy way. (A few years ago, another organic farmer, when asked about Cannard by a Bay Area weekly, warned other women to "beware of his charismatic power.")

He also has an intimidating, off-the-grid quality—one writer described him as having the eyes of a "nineteenth-century abolitionist." After I sputteringly described my reason for coming—a version of the Georgeanne Brennan Trickle-Down Theory—he just sat silently, hands on knees, staring at the mud on his boots. No response. Unnerved by the long silence, I just started talking, nervously. At some point a question formed, a softball.

"Do you feel vindicated?"

Cannard looked at me, not angrily.

Bob Cannard is among the more vindicated humans alive today, overflowing with "I told you so" cred. He was preaching the organic, local, small farming message to skeptics when Michael Pollan was a turtleneck-wearing creative writing major at Bennington College. Cannard didn't actually form a smile, but he was pleased to talk about ways in which he was proved right. He mentioned that Grimmway Farms, a gigantic grower best known as maker of preprocessed baby carrots, was now experimenting with volcanic dust fertilizer. He pointed out that large growers were adding cover crops, a practice he's advocated for thirty years. He's a microfarmer—who believes like the farmer-poet Wendell Berry that "small is half the battle"—but still he's heartened by the surging interest in organic even if it's driven by industrial-scale organics like Earthbound Farms. The Organic Revolution would, he believed, continue in other areas of food production, a kind of domino effect. "It's beef, it's chicken, it's eggs. It's goats. People care about how food is prepared and what they feed their babies." He paused. "I'm very encouraged by the trend."

Still, it didn't take much—just mentioning "I've spent a lot of time in Salinas looking for the next bagged salad revolution"—to stir the old revolutionary. Mentioning Salinas and bagged salad to Cannard was silly: Salinas is the antithesis of the permaculture microfarm. And bagged salad, as wonderful as it is, is the antithesis of local, seasonal, connecting-humans-to-nature farming. Longer shelf life, thanks to modified atmosphere packaging, means refrigerated trucks can travel farther (more food miles) and burn more greenhouse gases (more global warming). And bagged salad also means that Salinas Valley megafarmers can continue to dominate the small local farmers, further distancing people from their food sources.

Cannard delivered an extended sermon—at times fire and brimstone, at times poetic—about the evils of large-scale agriculture, the ongoing threat of petrochemicals and genetically modified organisms (GMOs), the perils of excessive antibiotic use. He talked about young girls going through puberty at the age of six, and offered a short lesson on tomato economics and a poetic description of something he called "vegetable dreams." All from a guy who had seemed heavy-lidded and listless twenty minutes before.

The tomato economics lesson is something familiar to any member of the Pollan flock. It's the rationale for spending four dollars for a pound of farmer's market tomatoes rather than one dollar for the Safeway tomato. Cannard produces 15 to 20 tons per acre; the big Salinas growers (it's actually not Salinas; the hotter Sacramento Valley is where most tomatoes are grown) can produce four to five times as much—something like 90 tons per acre. One compelling argument, for which there is substantial scientific evidence, is that the natural method is far kinder to the land. Others argue that it reduces food miles to eat locally, that it supports the community to invest locally. But Cannard took another approach.

"Do you want to buy one tomato, fully formed with all the refined essential sugars and compounds, including flavors that give you a burst?" he said. "Or do you want to have five tomatoes that have been commercially produced that have toxic residues and kind of taste like mush? Most people are instinctively choosing the tomato that makes them feel good, aids in their digestion, and causes them to sleep better." He then went on to explain that he believes the value of eating this natural tomato manifests itself at sleep time, producing a happy subconscious state that he calls "vegetable dreams."

Not long after this vegetable dreams talk, and after thinking about what a Cannard heirloom tomato might taste like, I started gazing out at my surroundings. Even from the porch you could see a wildly biodiverse land—row crops of salad greens, persimmon trees, apples, oranges, with oak trees presiding magnificently over it all. It was a rare case where *Edenic* was the spot-on adjective. Admiring the beauty, a question welled up.

"If you weren't here, in farmer heaven, with a fifty-week growing season and a perfect climate, where would you want to farm?"

"The Sahara," he said, curtly and without hesitation.

I looked at him, waiting for the smirk, the chuckle. Nothing. Are you serious?

"I'm dead serious!" he said angrily.

He got off the picnic table and led me over to the other side of the porch. We stopped in front of a boulder. He pulled out a buck knife and started stabbing into the rock. "This is not dead!" he said, as a kind of white talc substance flaked off. "This rock is alive with nutrients. People just don't understand. The desert is not dead, either."

This object lesson (he's a veteran ag instructor, after all) then led to another sermon; this time on how petrochemical overuse and water mismanagement have "totally fucked up" the San Joaquin Valley, as well as some talk about how he has been interested in working on desert revival projects for years. Desert revival was a sore subject. He said he had talked with the Chinese about doing some work in the Gobi Desert near Beijing, but it never happened. ("They're too damned corrupt.") I asked about another source of desert agriculture, the Middle East. "The Israelis? Please, they so fucked up the Negev. That place could be so beautiful. It was BEE-yoo-tee-ful."

It became clear that Cannard would have been willing to talk animatedly about desert reclamation for some time. But during a lull, I tacked back to my more mundane interest. "The important thing is not the varieties," he told me, "it's that people care more about their food source, about how it's prepared, not what it is." He then started patting his shirt for a piece of paper.

"Eggplant and carrots and turnips and chervil and bok choy and tatsoi and rocket and kale and radicchio and cauliflower and curlycress." About a minute into the memory exercise, right after curlycress, he stopped and threw his hands up. "I don't know. I can't keep track of it all. It's like two hundred crops a year."

A long pause. I pressed: "Could you just tell me some of the lesser-known ones?" He tipped his head back and, again, a grumpy roll call.

"Chickweed. Nettles. Amaranth. Cardoon." (When he mentioned cardoon, he turned to me, as if I knew cardoon, "the stems, not the flowers.") "Thistles. There's purslane. We have them in the garden, but most people would classify them as weeds," he said with evident disdain. This "weeds" classification was "ridiculous."

"Purslane grows all over the place, they just pull it out and throw it away. It's a wonderful vegetable."

I asked if any of these so-called weeds could become popular.

"Yes. Absolutely," he said. "You said twenty years or more, didn't you? It takes a while for people to catch on, to learn how to use it . . . There's a lot more people willing to try new things these days. Twenty years ago, there were only a few who would even try rocket [another name for arugula]."

I asked if any of these so-called weeds could be the Next Great Green.

"I just put the stuff out there. I have no idea. If it sticks, it sticks."

The Weed Period and the Greenmarket Fugue

Weeds as the greens of the future?

They take away valuable nutrients from your cherry tomatoes. They mess up your beautiful lawn. They grow at unimaginable rates, costing farmers millions of dollars annually, driving them to use dangerous herbicides. And as if things could get any worse for what the *American Heritage Dictionary* defines as "plants considered undesirable, unattractive, or troublesome," ecologists now often call invasive species simply "weeds."

But there is this other glass-is-half-full view of weeds. "What is a weed?" Ralph Waldo Emerson wrote, "but a plant whose virtues have not yet been discovered."

The Cannard-Emersonian view has, I learned, proved out in the food world. In seventeenth-century France, mâche was dismissed as a "troublesome coarse weed." Two hundred years later the French were calling the beloved green "lamb's lettuce" and Balzac was cooing about it in his novels. More recently, the Jerusalem artichoke, a sunflower species, has made the move to the produce section, rebranded as the "sunchoke." In 2009, the *Wall Street Journal* noted that dandelions, the scourge of suburban lawns, are a fast-growing $2 million-a-year business. Along with dandelions, the *Journal* listed several promising weeds, including two Cannard garden favorites—purslane and thistle—under the headline "The Next Arugula?"

But to me, the most stunning example of weeds-to-table potential came from René Redzepi. The barely thirty-year-old owner of Noma, a restaurant in Denmark, was named Best Chef in the World in 2009 by some of the world's top food pundits, beating out the likes of Thomas Keller, Ferran Adria, and Heston Blumenthal. Redzepi, wunderkind chef, the subject of fawning profiles in every food publication on the planet, is the pioneer of the New Nordic Cuisine, an Alice Waters–esque locavorism applied almost religiously to the natural bounty of Scandinavia. Virtually every profile of Redzepi celebrates his foraging. He scours Copenhagen and environs for forgotten and overlooked ingredients. One of his signature dishes uses scurvy grass, a weed, which he says "is how the Vikings used to get their vitamin C."

After visiting Cannard's farm, and hearing about Redzepi's success unlocking the culinary potential of so-called weeds, my long-dormant fantasy of finding some spectacular, mind-blowing green came alive again. I hungered to taste some of the greens that had captured the fancy of the salad avant-garde.

But there was a problem. It was now December, and I lived in Chicago. As anyone who has attempted an "Eat Local Challenge" here in winter can tell you, it's not easy to find locally grown heirloom tomatoes. It's also not easy to find purslane and thistle and cardoon. It was my first head-on encounter with the privations of seasonality.

During the long, purslane-less winter, I sated my curiosity by spending time on forager websites and bulletin boards, reading tips from forager gurus like Wild Man Steve Brill and Ava Chin, and collecting recipes for dishes like ramp risotto and buttered fiddlehead fern. Amid the plant guides and Euell Gibbons quotes (the author of *Stalking the Wild Asparagus*, aka the wild green eaters' bible), it became clear that the foraging-weed-eating people had some striking similarities to raw-milk people. (Being from a dairy-centric state, where margarine was outlawed until 1967, I was familiar with raw-milky rhetoric.) Like people who talk about unpasteurized milk as being a possible solution to allergies, anemia, hair loss, fatigue, and the Israeli-Palestinian crisis, pro-weed types talk about the miraculous powers and amazing history of greens that are the unfortunate victims of "horticultural snobbery."

Purslane, a native of India, was Gandhi's favorite vegetable. According to the enthusiasts, this member of the Portulacaceae family is a cure for arthritis and inflammation, will lower your cholesterol, and provide more vitamin E than spinach, more beta-carotene than carrots, and more omega-3s than almost any other plant. Amaranth, a member of a family that has 160 genera and 2,400 species (there's always taxonomic detail), can be eaten as a green or a grain, had a great backstory (the Aztecs thought it had supernatural powers and used it in sacrifice rituals, so spooking the Spanish Conquistadors that they banned its use for hundreds of years). And amaranth was said to have "incredible nutritional content" and the ability to catalyze weight loss. Another wild green, nettles, described as being chock full of wonderful health benefits ("more nutritional than kale!"), was apparently so powerfully good that it was also potentially bad: "Don't eat this if you're pregnant," one site warned. "It may cause miscarriage." While some of the health claims are exaggerated, there is evolutionary logic behind the argument. Weeds are survivors, strong plants throbbing with vitality—they're not denatured like their cultivated relatives.

Many of the weed testimonials went beyond health, suggesting that the weeds/foraged greens were also tasteful. "If you like spinach, you'll LOVE amaranth . . . Purslane adds a whole new dimension to summer salads."

IT ROUGHLY PARALLELED the baseball season, starting in early April and ending in mid-October. It involved roughly twenty different greens, cost on average twenty dollars a week. It required some entry-level foraging, but mostly it was dependent on Henry Brockman. There were moments of ecstasy, some sadness, one injury, and a short period that you might call a "greenmarket-induced fugue."

Exhilarating is not a word most people use to describe a tour through the produce section, even a good one. And even though I love a good salad, and my pulse rate increases upon entering Whole Foods, I still regard shopping for kale or lettuce as a tier below searching for ahi tuna or the latest frozen Indian entrées.

But what happened was a palpable shift in attitude. In early spring, bloggers reported that ramps—wild leeks that taste somewhat like onion—spurred a rush at the Madison, Wisconsin, farmers' market. Sold out in fifteen minutes! The news affected me much as reports of impending snowfall might stir a backcountry skier.

After six months of being forced to subsist exclusively on corporate, industrialized, Salinas-controlled greens, I received an email from Henry's Farm. The "Field and Farm Notes" announced that early spring greens were coming. Henry had lovage and sorrel, two greens I had never tried.

Thus began the weekly suspense. What would Henry have this week? Henry's Farm Notes email would typically come on Thursday afternoon. Was it good news or bad? Once he had a photo spread of a new find—something called Hopi Red Dye Amaranth. Another time he reported the arrival of his first crop of radicchio.

Yet it could also be gloom: an August email announced that most of his heirloom lettuce seeds didn't germinate. Bad weather. Too much rain and a heat wave. It was crushing. Now, many of you are surely going to say, "Wake up, idiot, this is how farming has worked for like ten thousand years." But keep in mind, I come from bagged-salad-eating, microwave-dependent people and had been largely detached from seasonality. It was exhilarating to simply encounter the ephemeral nature of nature. I wasn't used to not-having. One day, after resigning myself to a puntarelle-less summer, I found a farm in northern Indiana, Green Acres, that was growing it. A happy morning. Another time I arrived at the farmers' market only to see that the last of Henry's purslane was gone. (Note to self: arrive at farmers' markets early.)

The other obvious source of excitement was the next step. You come home with the loot—the elusive southern Italian chicory, the freshly harvested lamb's-quarters—then there's that now-what moment. You could treat it like your green leaf lettuce—eat it straight up, with some olive oil and coarse ground pepper. You could pair it as part of a spring mix. And then there's the sautée-ing, the boiling, the pickling, the baking, and, having been through the radicchio period, the grilling. When totally flummoxed by what-to-do-with-this-lovage, there's the gurus. Deborah Madison, Georgeanne Brennan? Is there anything in Alice's oeuvre? How about the Wildman (Steve Brill)?

All of this was, of course, a mere prelude to the ultimate excitement. It wouldn't be enough to rely on my taste alone; a green had to be presented to a focus group. I had some difficulty finding, in my small circle, people ready to try sautéed amaranth or nettles and potato soup on short notice. So the focus-grouping relied heavily on one particular person: my wife. Kristi had the right attitude—adventurous, open-minded, a willingness to drop whatever she was doing to test milkweed or a French merlot lettuce "for research."

The weed/foraged greens search was a happy time. I loved trolling around the forest preserve with a copy of *Stalking the Wild Asparagus* or a *Field Guide to Edible Plants*. I loved learning about milkweed. I loved feeling like I could know the earth, and survive on wild greens someday. I loved going to the Evanston Farmers' Market, or the Green City Farmers' Market or the Madison Farmers' Market—scouring the stalls, with that lingering possibility of finding something new. I loved trying to figure out what to do with a green (stems? leaves?).

Purslane—after my first encounter, I thought I'd found it. The leaves had a mild flavor and great texture, and it had an unusual fatty quality, a density rare among salad greens. It made a wonderful base for a salad—it made a wonderful pesto, better than basil-based pesto.

Lamb's-quarters? Forget about spinach; it's just as good, and more healthful. I was wild about the whole universe of Asian greens and herbs—shiso was my favorite. It seemed to have miraculous properties to energize anything. Kristi seemed to share in the joy of this greens adventure.

Seemed—that is key. In retrospect, things started turning sour after the stinging nettles incident. It was August. I had returned from the Evanston Farmers' Market with a good haul. My fateful gaffe: in the mad mess of heirloom lettuce and chicory varietals, I hadn't properly announced—or labeled, or segregated—the stinging nettles.

We'd tried them before—they're tasty, excellent cooked vegetables, a fine spinach alternative, but, true to the stinging part of the name, you must cook them to disable the tiny, nearly invisible hairs, which are like hypodermic needles. (The generic name for nettles comes from the Latin word *uro*, which means "I burn.") To the naked eye they look like an ordinary, nonstinging green. Needless to say, Kristi, well trained in the greens-testing ways (eat it raw first), dug into the heap, encountered the nettles, and, as predicted by forager gurus, suffered redness and burning on her hands for several days. She also had one other negative reaction. Sorrel, sometimes called "sour grass," has a stunningly pungent taste, bordering on vinegary. It was the first time I have ever seen a bed of salad greens provoke a gagging reflex; we tossed out a perfectly nice salad mix for fear of sorrel.

Still, it wasn't until the end of the season that I detected an attitude change. Even though we had an overstuffed crisper (CSA greens, foraged finds), I had to go the farmers' market—research, after all. And could this be our last chance at Treviso? On the way to the market, I asked Kristi if she had any particular requests. She said, wearily, "Greens that I have heard of."

I had been foisting greens on her all summer, and she had gamely tried them, so some weariness was not surprising. But the negative reaction led to a series of follow-up questions, which led to a series of admissions: she didn't like lamb's-quarters, didn't care for amaranth.

At first I blamed myself—overexposure? My own lack of culinary skill? I was no René Redzepi. But I started thinking about her reaction. And it dawned on me that the only green she'd really shown genuine, cheerful enthusiasm for was Treviso—grilled. Later I asked her point blank if she thought any of the many greens we had eaten had breakthrough potential. "Purslane, maybe."

She looked at me. "Do you *really* like amaranth?"

THIS WAS A WAKE-UP MOMENT. And ultimately, after some reflection, some consultation with my wife, some retesting of amaranth and lovage, I started recognizing that, indeed, there was a problem.

I was so excited by my first meaningful experience with foraging, my first real sense of connectedness with the land. I wanted so badly to believe in one of Henry's heirloom revivals, or, better yet, in some plant sprouting from a sidewalk crack. I wanted so badly to find something, something wonderful lurking in the minor leagues of salad, that I had lost sight of my original aim.

I needed to go back to my pre-Cannard, pre-Lucio self. Meat-headedly simplistic, food-source and food-mile ignorant, the naive bagged salad eater looking for taste, first and foremost, and broad consumer appeal. What follows is a highly subjective attempt to summarize the Summer of Greens Exploration—with an eye to the ur-question: What might make it to the big time—i.e., Safeway?

The Next Great Green?

Purslane. Of all the "weeds" being rediscovered by foragers these days, the one that appears to have the mark of greatness is *Portulaca oleracea*, or purslane. Purslane has great flavor and texture. It's easy to prepare (mix it with lettuce and sea salt), it's popular with chefs, it's sufficiently different. But probably the biggest reason it's destined for Safeway: health. Gandhi's favorite green has six times as much vitamin A as spinach and seven times more beta carotene than carrots. In short, purslane seems fated for "next super food" billing.

The Radicchios. Grilled radicchio—Treviso, when available—became a favorite at my house. Even my initially radicchio-phobic step-daughter was won over by the less bitter taste of grill-enhanced radicchio. Some of Treviso's relatives (particularly Castelfranco, potentially the world's most beautiful salad green) deserve more space in the produce section. Will it revolutionize the American salad? Will Lucio and Carlo go down in the annals of salad history right next to Todd Koons? Probably not. But as Donohue pointed out—during my second visit, during a moment of radicchio realism—the red chicory might not become a romaine or iceberg rival, but it could at least become more like artichoke: that is, a higher-volume, second-tier vegetable. And a Whole Foods with affordable and accessible Treviso and Castelfranco sounds good to me.

The Central Asian Mix. I never got a chance to try a Central Asian mix, but I did discover the dizzying world of possibilities (Asian greens, French and Italian heirloom lettuce, chicories, mustards). Henry Brockman's mesclun mix, drawing on his vast catalog of greens, made all other mixes I had tasted previously seem bland and flavorless and limp. Encouraging message: There is limitless potential for continual improvement and novelty within the salad-mix genre.

Shiso. Shiso, a relative of mint, whose leaves look unsettlingly like stinging nettles, pops up at American sushi restaurants. It's used to wrap raw fish and to inhibit bacterial growth. But outside of sushi land, it's not well known. Fortunately, Henry, who lived in Japan and is married to Hiroko, grows several shisos (green, purple, Korean). Shiso has so many applications beyond fish wrap. It brightens a salad, it energizes an ordinary chicken dish. It lifts a soggy salad, or a pitiful hot dog. I came to describe shiso as a kind of turbocharger. In Japan, shiso's homeland, there is even a shiso-flavored Pepsi.

Colored Carrots. Put your money on colored carrots—if you're looking for a safe bet on what will be new in the produce section in the next decade. You can already find colored carrots at most farmers' markets. The reason colored carrots are certain to take over Walmart is not simply because they look cool (they do) or even because they taste different (they don't). Like purslane, it's because of health. Each colored carrots does a different, good thing. For instance, yellow and orange carrots have beta carotene—good for eyes. Red carrots are full of lycopene, the heralded antioxidant in tomatoes. Purple carrots have a whole other set of pigments called anthocyanin.

"IT'S ABOUT ONE OF THE HAPPIEST DEVELOPMENTS of our time, a quantum leap forward in food choice, food quality, and culinary sophistication in America."

That's how the writer David Kamp described his book *The United States of Arugula: How We Became a Gourmet Nation*.

That's more or less how I felt after spending several months in the salad universe—even before I started investigating the eight-hundred-pound gorilla in the future of produce.

I never quite had a second bagged salad moment, but I'm certain that the next twenty-five years will be, for salad lovers, a wondrous time.

There are two reasons for my optimism.

First, there's a whole culture of adventurers, born out of the small farm and local foods movements, allied with crazy chefs, scouring the flora of the earth for better flavors and more complexity. René Redzepi, the Danish chef who pillages Scandinavia for sea buckthorn and scurvy grass, might strike some as the type of culinary stunt artist that only the elite foodie could appreciate. But thirty years ago, Alice Waters served a mesclun salad that was disparaged by many as "weeds." In other words, what may seem charmingly baroque today could be the salad of the future. My original fantasy of eating some Afghan blue-green lettuce is not just plausible—it seems inevitable. The only flaw in my dream: it's not some obsessed scientist searching the steppes of Afghanistan for an elusive green, it's an obsessed foodie.

Although my search focused on my peculiar interest in salad greens, this explosion of variety is rippling throughout the produce section. There are farmers specializing in introducing heirloom varieties of dates. Farmers trying to figure out how to bring us more types of mushrooms. The proliferation of new citrus varieties is mind-boggling.

The second reason why greens lovers should be excited about the future? The agrigiants in the World's Largest Fresh Valley. These are fractious times in food politics. Great efforts are being made to create a Hatfield versus McCoy situation, small farm versus big, local and organic versus chemicalized and corporate, Alice Waters versus Fresh Express. But the trickle-down seems to be working fine.

The small farms are the first place you'll see the greens of the future. And if fiddlehead ferns and ramps and amaranth prove wildly popular, if Americans can't live without them for a season, the Salinasans will figure out how to grow it, scale it, bag it, and keep it shelf-stable for an ever-increasing time. Modified-atmosphere packaging is improving—biodegradable packages are on the horizon. Packages designed with antimicrobial agents to reduce the risk of E. coli are coming. The convenience salads of the future will not be limited to just leafy greens: they'll have cucumbers and tomatoes and protein.

In short, both small farms and multinational corporations are contributing to a future of safer, better, more diverse salads.

5.

The Culinary Potential
of Frankenfood

THE BETH EMET SYNAGOGUE BULLETIN BOARD DOESN'T ordinarily attract my attention, let alone send me into an angry, expletive-strewn rant about food production. But one spring day, as I was picking up my three-year-old daughter from preschool, I spotted, not far from the rabbi's office, in a rack filled with the usual pamphlets (camps for Jews, fun things for elderly Jews, plays of interest to Jews), an anomalous brochure.

It proclaimed in bold letters "Unintended GMO Health Risks." Above the text, a cartoon-like Casper the Friendly Ghost character, with a smile and fork, added "Healthy Eating Starts with

No GMOs." I scanned the contents: some do-you-knows about health risks associated with genetically engineered foods. Organ damage, sterility in animals, allergies, and other unknown consequences. The brochure was produced by the Campaign for Healthy Eating.

I stuffed it in my pocket, greeted my daughter, smiled, said good-bye to the other parents, and as soon as I got into the hermetically sealed comfort of our Subaru Outback, I thrust the brochure in front of my wife, and said, "Why would Beth Emet promote this shit?"

My wife glanced at the pamphlet and said nothing.

"Organ damage? Sterility in animals? This is utter nonsense."

Again, no discernible spousal reaction.

"You know, genetically engineered foods are kosher."

We drove quietly, and I stewed, and started envisioning an encounter with the rabbi, in which I would point out that Beth Emet has a soup kitchen that feeds hungry people with nutritional deficiencies, and that by giving voice to this anti-GMO nonsense you are effectively perpetrating an idea that is thwarting a technology that could save millions of people from starvation.

The Beth Emet Incident occurred six months into my examination of how genetic engineering might impact the salad bar of 2035. When I started this project, I had a healthy suspicion of GMOs. I thought the idea of transferring genes between sexually incompatible species was creepy, and I was deeply troubled by the notion that large multinational corporations were patenting and profiting from genes.

But after my biotech immersion, I found myself intentionally redirecting conversations with friends and family to agricultural biotechnology (I don't call it Frankenfood anymore), so that I can say things like "Vitamin A–enhanced golden rice could save half a million people from blindness each year."

I didn't totally fall under the spell of Monsanto—it's not an unequivocal embrace. And although my attitudes change, I do not deviate from the mission. We make a brief detour for some lobbying work, but then resume our look at the Whole Foods salad bar of 2035.

Frankenfood City, USA

To the naïve mind, unfamiliar with the frontier of American agricultural research, Davis, California, might seem an unlikely ground zero for Frankenfood making.

It's a leafy, mellow college town, full of bookstores and coffee shops, the American Bicycle Hall of Fame, and one of America's best farmers' markets (yes, they rank farmers' markets, too). Davis was one of the first Nuclear-Free Zones (two years before Berkeley). And the city has famously built special tunnels so toads wouldn't be squished crossing a highway. But in spite of the hippie Berkeley-Boulder vibe, America's most bike- and toad-friendly city is also probably home to more plant geneticists with gene-splicing skills than any other city in the United States and, quite possibly, the world.

And it's Davis that's home to two of the most important sites in the history of genetic engineering.

The Plant Transformation Facility at the University of California–Davis has been the scene of more than 15,000 "transgenic events," which is the term molecular biologists use when they blast DNA from one life-form into another. In room 192 of Robbins Hall, a brick building not far from the student union, thousands of microscopic plantlets grow in Petri dishes bathed in pink and fluorescent blue light.

Here molecular biologists can mix what were previously sexually incompatible species together using a gas-pump-like tool called the Helium Particle Delivery System. Using bullets (literally) made out of gold, they fire genes from one species into another in a bombardment chamber. The Davis lab has given birth to grapes spiked with jellyfish, tomatoes spiked with carp, transgenic squash, transgenic carrots, transgenic tomatoes.

The other hallowed spot in genetic engineering history, an innocuous office building about a ten-minute drive from Robbins Hall, is the birthplace of the most audacious plant in the history of high-tech plants. Among biotech people and anti-biotech people, this plant, a tomato, needs no introduction. The so-called Flavr Savr was supposed to be the game changer. It came with Bagged Salad Revolution–like promise—longer shelf life, better yield, and better taste. Calgene, the company that created the Flavr Savr, claimed it could bring "backyard flavor" to the supermarket tomato. Achieving "backyard flavor" in an industrial-scale, California-grown tomato has long been one of the Holy Grails of the $4 billion–plus tomato industry. During the pre-tomato launch hype-a-thon, Roger Salquist, the president of Calgene, claimed that genetic engineering could not only bring us the tomato of our childhood dreams, but also remake the taste of the tomato, tailored to our every desire. "Eventually we're going to design acidic tomatoes for the New Jersey palate and sweet tomatoes for the Chicago palate."

The Flavr Savr turned out to be the Edsel of the produce world, a spectacular failure not just for Calgene, but for the whole biotech industry. This purportedly longer-shelf-life tomato became the lightning rod for much of the anti-GMO movement. People learned about other transgenic crops—a potato with a chicken gene, tobacco with a firefly gene, and, perhaps most notoriously, a tomato with an Arctic flounder gene, which provided an image for a Greenpeace anti-GMO campaign. NGOs cried foul. Consumers were alarmed. It was an op-ed about the Flavr Savr where the term *Frankenfood* first appeared. As for the tomato's taste, most reports said that far from achieving backyard flavor, it was not that great.

By 1997, supermarkets stopped stocking the tasteless tomato. The Flavr Savr was a financial disaster for Calgene.

But that was almost fifteen years ago.

One fall day, across campus from the Helium Particle Delivery System, I went to visit Kent Bradford, the director of UC Davis' Seed Biotechnology Center and presumably among the best-positioned people at Davis to answer my burning question:

Whatever happened *after* the Flavr Savr?

Genetic engineering didn't stop with the Flavr Savr debacle. As anyone who has watched *Food, Inc.* or *The Future of Food* by Deborah Koons Garcia (Jerry Garcia's widow) can tell you, the use of GMOs has exploded. Many genetically engineered foods can be found throughout our food supply. Genetically modified soybeans and canola dominate the market—which means that most processed food, everything from your spaghetti to your Snickers bar, has GMOs. More than 90 percent of American cotton and 80 percent of corn crops come from GM seed. All of these crops, though, are what are called "commodity crops." They're not what you pick up at your local greengrocer. They're industrial crops, secondary ingredients. Not what interested me.

What I wanted to know is what was happening with the tomato with the flounder gene, especially the quest to achieve "backyard flavor"? And what I couldn't get out of my head was this claim that tomatoes could be engineered for precise tastes—"acidic tomatoes for the New Jersey palate and sweet tomatoes for the Chicago palate."

I had searched for some signs of genetically engineered fruits and vegetables aimed at consumers, but there wasn't much. Most Hawaiian papayas, it turns out, are genetically modified (for disease resistance), but they've been around for fifteen years. A team of Israelis married two sexually incompatible plants—a lemon basil plant with a cherry tomato—and it impressed a group of taste testers. But I learned that tomato wasn't heading to market anytime soon—it was a mere test. One day I found something online about a biotech company rumored to be working in "stealth mode" on something called the "applesteak," billed as the first ever plant-animal ("it would combine the nutritional profile of beef with the low cost and wide appeal of the common apple," the article said). After two minutes of excitement, I discovered that it was an Internet hoax.

What was going on? Did they just stop working on "sweet tomatoes for the Chicago palate"? Wouldn't the Flavr Savr creators be hell-bent on redemption, going back to the bench to try again? Or did everything just stop?

That's why I had come to the UC Davis Department of Plant Sciences, to visit a genetic engineering insider.

Strangely, Bradford, a tall, genial Texan, who has been a professor at Davis since the early 1980s, shared my curiosity about the post–Flavr Savr world—he just had a different way of explaining it. "Yes," he chuckled. "Where are all these output traits?" (Input traits are breederspeak for what's so often critical to agriculture—disease resistance, insect resistance, adaptability to particular environments. An output trait is breeder parlance for what I was looking for—traits that improve taste and texture, traits that could change the dining experience of the yuppies of the future.)

Bradford and some Davis colleagues had observed that almost twenty years after the biotech revolution began, there were few signs of any "Second Generation" crops. The First Generation was the commodity crops from the giant seed companies—soybean, maize, cotton, canola, sugar beets. But Bradford expected that after the first wave of insect- and pest-resistant crops proved their worth, the next wave would come, and it would be more consumer focused—that is, better tomatoes, tastier lettuce. But biotech specialty crops (that's the ag scientist term for produce) hadn't appeared. In fact, a GMO specialty crop hadn't been commercialized since 1998. Even Bradford, a longtime biotech believer, considered, "Maybe the genes weren't working?"

Bradford's initial hypothesis was that what he calls "the pipeline" had dried up—that spooked by fears of a consumer backlash, scientists had simply stopped trying to create tomatoes for the Chicago palate.

A few years ago, Bradford and his collaborator Jamie Miller set out to find out "what was going on" with bioengineered specialty crops. Using a simple methodology, they surveyed the leading plant science journals and tracked GM crop field trials—all subject to government regulation—from 2003 to 2008. Searching for citations related to specialty crops, they found that research not only had never stopped but was thriving. "There was research on forty-six different species," he said. "More than three hundred traits were being tested." A lot of it was on input traits (disease, weed resistance), but breeders had also experimented with output traits. "It was happening at the research level, but it just didn't move to the next step. It just stopped there."

There was an obvious explanation, Bradford said, sighing. "It was regulatory."

Post–Flavr Savr, in response to consumer concerns about transgenic breeding, a regulatory process was created that treated genetically modified foods differently than conventionally bred crops. If you have an Ed Ryder–bred iceberg lettuce, using classic plant-breeding techniques (crossing, back-crossing), the assumption is that the resulting lettuce is safe. There's no requirement for pretesting. You just introduce the product into the market.

But with GMOs, Bradford said, the attitude was "it's guilty until proven innocent." A genetically engineered crop must pass review by the USDA, Environmental Protection Agency, and Food and Drug Administration before it is commercialized. The cost could range from $50,000 to tens of millions to win regulatory approval. For every "transgenic event," the genetic engineer must show exactly what genes went into the plant, how they function, and then prove how the plant makeup has been altered. That research is costly. So is plant storage, oddly enough. Once a transgenic creation is spawned at the Plant Transformation Facility, it is whisked to the UC Davis Controlled Environment Facility, a sort of supermax for plants, where it will stay in a tightly secured warehouse. Or they'll be airmailed to some other place, where they'll live out their lives in another intensely biosecure environment. The process is costly and time-consuming, which partly explains why biotech crop development is largely in the hands of the agribusiness giants, the Monsantos, Syngentas, and Bayer CropSciences of the world—who have the resources to undertake the process. With such high approval costs, big companies have favored commodity crops with market potential for hundreds of millions in sales, not tens of millions.

To illustrate this point about why bioengineered specialty crops haven't appeared—and hence no glow-in-the-dark arugula—Bradford told me a short story about a tomato. About a year earlier, Bradford and other UC Davis breeders had cooked up a way to challenge the status quo.

They would genetically engineer an heirloom tomato.

This strikingly oxymoronic idea was devised partly to create a kind of forbidden fruit. Bradford knew that the people who most fiercely oppose genetic engineering are also the people who often covet heirloom tomatoes. They go to farmers' markets, buy organic food, and their hearts race when they see yellow and pink Brandywine tomatoes. A Davis geneticist had identified a gene, in another tomato, the Red Sun, that could solve one of the biggest problems anyone who has tried to grow a Brandywine knows—they're vulnerable to nematodes, tiny plant parasites. The reason why lots of farmers abandoned Brandywine generations ago—why they're called heirlooms, and why they sometimes cost four dollars a pound—is that, among others things, the nematode weakness often kills them. "It was easy to solve this. We had the gene . . . We would simply drop in this one trait, and then"—he snapped his fingers—"we would say, 'Here's your Brandywine tomato. Do you want to stick with your anti-GM thing, or do you want this tomato?'"

Bradford explained that, even more important, this genetically modified Brandywine had another virtue: It's not interspecies. You don't have to use genetic engineering to pull traits from bacteria or viruses or Arctic flounder. You can also use it to do the same things you could do in traditional plant breeding—only faster. "All this was doing was moving a single gene from one tomato to another tomato. We thought it would be the easiest thing to move through regulatory."

But then Bradford shrugged and explained that even with the minimal requirements—and the possible upside—they ended up scrapping the idea. "It was just too expensive. It wouldn't have been millions but it would have cost hundreds of thousands at least (storage costs, research, lawyering)."

Bradford's tale about the demise of the genetically engineered heirloom tomato was intended to function as a depressing parable about the purgatory that much of the ag-biotech world is in—they have the technology, it's been vetted by the scientific establishment, yet most of the work is for naught, left languishing in the pages of plant science journals.

We talked about the reasons for what he calls "the bottleneck." Bradford painted an upside-down picture—it was NGOs such as Greenpeace and the Union of Concerned Scientists that were the boogeymen. Andrew Kimbrell—the crusader, one of the good-guy stars in the *Future of Food* documentary—was fighting technologies that could save lives. Big Organic, a $20 billion industry, had a vested interested in stopping GMOs. The Europeans were also a problem. Bradford rolled his eyes at the mention of the notoriously anti-GMO French. "I've been to a French cheese market. And you say you're afraid of eating anything strange? I'm sorry."

After some ventilating about fungal cheese-eating anti-GMO Europeans, Bradford brightened. He had a possible solution.

"Three words. Biotech and sustainability. Biotech and sustainability."

It was the genetically engineered heirloom strategy again.

Bradford's idea, which sounded like the work of some James Carville of biotech, was that the environmental virtues of genetic engineering will sway the hearts and minds of Prius drivers in San Francisco and Berlin.

Bradford suggested that organic and genetic engineering should *not* be viewed as enemies. In fact, he said, back in 2000, when the USDA was developing the National Organic Program standards (the NOP is like the kosher law of organic; defining what is and isn't organic), the first draft did not prohibit genetically modified foods. But then activists launched an anti-GMO campaign, flooding the USDA with a tidal wave of letters—275,026, to be exact. The USDA then determined that genetically modified organisms would not be included under the standard for organic produce. Being deemed unkosher in the organic world is a hard stigma to overcome. GMOs are thought by many to be the antithesis of environmental responsibility.

But Bradford thought that that perception should—and could—change. "Biotech and sustainability. If we could just get those three words out there . . .

"Pam's book," he said, "it's the message we really want to get out. It's starting to get through. You've read it?"

I nodded. I had read Pam's book—sort of.

How I Learned to Love Frankenfood: The Revelatory Text

She's into yoga. She's in a writing group. Her children were midwifed by a former Buddhist priest who manages a food co-op. She drinks chardonnay and vacations in Tahoe and hangs out with eco-conscious lawyers from Marin County. She's married to an organic farmer.

And she's a genetic engineer.

The basic gist of this seeming paradox—yoga-loving, soy-milk-chugging northern California stereotype who believes that the slicing and dicing of genes can save the world—was apparent in the Lame Read.

By Lame Read, I mean the sort of read that a freshman might do two hours before an exam. Veering into the world of biotechnology, with its own lingo (molecular markers and base pairs), I needed a source sensitive to the questions of laypeople, and in the search for a genetic engineer who spoke English I discovered Pam Ronald. *Slate* ran a piece about her book, *Tomorrow's Table.* I got it from the library, blitzed it. It included definitions of terms such as *gene.* It seemed accessible. I queried her.

We talked. And it was enormously embarrassing. Ronald, who is a professor of plant pathology at UC Davis, is a geneticist whose research is primarily focused on rice, specifically, developing flood-tolerant rice that can help feed people in poverty-stricken, flood-prone places like Bangladesh, where the average salary is a dollar a day. I was interested in what kinds of tasty greens might show up in the Whole Foods produce section in twenty-five years. A dissonance became apparent quickly. Ronald pointed out, not impolitely, that what I was looking for would impact the wealthiest 2 percent of the population. Not her specialty. This was an awkward moment. I then qualified, saying it was actually not Whole Foods that I was looking at, but "more like Safeway." She was perfectly nice, offered a few suggestions, tried her best to help my quest for genetically modified yuppie greens.

A few months after this talk, and after visiting Davis (and not seeing Ronald in person), I was eating a whole wheat bagel and drinking hazelnut coffee at a Panera Bread in Wilmette, Illinois, when I began my second read of her book. I remember the circumstances exactly because it was one of those handful of reading experiences in my adulthood that was a consciousness changer.

Tomorrow's Table is a peculiar book—it's part narrative, part textbook, part travelogue. At times it gets stiffly scientific, yet it can also be stunningly personal. It has two authors. It's constantly disrupted by these lengthy sidebars and graphs. It has ten recipes—some of the most ordinary stuff possible (cornbread and oatmeal), but also there's Sticky Mutant Rice with Genetically Engineered Papaya and a ten-step guide to "Isolating DNA from Organic Strawberries." (All you need is a Ziploc bag, some organic berries, and some ice-cold ethanol.)

The book's core argument is not really that new. Since the 1970s, biotech proponents have been telling us that genetic engineering could reduce the use of chemicals in agriculture—fewer herbicides, fewer pesticides, fewer bactericides, fewer nematocides.

But *Tomorrow's Table* is conspicuously different. We've heard about biotech ad nauseam from the scientists, agri-multinationalists, and the government, but this pitch is coming from the tofu-eating, writers'-group-going Ronald and her husband, Raoul Adamchak, formerly a partner of of Full Belly Farm, one of northern California's most-celebrated organic farms. Yes, Adamchak, who teaches organic farming at UC Davis and formerly served as head of California Certified Organic Farmers, is on board with GMOs. This is an organic farmer who says that he doesn't think organic alone can feed the world, and who suggests that if Rudolf Steiner, the nineteenth-century German ecologist, a godfather of the organic movement, were alive today he might embrace genetic engineering "as a sort of biodynamic, homeopathic cure." That's a head turner.

That's a head turner because many people, *particularly* the hard-core organic, have serious worries about GMOs. Some think that artificially transformed genes open up a Pandora's box of environmental problems. Others fear that GMO crops pose myriad human health risks, such as increased allergens, new toxins in the food chain, and the possibility that bacteria in our guts could pick up antibiotic-resistant genes found in many GM foodstuffs.

Given the widely held concerns about GMOs, much of *Tomorrow's Table* is devoted to countering fears.

The Ronald-Adamchak thesis is that there is a false, sensationalized dichotomy that misleads people into demonizing GMOs. Ronald points out that the Mesopotamians were altering the genetic makeup of wheat ten thousand years ago when they crossed two plants, and notes that the genes she's moving around in her lab are not some new, different material—they're made of exactly the same chemical building blocks that we eat every day. "They're the same components that the Buddha ate twenty-five hundred years ago."

But the genetically modifying Mesopotamians couldn't breed Arctic flounder into their wheat.

The technology in Ronald's lab—using genomic knowledge, agrobacterium, and molecular markers—doesn't just make things more efficient, it also opens up a whole universe of interspecies breeding, a realm that many fear, myself included. On this radioactive issue of interspecies potential, Ronald's counter is basically that, again, there's a false dichotomy. Genetic engineering is a process, and just like conventional agriculture, it's a process that can be used safely or unsafely. "It's not the process that's bad or good," Ronald says. "It's the product."

Ronald has a similar response to another widely cited reason to fear Frankenfood: it's a tool of The Man. In a scene from *Tomorrow's Table*, where she's driving to a yoga retreat in Sonoma, Ronald gets into a conversation with the manager of her local food co-op, addressing the concern that multinational biotech companies like Monsanto and Bayer CropScience and Syngenta will own patents on every ear of corn and head of lettuce on earth. Ronald acknowledges that many people just don't feel comfortable with Monsanto, maker of Agent Orange and DDT, dominating their food supply, and that many folks are concerned that the GMO business is nothing more than a big corporate grab. Here again she claims that this argument is a caricature. She asks her co-op friend if she'd like GMOs better if she knew their history—the early days when non-profit partnerships and university researchers were helping small farmers and addressing humanitarian problems. A university scientist named Dennis Gonsalves, she later tells us, got a $60,000 public grant and went on to develop a papaya variety, the Rainbow, that's credited with saving the Hawaiian papaya industry. Instead of licensing his disease-resistant papaya to a seed company, and making millions in royalties, Gonsalves, a Hawaii native, simply released the seeds for free.

Not surprisingly, a sizable chunk of *Tomorrow's Table* focuses on the almighty question: Is this stuff safe? Ronald can be talking-pointy, noting that we've been eating GM products for years (it's in 70 percent of processed foods) and there's not a single reported instance of health problems or harm. She points to exhaustive scrutiny by scientific bodies, such as the National Academy of Sciences and the British Royal Society: They have studied GMOs for a quarter of a century and have concluded that biotech crop modification is safe; no more dangerous than other methods. She counterattacks. *Seeds of Deception*, an anti-biotech activist favorite, charges that GMOs cause health problems such as sterility, endocrine disruption, and mood swings. Ronald says that author Jeffrey Smith is a member of Iowa's Natural Law Party (translation: kook) who has no scientific training and who bases many of his claims on anecdotal evidence.

But undoubtedly the most powerful part of Ronald's defense of GMOs—a kind of thunderous closing argument—is the highly personal revelation of her miscarriage.

Yes, Ronald describes how she carefully avoided risky foods when she was pregnant with her first child—even gave up eating her beloved raw cookie dough. But as cautious as she was, her child was stillborn because of an unpreventable umbilical cord accident. It was a less than 1 percent chance. While this is a stretch from the world of flood-tolerant crops, her point is that you can't *totally* eliminate risk. There is some risk inherent in the essentials of life. One of the issues that frustrates biotech people is what some call a "zero-tolerance" application of the precautionary principle—that's the precept that an action should not be taken if there is any uncertainty. Of this Ronald concludes: "In the end we can only gather the most information from the most reliable sources and make the best choice possible. I know that GE [genetically engineered] crops currently on the market are no more risky to eat than the rest of the food in our refrigerator."

Ultimately, the stunning wager of *Tomorrow's Table* is this: Ronald and Adamchak are basically saying that if we can get over this stigmatization of GMOs—if we can take a science-based, rational, pragmatist view and see that genetic engineering and organic farming are not mortal enemies—then we can do something that's really never been achieved before in human history: feed the world and save the planet.

Crop scientists figured out half of this equation in the 1960s. A young agronomist and former wrestler named Norman Borlaug bred wheat with a thicker stem and bigger seed heads. His innovation increased yield by a staggering 30 percent—turning once-famished Mexico into a net exporter of wheat. Borlaug then shifted his work to Asia, where many were predicting a future of catastrophic famines. His crop improvements are estimated to have saved hundreds of millions of lives. He won the Nobel Peace Prize. He inspired a legion of idealistic agricultural scientists who fanned out across the globe to vastly increase productivity in what was known as the "Green Revolution."

But Borlaug's "Green Revolution" wasn't green in the present sense of the word. The yield increases came at a cost, requiring farmers to make liberal use of chemical fertilizers and pesticides, which bled into the land and seas, poisoning farmers and wildlife and creating nitrogen-rich dead zones in the ocean.

There was, of course, an alternative to this approach: organic farming. It's better for the soil for farmers to rotate and diversify crops, to use cover crops, to use volcanic dust fertilizer. It's better for wildlife. But organic farmers with their pesticide-herbicide-nematocide-free commitment struggle to combat certain pests and diseases. It's more costly, yields are lower. Even today, organic farming amounts to less than 1 percent of American agriculture. At a time when demographers expect the world's population to add 3 billion people by 2050, Adamchak and Ronald don't believe that organic agriculture alone is a viable means of feeding the world.

Enter genetic engineering.

The stump speech example of genetically engineered environmentalism comes from an unlikely place, a place whose capital city has a smog problem so bad that some call it Beige-ing.

China shifted in the 1990s to Bt cotton, a GMO form of cotton. "Bt" means *Bacillus thuringiensis*—a bacteria that produces a toxin that organic farmers have been using for decades. Organic farmers spray a liquid version of Bt on their crops. They like Bt because it's natural—it's what's called a biological control, using a live organism to combat a pest—and it's remarkably efficient in taking out crop killers such as caterpillars and beetles. In *Tomorrow's Table* we learn about Bt from organic farmers, and then we hear about what happened when the Chinese took this bacteria and bred it into their cotton. Within four years the Chinese reduced their pesticide use by 156 million pounds—that's as much pesticide as is used annually in the entire state of California. Overall, China has reduced pesticide use by more than 80 percent. The reports of pesticide-related injuries declined from one thousand each year to fewer than a hundred.

But in the Ronald and Adamchak view, pesticide reduction—a common biotech brag point—is just the beginning. They tell us that genetic engineering—paired with organic agriculture—could help preserve wilderness, enhance biodiversity, protect our oceans, and stave off climate change. It's an extraordinary gulp of claims, but here's the logic:

- More productive farmland, farmed with higher-yield varieties, spares the need for yet more farmland—which means more room for wild spaces. GMO crops could increase per-acre yield—at a far faster rate than conventional tools, and GMO crops, Ronald argues, could expand arable land. Crops could thrive in deserts, in colder areas, in areas with saltier soil.

- A GMO-based farm economy reduces heavy pesticide use, which means protecting biodiversity and potentially saving millions of birds, insects, and endangered species. Ronald points out that pesticides kill more than 70 million birds a year, as well as billions of insects. Herbicide use has led to a drastic reduction in the global frog population. The inference: Frankenfood could save the African horned frog.

- Frankenveggies could protect the health of the Gulf of Mexico. One of the side effects of heavy-duty fertilization of conventional agriculture is that plants can't properly absorb all the nutrients in the fertilizer. In the Midwest, excess nitrogen leaches into the water table, travels down the Mississippi, and pours into the Gulf, where it's created an area so choked with algae that marine life is dying. It's called the "dead zone" and it's growing. But some biotech companies are engineering crops such as potatoes, rice, and wheat to improve their ability to absorb nitrogen, which would potentially reduce the amount of nitrogen reaching the Gulf and slow the dead zone effect.

By the time I left the Panera Bread café, I was confused. On the one hand, all the characters and scenes in *Tomorrow's Table* seemed too perfectly cast. We're talking about "gene flow" with a doula. We learn that GM cheese is kosher (because they don't have to take enzymes from slaughtered calves) at a writing group. I groaned when, in the chapter "Conserving Wildlands," Ronald's son complains of being served "too much tofu." It just seemed so smartly targeted to the yuppie-hippie milieu. Did Monsanto arrange for this marriage?

On the other hand, I was profoundly intrigued. The book undermined a lot of the fears that I'd heard—suggesting that they may be traced to dubious sources. And the book also introduced one of the most exciting food production ideas I'd heard since open-ocean aquaculture—open-sourcing genetic engineering. Instead of patenting traits, licensing them to Monsanto, and collecting royalties, Big Pharma–style, the open-source scientists could work together, like, say, Linux programmers, on projects that aren't necessarily a pure cash grab.

REELING FROM MY Panera read, I called my friend Scott, an ecologist. I'm curious if he's heard of Pam and Raoul (he hasn't) and if the biotech-for-sustainability view is growing popular among his peers.

Scott snorted. He said that GMOs are still a concern of many ecologists who fear that it could disrupt ecosystems. He had also never heard of open-sourcing GMOs.

At dinner with Kara Nielsen, a Bay Area food trend expert, I raised the idea of the genetically engineered heirloom tomato, wondering if an all around überfoodie would be tempted by this lab creation. She scoffed at the thought. "That wouldn't be an heirloom tomato, it would be a genetically engineered tomato."

I wanted to know Michael Pollan's opinion on all of this. I

hadn't noticed initially, but he had actually contributed a one-sentence blurb to *Tomorrow's Table*. It was a kind of nonstatement, the type of inscrutable remark a Supreme Court nominee might make. "Whether you ultimately agree with it or not, it's a fresh approach to the debate on transgenic crops." I searched for something clearer. *Food, Inc.*, a movie he co-narrated, which focuses to a great extent on Monsanto, does not have a pro-biotech message. There was an interview on a website called Fora TV in which Pollan basically offered a longer version of his nonopinion on the book jacket. In the clip he starts by expressing a willingness to hear fresh ideas on transgenes, and at one point says he's open to the idea of "open source genetic engineering," but then he backs off and seems to show a favoritism for Ed Ryder–style breeding. "Most of the advancements in yield are not because of GM, but because of conventional breeding." I found a passage in *The Botany of Desire* in which he notes that Monsanto's New Leaf potato reduces pesticide use (a good thing), but the overwhelming message is negative because of the intellectual property consequences (corporate ownership of building blocks of life, Monsanto making a lot of money) and because Pollan ends his discussion being unable to eat a GMO potato. Still, even though Pollan can't get himself to make GMO au gratin, he never condemns the actual technology or raises Jeffrey Smith–like safety concerns. In other words, the Ronald-Adamchak point—genetic engineering doesn't have to serve corporate designs, it *can* be used for good purposes—still holds.

A FEW WEEKS later, Terra Brockman, sister of Henry Brockman—that's my heirloom radicchio dealer—came to a suburban Chicago library to talk about her book *The Seasons on Henry's Farm*, a beautiful back-to-the-farm memoir. After a short slide presentation, Terra invited questions. I had *Tomorrow's Table* on my mind and was curious what Terra, who is not only Henry's sister but also a local farms activist, thought of the idea. Before I asked my question, though, a woman asked Terra the gene flow question—that is, whether Henry's Farm was at risk to be infected by allergens from neighboring farms that grew GMOs. Henry's Farm is smack in the center of the Corn Kingdom, a part of central Illinois where many farmers use genetically modified crops, like Roundup Ready corn and soybeans. Terra smiled and informed the woman that "fortunately" the farm was in an organic enclave. She even had a slide, an aerial shot, of the farm's location as evidence. "So, no," she said, with relief, "we aren't at risk—none of our neighbors grow GM crops." She wasn't likely a supporter of the Adamchak-Ronald approach. When my turn came, I held my GMO question and instead asked about the portability of fragile heirloom crops. After leaving the library, I felt strangely bad, ashamed for being cowardly.

It took a while—some reading about non-oligarchic GMOs, some more conversations with people with unthinking, fundamentalist views on biotechnology based on shoddy science possibly sourced to a swing dancer. (Jeffrey Smith, *Seeds of Deception* author—no formal scientific training, *but* he was a professional swing dance instructor and has advocated "yogic flying" to reduce crime.) You can probably see where this is going. I had my post-preschool outburst.

Needless to say, after calling anti-GMO talking points "shit," I became progressively more open about my opinion. I found that it was not easy to change minds. Plenty of extremely intelligent, otherwise reasonable people have no interest in learning about the virtues of new plant breeding technologies or hearing about why open-source genetic engineering is so great. My wife—atheist, reasonable, science-literate and science-centric (climate change, vaccines)—is unpersuaded. And why take a chance? Why not, she argues, stick with what we know is safe? End game.

The notion that large multinational corporations like Monsanto and Bayer CropScience are patenting genes and profiting from it is unsettling. The idea of inserting DNA from bacteria or an Arctic char into a tomato is creepy. There's ample risk in the unknown—inserting a transgenic gene does deserve a higher level of scientific scrutiny than old tried-and-true methods of cross-breeding. And there is good reason to be wary of large corporations' grandiose promises of changing the world. We've heard it before, and we've been burned before.

But I had come to believe that categorically rejecting genetic engineering was reckless, dangerous, and inhumane.

I promised that I'm not going to turn this into a food politics rant, but let me just point out one of the biggest reasons why my mind was changed—and why you should reconsider blithely following the advice from otherwise excellent guides of food choices, like Mark Bittman and Alice Waters and your synagogue pamphlet: According to the World Health Organization, a quarter billion children worldwide, mostly in the developing world, have diets lacking in vitamin A. Between 250,000 and 500,000 of these children go blind every year—with half of those dying within twelve months. There is a crop, developed in 1999, that is fortified with vitamin A compounds. If children unable to get vitamin A from other protein sources simply eat this crop, they will not go blind and die. It is named "golden rice" because of its yellowish hue, and every health organization in the world has declared it to be safe to eat. But golden rice was not bred through traditional means; it was bred in a lab. So golden rice is, by its opponents' definition, Frankenfood, and therefore it's been ferociously opposed. There is no "natural, traditional" alternative means of creating golden rice. You cannot use classical plant-breeding techniques because vitamin A compounds are only found naturally in the green parts of rice, not in the seed. In order to create a rice seed containing vitamin A compounds, you splice two daffodil genes and a bacterial gene into the rice genome.

Genetic engineering, as yucky as it can sound, and as Monsanto-dominated and profit-oriented as it currently is (thanks to the Supreme Court),* presents opportunities to develop crops to respond to a changing planet. And as the globe warms, as more areas become flood and drought prone, as population grows, we must consider how to integrate biotech tools into our food production methods.

The Search for Genetically Engineered Brandywine Tomatoes and Glow-in-the-Dark Peruvian Potatoes Resumes

After going through a Frankenfood conversion, the news that I had really been waiting for came, serendipitously, via email from Prakash's AgBioView.

AgBioView is an email list I'd subscribed to as a way of getting a sneak peek at the transgenic pipeline. Edited by C. S. Prakash, a plant geneticist at Tuskegee University in Alabama, AgBioView features the latest ag biotech research news. If you want to hear about the latest research on Frost Resistant Eucalyptus or Bt Corn with resistance to Rootworm, AgBioView is indispensible.

But this list was far more than a research update. AgBioView is like a political hotsheet. If you know about GMOs largely through the NGOs and *Food, Inc.*, AgBioView would seem like a parallel universe. Instead of plucky farmers who fight Monsanto, AgBioView's heroes include "Brave Italian Farmer [Who] Plants GM seeds," and "Peruvian scientist who was jailed for speaking up *about* GM crops."

Diamond v. Chakrabarty is one of the worst decisions in Supreme Court history. The 1980 decision ruled that genes could be patented. Combined with 1980's Bayh-Dole Act, which gave universities the right to patent and commercialize to corporations, this decision unleashed the race to own the essential building blocks of life. The results are tremendously stifling. Not only are corporations dominating ownership of genes, due to the high biotech costs, but independent scientists are not allowed to study patented GM crops without prior permission of the owner.

Prakash's weekly emails linked to op-eds with headlines like "Lack of GMO Costs Lives" and "Higher Food Prices Because of No GM" and "Frankenfood is good for you."

One morning, skimming this variety show of biotech news, I found an alert about an upcoming gathering of the biotech world. It was, serendipitously, in Chicago. And one of the featured events was, miraculously, a seminar titled "Game Changing Output Traits." Those are the four magic words—that signaled gene-spiked fruits and vegetables that might wow consumers.

It was strikingly clear that BIO, the McCormick Place, Chicago edition, was not going to be an ordinary ag/food show. I had spent a lot of time in trade show land and had grown accustomed to the speakers—who invariably focus on innovation, the future of the industry, how to build teams and enhance creativity. I'd seen Ted Allen, Temple Grandin (the autistic meat scientist), even a big name—Dan Pink.

And BIO? Day one's keynote was Bill Clinton, day two it was Dubya and on day three, Al Gore. Fareed Zakaria was relegated to a mere three o'clock teatime talk.

The five-day meeting, attended by fifteen thousand people, was about far more than output traits. BIO was Big Pharma's show (Abbott, Baxter, Pfizer, Novartis, AstraZeneca, Merck) and it featured a whole wide world of Next Big Things—cancer therapies and biofuel solutions and synthetic biology breakthroughs.

The bio-aggies, though not the show's centerpiece, were well represented on the floor. One booth had two cows and two pigs, lazing around on some hay in a makeshift pen. Two teenage 4-Hers told anyone who would listen that those cows will never get BSE (mad cow disease) because they've been genetically engineered for immunity. The pigs, they said, were genetically engineered to grow five times as fast as your ordinary porker.

A few steps away, a vendor hawked "pond scum cookies" with yeast made out of algae. (They tasted pretty good.) Two eight-foot-tall corncobs were on display in the Ag Pavilion—one looked horrible, missing kernels, mottled, while the other was perfect, plump, with a full set of kernels. The healthy one was GMO corn with insect resistance. I took a quiz to test my knowledge of animal livestock biotechnology and won a prize—not a stuffed animal, a stuffed E. coli. It felt, at times, like a biotech county fair.

The "Game Changing Output Traits" seminar was far from fairlike. They didn't serve half-tomato, half-lemon-basil tomatoes, and there were no testimonials about blue bananas that build muscle mass. We were years away from Safeway, still in the realm of the field trials and journal articles (the pipeline) and theoretical models. One presenter showed a carefully choreographed slide show on how zinc fingers (not the zinc in your Centrum, but naturally occurring proteins) would improve the speed and accuracy of moving stacks of genes. Another presenter talked about a more efficient process of "tuning" genes.

By far the most intriguing and intelligible of the purported game changers came, strangely, from J.R. Simplot. Simplot is perhaps best known as one of the world's largest suppliers of French fries. You might not think of an Idaho-based potato-processing goliath as a likely biotech pioneer. Neither do the biotech people. As soon as Caius Rommens, Simplot's lead genetic engineer, got his turn, he surveyed the audience. "How many of you work for food companies?" No one raised a hand. By and large, food companies try to distance themselves from the faintest association with genetic engineering. This wariness stems back to the early 1990s, when several companies, such as Campbell's, that were exploring GMOs received boycott threats from anti-GMO groups. It's one thing for Monsanto to get involved with a controversial technology. But for food companies, who sell wholesome foods to moms and babies, it's reckless brand management.

But Simplot was plowing forward. The company has a tradition of pioneering work—a Simplot chemist's discovery led to the introduction of frozen french fries in the late 1940s. And now they believed that biotechnology could create a new generation of superior potato products. Rommens, formerly of Monsanto, demonstrated Simplot's approach. "We're not adding genes, we're subtracting." Instead of adding traits, Simplot was silencing genes and achieving many of the same goals. It was cleverly pragmatic. By using the silencing approach, Simplot was hoping to avoid many of the regulatory steps.

Rommens spoke enthusiastically of a brave new future for spuds. In only five years, he predicted, the Russet Burbank, the world's biggest-selling potato—sold by the billion to fast-food restaurants around the world—will be obsolete, replaced by Russet Burbank 2.0, called the Russet Ranger. He claimed it would have 7 percent more healthy starch and a stronger flavor.

Lower-cholesterol potatoes, allergen-free potatoes, color-enhanced potatoes, potatoes that are less greasy—even safer potatoes. "We can take out acrylamides [potentially carcinogenic chemicals that bond with sugars when you fry potatoes]," Rommens said. And all of this didn't even require a gene from another species—it's all within the potato genome. It's just using more precise selection. "The potato hasn't been much improved by breeders since the nineteenth century," he concluded. "It's time for a change."

The Biotech Cowboy Country Fantasy

It's hard not to think about the world of possibilities at BIO. McCormick Place was filled with country and region and city pavilions all vying to become some bio-version of Silicon Valley. I passed booths with names like BioBasque (yes, Pamplona, Spain, home of the running of the bulls, wants your biotech start-up) and BioLake (a lakeside city in Szechuan province). There was a Dutch booth that boasted "Collaboration is in our genes." There were Brazilian bio-centers, and

German bio-valleys, and bio-clusters in Seoul suburbs. All trying to out-bio each other. Surely, most of them wanted pharma money, but seeing the profusion, in this world's fairish environment, it awakened the idea that perhaps there was a lawless place—without an FDA, USDA, Greenpeace, and Food & Water Watch—a place where the work of the UC Davis Plant Transformation Facility could actually be tested, not sentenced to life in a bio *supermax*.

There is no such place, and this was unfortunate, because months were wasted nagging Israelis in hopes of finding this libertine place that didn't exist.

Israel? It made sense: precarious natural resources (desert, limited farmland), history of agricultural innovation, a strong biotech industry. And Israeli farmers were famous for running wild with "weird crops" (star-shaped zucchini, strawberries shaped like carrots, worm-shaped berries). Add to that the one gleaming example of genetic engineering for taste: the lemon basil plant married with a cherry tomato. But Israel was just as restrictive as the rest, just as thwarted by patents and prohibitively costly regulations. That Israeli-bred lemon basil tomato, the flora cocktail that excited me so much? "There was interest," Efraim Lewinsohn, the plant's breeder, told me when I reached him, "but because it's GMO, companies lost interest in commercialization. And there are no prospects in the near future."

It became clear that Lewinsohn's half lemon basil, half tomato was an extraordinarily anomalous creation. Most transgenic work focused on the commodity crops. As of summer 2011, a grand total of two bioengineered crops appeared on their way to Safeway. There's a disease-resistant plum that got the FDA's approval, but is awaiting EPA sign-off. And Monsanto announced its plans to bring us GMO sweet corn. The genetic engineering of "specialty crops" was, as Bradford told me months previously, overwhelmingly focused on input traits (yield, disease resistance, etc.), and when bioengineers did turn their attention to consumers' wants, they favored health traits. Bananas and apples spiked with antioxidants. Tomatoes with more vitamin C. Scientists have created soybeans with lower oil, and they're engineering peanuts to be hypoallergenic—which will, if they are successful, reduce the most common cause of fatal allergic reactions to food in the United States.

But culinary applications? Playing with flavor or texture?

There's Simplot's superpotato. There are university researchers modifying the acidicness of tomatoes. Monsanto is rumored to be planning more consumer-oriented products—if the sweet corn succeeds. But nothing was approved for consumption, and they probably wouldn't be for at least five years. The GMO market was, in other words, not open yet.

And What if the World Embraced Agricultural Biotechnology? The FAQ

Let's say that golden rice saves millions of children from starvation in Asia. Or bioengineered crops slow down the creation of algal dead zones in the Gulf of Mexico—or a low-fat, anti-cancer potato becomes a smash hit at McDonald's.

Consumer worries about GMOs evaporate, becoming as anachronistic as fears of microwaves causing cancer. The regulatory barriers are gone; transgenic plants are treated the same as any other. The Monsanto juggernaut is over; small, boutique companies, open-source breeders, plant breeders from the comfort of a Brooklyn loft have a chance to contribute to the vegetable economy. Then what happens?

Would it look different? Yes. There will almost surely be more varieties. Austrian heirloom varieties like Forellenschluss; heirloom tomatoes like the Brandywines and Cherokee Purples; Green

Zebra tomatoes; and hard-to-get radicchio—currently only available from farmers like Henry Brockman—could become readily available. So many vegetables today aren't commercially viable because of disease vulnerabilities or production inefficiencies. But in a genetically engineered future, all the flaws that make them ill suited for commercialization become mere speed bumps. "You could have disease immunity almost immediately," said Bradford. "And it would be very easy to take care of these other variables. Instead of taking a decade to ready a crop for commercialization, it will take a matter of months."

It's possible that colors would change. You could find pink lettuce and blue arugula—maybe with a green orange slice for St. Patrick's Day. Color becomes malleable because it's often a single trait.

Would it taste different? Yes. It is also likely, some geneticists say, that in 2035 some lettuces won't taste anything like lettuce.

The Flavr Savr–era notion of tomatoes with customized flavor was a reckless ambition in the 1990s; modifying taste is among the most challenging tasks for plant geneticists. You can silence a gene in the potato genome, tuning down the bitterness or acidic quality, but it's still a fractional impact on taste. Taste is complex. A tomato, for instance, has between five and twenty compounds that influence flavor. Changing flavor requires not one gene, but packages of genes, and the genes must be placed precisely. Then there is texture, inextricably linked to flavor.

Modifying taste eludes technologists today, but in the next ten years, that could change. In the 1990s, it took years and millions of dollars to sequence a genome. Now it's a task that can be completed in minutes. They'll be able to choose from a genetic cassette—stacks of genes that together confer desired traits. With a few mouse clicks, geneticists say, they could choose from a range of flavors, textures, colors. "Think of it like Photoshop," said Prakash. "At some point that won't be a far-fetched metaphor."

It will be technologically possible, therefore, to create a Caesar salad—without the Caesar dressing. The flavor of the Caesar could be bred into the lettuce. You could also have a banana that looks like a banana but tastes like a banana sundae.

Textures would be far easier to change. You could bite into an apple that has the consistency of a banana.

Bananas that taste like curry. It sounds far-fetched and truly Frankenfoodish, but some say it would inevitably happen. Fruits and vegetables would merely be another frontier for adventurous and often mind-bending culinary pioneers. The culinary sleight of hand is already happening today. "Surely, you'll see culinary minds play with foods in the same way they mix spices and pair dishes," predicted Bruce Chassy, a professor of microbiology at the University of Illinois. "The question is whether people will want such inventions." Marketers and plant breeders will work together, he predicted. It will become more of a food marketing question than a technology one.

Produce that doesn't spoil. In a biotech future, the sell-by dates will be different—instead of rushing to eat your lettuce in a week, looseleaf lettuce could languish, unsealed, for a month—or more. One of the huge problems in the produce industry is perishability, with close to one third of all fresh fruits and vegetables produced lost to overripening or damage during shipment. But bioengineers are already making progress in changing the post-harvest behavior of plants. By shutting off an enzyme, an apple has been modified so that it won't turn brown after it is sliced—and a banana has been engineered to ripen more slowly.

Although small organic farmers are often the most hostile to technologized solutions and may be the least likely group to adopt high-tech crops, it's possible that GMOs could change the farmers' markets in places like Chicago or Buffalo. "In New York and Illinois, it's pretty hard to grow a lot of crops because they're going to freeze," explained Dennis Miller, a food scientist at Cornell University. "But you could engineer in frost tolerance. You could extend the growing season and bring in more exotic crops into new regions. I don't know if we'll be growing bananas in upstate New York," said Miller, "but it would expand the options for locally grown fruits and vegetables."

How Frankenfood will Improve Health

Most breeders expect that the biggest change for consumers would be something that's already familiar to any Whole Foods shopper. We already have calcium-fortified orange juice and herbal tea enhanced with antioxidants, but in an ag biotech-friendly world, the produce section would likely be overflowing with health enhancements.

Orange potatoes, enhanced with beta carotene, calcium-enhanced carrots, and crops with enhanced antioxidants are already in the pipeline. By the 2030s, vegetables and fruits will be vitamin, nutrient, and beneficial-gene delivery vehicles. To illustrate how this would play out, Prakash pointed to the work of Cynthia Kenyon, a University of California–San Francisco molecular biologist, who extended the life span of a ground worm by six times by changing a gene called "def 2." While this is in the realm of basic science, C. S. Prakash also suggested that if something like a "fountain of youth" gene is found to benefit humans, it could be bred into vegetables. By combining genetics and plant science, a whole new realm of products would likely appear.

Some geneticists envision a future in which crop development would become a highly collaborative process: nutritionists, geneticists, physicians, chefs, and marketers would work to develop new fruits and vegetables aimed at various consumer wants.

PART
THREE

MEAT

6.

Why Not Cow, Goat, Emu, or Rabbit?

WHY IS THE LOCUS OF THE NEXT GREAT MEAT search a lab in Utrecht, the Netherlands—rather than, say, the grasslands of the Argentine Pampas or a small, experimental commune of insanely creative farmer-chefs in northern California or western Massachusetts?

It was a painful process of elimination.

First, the Big Three and turkey—all of them—were immediately disqualified. Three meats have dominated American meat consumption for over one hundred years: chicken surpassed beef in the 1970s (after the red meat-is-unhealthy message gained traction), pork has slumped, and turkey, due to its spectacular popularity as a deli meat, has become a solid fourth candidate. There is remarkable, untapped diversity within the Big Three that is being revived right now. If you go to the Davis farmers' market, you can get four different kinds of heirloom chicken—the Cornish Cross, the Golden Ranger, the Dark Cornish, and the Red Broiler. There's a chicken called the Arakuan that lays green eggs. You can join a "pork CSA" and begin exploring various porcine tastes each week—Berkshire, Tamworth, and if you're lucky they might have some of the nearly extinct Red Waddle. There are of course dozens of bovine varietals.

The same mind-expanding process that happened in the vegetable and fruit world is coming, albeit a bit slower, to meat. None of these heritage pigs would thrive in a CAFO—that's a Concentrated Animal Feeding Operation. They're available because of the revival of smaller-scale, less widget-like livestock farming. If you're stuck in a place without Brahmans or Arakuans, don't worry. Trickle-down applies here, too.

Few things could have been more appealing than an heirloom meat–eating odyssey, poking through the subculture of grass-fed, free-range pioneers, visiting Ted Turner at his ranch in Montana, heading down to an Argentine estancia. But it was too redundant. Check out Mark Schatzker's *Steak* for a beef-eating odyssey.

Second, the RMAs and the hybridists and revivalists were tempting, but ultimately resisted. Emus, ostriches, and rheas—they're called "red meat alternatives"—constitute less than one-half of 1 percent of all meat consumed in the United States. Emu farmers tout the five-foot-tall flightless bird: "It's leaner, tastier, and uses less land." Ostrich proponents will tell you that "Darwin loved it" and that ostrich meat is lower in fat and lower in cholesterol. There are the hybridists who believe the beefalo, a mixture of cow and bison, could be the meat of the future. I tried a grilled emu burger and liked it. You can get it through mail order in a matter of days.

Then there were the revivalists. Thanksgiving in Chicago in

1850 featured not merely turkey, but buffalo, jackrabbit, black and cinnamon bear, elk, sandhill crane, butterball duck, redwings, marsh birds, antelope, wild goose liver, and spotted grouse. The notion that some wonderfully tasty species of fowl or mammal that fell into obsolescence could be revived, domesticated, and brought to the Safeway meat section fascinated me. In *Guns, Germs, and Steel* Jared Diamond addresses the question of why, in a world with hundreds of possible meats, our species chose just a handful. Diamond attributes it to what he calls the Anna Karenina Principle. In brief, the AK principle dictates that if a prospective animal has one flaw (slow growth rate, eats too much, has a nasty disposition), then it's eliminated. But those choices were made thousands of years ago. With new technologies, in our era of cloning, what could this mean for the meat section?

Ultimately, what steered me toward a very different path—the path of plants and rabbits—was Michael Pollan. *The Omnivore's Dilemma* didn't turn me into a grass-fed-beef monogamist or radically alter my food choices. And *In Defense of Food*—best known for the mantra "Eat Food. Not Too Much. Mostly Plants."—didn't change my diet, either.

But *Defense* did change my search for the *future* of meat. After spending months learning about crop science and biotechnology, I was paying much closer attention to the enviro-food intelligentsia. I was reading *Defense*, the "Mostly Plants: What to Eat" chapter, when I spotted this footnote at the bottom of page 166:

"A 2006 report issued by the United Nations stated that the world's livestock generate more greenhouse gases than the entire transportation industry."

Now, the notion that meat eating contributes to global heating is not a new idea, but it was a revelatory concept, at the time, for me. I knew about the global warming costs of my Subaru but had never seriously considered how my appetite for burgers was also heating the earth. In the months following, I started to read through the growing Meat = Global Heat literature. Anna Lappé's *Diet for a Hot Planet: The Climate Crisis at the End of Your Fork and What You Can Do About It* and Tom Friedman's *Hot, Flat, and Crowded* sounded the meat/climate change siren; a paper by two University of Chicago researchers detailed the methane and nitrous oxide emissions produced by a carnivorous diet. And our meat appetite, obviously, does more than just warm the planet. Cattle consume nearly 10 percent of the world's fresh water. Eighty percent of the world's farmland is devoted to meat production.

Already, my simple culinary journey, with its seemingly straightforward question, "What will the future of salad look like?" had become mucked up with thorny questions about things like bioethics, nitrogen fertilizer, and cultural politics. After the salad odyssey, I saw that the foods-of-the-future question was inextricably linked to the future-of-the-Earth question.

The Anna Karenina Principle 2.0

So, at the outset of this search for the future of meat, I made an Amendment to the Anna Karenina Principle. Ten thousand years ago humans considered six key factors when choosing animals to domesticate: diet, growth rate, problems of captive breeding, disposition, tendency to panic, and social structure. This mind-set ultimately resulted in today's dominance of the Big Three. But that was before humans had suburbs, SUVs, Home Depot, and BP. Now humans, having evolved, are becoming aware of how destructive their choices can be. Now humans must consider global warming, soaring populations, and diminishing resources.

Greenhouse-gas-guzzling meat-eating will not disappear (people will be eating meat until the earth burns itself into a fiery ball), but The Next Big Thing in Meat, I concluded, *must* have some environmental logic.

I thought about rabbit. Rabbit, known to many as a pet or a carrot-eating cartoon character, is a popular foodstuff in France and Italy. It doesn't need much space. It's easy to store, cheap to feed. It grows fast, eats salad greens, and tastes like chicken. Urban DIY pioneers in places like Berkeley and Brooklyn are already starting to raise them at home. Rabbit was on my list.

I thought about the possibility that The Next Big Thing in Meat will not even be meat. A multimillion-dollar mock meat industry already existed. These companies were racing to produce plant-based products that would better mimic the taste and texture of real meat. Mock meat technologists were making a vast upgrade from the vegetarian substitutes of the past. They were trying to move from merely filling the needs of vegetarians to satisfying that next mass audience: carnivores.

There was, however, a problem with the idea of exploring the fake meats of the future.

I tried them. I tried Tofurky, Yves, Boca Burgers, Gardein, mock bacon bits, mock meatballs. I wanted to like them. But after a self-satisfied purchase, an initial taste, a satisfactory meal, followed by a euphoric thought, "this is not so bad," the mock meats would invariably languish in my refrigerator. Maybe the next generation of mock meats would be much better? A University of Missouri food scientist was purportedly getting closer to achieving the perfect mock chicken—a real chicken flavor profile with the fibrous texture of real chicken flesh.

But my interest in rabbit and mock meat was only modest.

There was one too-good-to-be-true idea out there on the Food Frontier, circa 2009. It's an idea that promised to combine the benefits of a vegetarian diet (more healthful, less damage to the environment) with the potential for an actual, real meat experience. The idea was controversial and unnatural, and there was only one team of scientists in the world working to make this happen.

7.

The Guilt-Free, Heart-Attack-Fighting Super Burger

HE CALLED IT "THE JURASSIC PARK SCENARIO." In terms of pure shock value, the JPS eclipsed anything I'd heard of in the Frankenfood world, ranking right up there in jaw-dropability with finding a herd of grass-fed Wagyu cattle on the moon or discovering a cheesecake recipe that instantly creates abs of steel.

The upshot of the Jurassic Park scenario is that the range of meats available for human consumption would expand exponentially. *Everything* is on the table. Endangered, taboo animals—zebras, giraffes, giant pandas, California condors. Extinct animals—

choose your epoch—Paleozoic or Mesozoic. The only thing required to get T. rex or brontosaurus or pterodactyl on the menu at Outback is a DNA sample.

Though I would normally have been highly skeptical about T. rex burgers, given the peculiar circumstances of this revelation—the source, and what I'd learned about the Super Burger—it actually sounded somewhat plausible.

Two hours earlier, in front of a bevy of ribeyes and New York strips at the Whole Foods on P Street in Washington, D. C., I learned that "we will soon have a hamburger that won't cause heart attacks, but will stop them." How? You'll just take out the saturated fat, and replace it with omega-3 fatty acids. I was told that this new hamburger will have the fat profile of "salmon or an avocado," and the burger will effectively eliminate any worries about nasty food-borne illnesses, like E. coli or mad cow disease or SARS, because "it will be the purest, safest meat ever." As for the taste of the Super Burger? You can truly have it your way—it's easy to engineer a flavor profile. You can mix fats and salts, you can vary the amounts of proteins, to achieve the perfect taste.

The man making these claims was not Craig Venter (genomics pioneer with the god complex) or Ferran Adria (the überchef and molecular gastronomist), and it wasn't Steve Jobs talking about Apple repositioning itself as a meat sciences company. The man offering this utopian meat future-view was Jason Matheny, a then thirty-four-year-old graduate student at Johns Hopkins.

Matheny is America's leading proponent of the idea that hamburger doesn't have to come from a cow. He founded and directs New Harvest, a nonprofit that promotes the eating of meat made in vitro. He's quoted in most news articles on in vitro meat. He coauthored the seminal paper in *Tissue Engineering* on how to make in vitro meat. He raises money for in vitro meat; he sends out monthly emails tracking every appearance of in vitro meat in the media. He manages the website. New Harvest is based in his apartment.

I spent eight hours with Matheny eating tofu, seitan, and soy nuggets for two reasons.

First, it was phase one of my strategy to get inside the Dutch meat-growing lab that might be developing the meat of our future. Meat spawned in test tubes, labs, and football-field-sized factories churning out sheets of pork certainly isn't, on first thought, as pleasing as grass-fed cows lazing in the tall grass of a Shenandoah Valley meadow. But as a way of reducing the impact of cow farts (methane, depleting the ozone layer), as a way of feeding a crowded, hot, increasingly meat-happy planet, as a way of resolving ethical dilemmas for people uncomfortable with giant feeding lots, as a way of helping wannabe vegetarians who loathe plant-based alternatives, lab-grown meat started sounding pretty damn pastoral, if not utopian.

Still, amid all the hype (PETA [People for the Ethical Treatment of Animals] offered a $1 million award to anyone who invents a lab-grown meat product), pithy quotes, best "Best Science Story" blurbs, something was missing. At the time no English-speaking reporter, as far as I could find, had examined the lab at the center of the commotion. What does in vitro meat-growing look like (one writer likened it to bread making), and what does the meat taste like? In one article, Matheny said coyly that the Dutch researchers can't actually say whether they have tried their product—due to some FDA-like gag order—but that "if you get them drunk . . . they might tell you." I wanted to get them drunk. Or at least I wanted to see the lab. And the best way to get access appeared to be through Matheny, the ambassador of the movement.

But there was another reason I wanted to meet Matheny. Matheny was, it turned out, a highly curious individual.

You might not pause at the grouping of the phrases "in vitro" and "tissue engineering" and "Hopkins PhD." (Hopkins, after all, has a world-famous medical school.) But Matheny's PhD program had nothing to do with tissue engineering, tissue growth, cell biology. He studied health economics at Hopkins. The coauthor of "In Vitro–Cultured Meat Production" in the peer-reviewed biomedical journal *Tissue Engineering* didn't appear to have any relevant expertise. Matheny went to the University of Chicago, where I had worked for many years. And in a phone conversation in which we established this commonality, he revealed—in a flurry of Hyde Park/U of C nostalgia—that he had lived briefly in the arch-hippie Kumbaya co-op and had majored in art history at Chicago.

I found a short article about him, in honor of his winning a public service scholarship, with another interesting fact. Matheny was so inspired by the philosopher Peter Singer's argument ("it's morally indefensible for people with means not to give 5 or 10 percent of it to charity") that he upped the ante, giving 60 to 80 percent of his income to charity, which meant extreme cost-saving measures. The article said Matheny only wears clothes from thrift stores, only buys used books, and seeks the cheapest housing possible—he lived in a hundred-dollar-a-month apartment in Oakland. Matheny clearly had a strong humanitarian-activist streak, but it wasn't at all clear how an art history major and former Kumbaya co-op resident could have hatched the test-tube meat idea.

MATHENY IS THIN, has short, closely cropped hair, wears black-rimmed glasses, and, though he's in his mid-thirties, seems much younger. With jeans and sweater ("You can get great stuff from thrift stores!"), he looks vaguely like a young Ron Howard, if Ron Howard listened to Moby. Matheny is exuberant and cheerful, and when he talks, whatever the topic—favorite vegetarian restaurants in Chicago, soy extrusion technology, or English moral philosophy—he's earnest and detailed. On utilitarianism, he launched into a twenty-minute narrative on his journey from Jeremy Bentham to John Stuart Mill to Peter Singer and then back to Bentham. Perhaps because of his Opie looks, and his sans-artifice delivery, everything he says, even when he's making proclamations such as "in vitro meat will be the purest meat ever," comes across as genial and reasonable.

We met at Java Green Organic Eco Cafe, a tiny six-table coffee shop in downtown Washington, D.C., that serves mainly soy-latte-quaffing vegetarians, but also revels in conversions (the owner bragged about tricking hard-core carnivores with his fake-beef bulgogi). When Matheny entered, the owner yelled out a warm hello. A couple wearing PETA T-shirts stood up and hugged him. After the commotion petered out, Matheny told me that he had invited a man named Ethan, who was trying to expand a faux meat product line, to join us. This surprised me. We were here to talk about in vitro meat, right? Matheny, in a brief departure from his usual glibness, gave a serious look and said that in vitro meat was not competing with soy or mycoprotein or seitan or tofu. "Any plant-based meat is fine. Conventional meat production is the problem."

In Matheny's view, there's no reason to worry about competition from other meat alternatives. The world consumes 285 million tons of meat every year—90 pounds per person. Sales of meat exceeded $150 billion in 2010. "There's an enormous audience."

If you've ever heard a friend explain how or why he or she became a vegetarian, then the first part of Matheny's in vitro meat narrative will sound familiar. Haunting early exposure to factory farming—in his case, a middle school trip to a chicken farm near his home in Louisville, Kentucky ("It wasn't Old McDonald's farm"), followed by a steady move away from meat and a growing awareness of the manifold evils of meat. A vegetarian in a carnivore family in middle school, he quickly graduated to veganism in high school. At Chicago he became more politically active, joined the Kumbaya co-op, and grew concerned about animal welfare and the environmental costs of factory farming.

Matheny had his second factory farm–related epiphany a few years later. In spite of his easygoing demeanor and boyish charms, Matheny has some pathology: he is either very productive or very indecisive. He has three advanced degrees: a master's in business, a master's in public health, a master's in agricultural economics. He is on the verge of getting a fourth—a PhD in health economics. And at one point he was studying for a master's in architecture at Berkeley.

While studying for one of his master's degrees—this one in public health at Johns Hopkins—he went to India as part of a six-month internship with the Bill and Melinda Gates Foundation to assess AIDS prevention programs. One day, a friend invited Matheny to tour a chicken farm about twenty miles outside New Delhi. Nothing unusual here—thousands of birds in cramped metal sheds, filled with noxious odors, being poorly cared for by poorly paid farmhands.

What was alarming to Matheny was that this was not in steak-eating Texas, or chicken-loving Kentucky: this was India, traditionally *vegetarian* India. For centuries Hindu-majority Indians had a plant-based diet. During his travels, Matheny saw more industrial-size chicken farms popping up on the subcontinent. "You could easily see why," Matheny recalled. "Walk into any McDonald's and there were tons of young people eating chicken sandwiches."

After this firsthand encounter with the global surge in meat eating, Matheny found some ominous statistics. Poultry consumption in India had doubled in the previous five years. In China, meat demand was doubling every ten years. The phenomenon was replicating itself throughout the developing world, where moving from a plant-based diet to a meat-based diet had become a symbol of the middle class.

Matheny knew the environmental cost of meat consumption—

the millions of acres of land needed, the animal waste, the smell, the water use, the fossil fuels required to power industrial-scale farms, the greenhouse gas emissions. Considering the Third World's growing meat appetite, Matheny concluded, "It just wasn't sustainable."

There's nothing unusual about Matheny's reaction yet. He cites "The Long Shadow of Animal Agriculture" as a source of his concern, the same United Nations Food and Agricultural Organization report that Pollan footnoted in *In Defense of Food*, the same report that spooked Anna Lappé, Tom Friedman, and countless others.

The point where Matheny deviated from the eco-mainstream occurred while he was working on his third master's, in agricultural economics at the University of Maryland.

Matheny felt a tremendous sense of urgency after reading "The Long Shadow" in large part because he does not believe in "the massive dietary transition approach." Some environmental and public health activists believe that people will be reasonable, that they'll be persuaded by the environmental logic of a vegetarian diet, or the health argument (a plant-based diet reduces the risk of heart disease, obesity, diabetes, not to mention that it reduces the chance of getting food-borne illnesses like E. coli, avian flu, or mad cow disease). Eating less meat would also reduce the public health danger of animal waste from industrial farms, which contains pathogens, including dust, arsenic, and antibiotic-resistant bacteria. Other activists believe that humanitarian concerns about animal treatment will win the day, that humans will become progressively more appalled by factory farming and will stop eating animals.

Matheny wasn't seeing it. "Only one or two percent of Americans are vegetarian," he said. In the United Kingdom, a place where the green message was purportedly succeeding, less than 5 percent of the population is vegetarian. In Matheny's view, none of these messages was having a measurable impact, and any change was far too slow. There had to be a faster means of solving the world's meat problem.

That's when Matheny started wondering if there was a "compact fluorescent lightbulb of meat production." Ever since his Berkeley stint, specifically a 2001 lecture series on green technology, Matheny held the techno-idealist's view that instead of getting people to change behavior, say, take fewer showers or drive less, we should just accept their lazy ways and satisfy them with more efficient technologies. The most famous example of this approach is the widespread adoption of compact fluorescent lightbulbs, which use 75 percent less energy than standard incandescent bulbs.

In his search for the carnivore's CFL, Matheny learned about several promising approaches. Plant-based meat substitutes were not new—Buddhist cuisine had featured faux meat like tofu for centuries—but a recent improvement in soy-processing technology, called "extrusion cooking," made it increasingly possible to mimic meat. Technology was also improving the taste of mycoprotein (made from an edible fungus), and microbiologists were making strides in farming algae, a high-protein source grown in salt water.

But the turning point came one day when Matheny spotted a short *USA Today* article about a NASA project. A team of bioengineers at Touro College in New York, trying to find a new food source for astronauts on long-range space missions, had grown goldfish meat. The idea, the article said, was that live-muscle cells, placed in a nutrient broth, could offer an alternative to the usual astronaut brain food, kelp and other plant-based protein sources.

Fascinated by the NASA idea, Matheny started looking for anything he could find about lab-grown meat. He soon learned that the idea of culturing meat as a food source was at least sixty years old. In the early 1930s, Winston Churchill (yes, *that* Winston Churchill) suggested that it would be more efficient to cultivate chicken wings and breasts in a growth medium than to raise an entire chicken. The British leader, at the time a journalist, was inspired by an earlier experiment by Nobel Prize–winning surgeon Alexis Carrel. Carrel kept a piece of chicken embryo heart muscle alive in his lab for more than thirty years.

Matheny also learned about a more recent instance when humans actually ate in vitro meat: in 2003 a pair of Australians grew two quarter-sized frog steaks in vitro, sautéed them in a honey-garlic sauce, and served them as part of an art performance. Four of the eight diners spit it out.

Matheny recognized a "yuck factor" issue with in vitro meat, but he also started thinking there might be a "ceiling" with plant-based meats—that mock meats from soy, gluten, or mycoprotein might hit a wall and never achieve a perfect replica of real meat. He already knew how hard it was to wean humans off meat. He believed an evolutionary factor was at play. "Our taste buds have evolved to like the taste of things like sugars, fat, and meat, which were important in our ancestral environment," he told me. "I hope they [mock-meat engineers] do succeed. But there's a real possibility that they'll never be able to match the taste and texture of real meat with mock meats."

A second factor shaped Matheny's thinking about meat-replacement strategies. Matheny is what you might call a utilitarian fundamentalist. Like Peter Singer, Matheny believes that it is our moral duty to reduce the amount of human suffering on earth. With this goal, he's extremely analytical about personal decisions, such as the use of his time, or expenditures, or where he lives. For example: Should he live in Oakland in a bad neighborhood and assume a higher personal safety risk, to save money that he could give to charity to reduce human suffering? Or should he live in Berkeley, and save less money, but lower the risk of getting mugged or killed, thereby increasing the likelihood that over a longer term he could give more money to charity? Those are the types of questions that Matheny considers very carefully.

He applied this cost-benefit analysis to solving the question of sating the world's meat appetite. Agribusiness concerns were spending millions trying to make better meat replacements. It was a robust industry. Meanwhile, virtually no one—beyond a boutique-scale NASA project at a place called Touro College—was examining cultured meat.

Matheny came to a utilitarian conclusion. "My time would be better spent working on in vitro meat. I could contribute more."

So, Jason Matheny, graduate student in agricultural economics, started studying the tissue growth technology that had inspired the NASA project. He found about two dozen papers on tissue growth in humans and animals in peer-reviewed journals. He started cold-calling and emailing more than sixty of the authors cited—the world's experts in muscle tissue engineering—with a simple query about tissue growth: "Can this be tested as a food idea?"

Many responded with generous feedback. Three were exceptionally curious about the graduate student's idea. They offered to coauthor a paper. A few months later, Matheny and Vladimir Mironov, a tissue engineer at the Medical University of South Carolina; Pieter Edelman, a cell biologist at Wageningen University in the Netherlands; and Douglas McFarland, an animal scientist at South Dakota State University, began trying to figure out how a technology largely thought of as an answer to organ and cartilage regeneration could be used to make hamburgers and chicken nuggets. After six months, they laid out for the first time a theoretical process to produce in vitro meat on a large scale.

How to Make Test-Tube Meat—The First Recipe

1. Cells—specifically precursors of muscle cells, called myoblasts, which proliferate quickly—are selected from biopsies of chickens, turkeys, pigs, lamb, cattle, or other animals.

2. The selected cells are put in a growth medium—a vat of nutrient-rich soup, including carbohydrates and amino acids, that fosters rapid cell growth. Here the cells proliferate into millions. Then the millions of cells are poured into a bioreactor, essentially a large fermentation chamber. The cells fuse to become muscle fibers that create thin sheets of meat.

3. To achieve the taste and feel of real meat, the cultured product has to be exercised, like real animals. (The Australian effort had skipped this step, creating frog steaks with a texture one person described as "reminiscent of snot.") One approach was to hang the thin sheets of freshly spawned meat on polymer scaffolding—the sheets would be moved mechanically every ten minutes to stimulate movement. After being grown and stretched, the meat sheets would be stacked to increase thickness. In a second approach, the meat would be grown on small, edible beads that would stretch the meat with changes in temperature.

Matheny had not anticipated the response a paper in *Tissue Engineering and Regenerative Medicine*, a biomedical journal with fewer than five thousand subscribers, could provoke. Almost immediately after "In Vitro Meat for Large Scale Food Production" appeared, reporters started calling. By the end of 2005 he had been interviewed by the *New York Times Magazine*, *Washington Post*, and *Der Spiegel*, and had appeared on the *CBS Evening News*, NPR, and the PBS program *Nova*. *Discover* magazine named "Lab Grown Meat" one of its best science stories of 2005. Because of the public and media enthusiasm, Matheny created New Harvest.

But the most important response came that spring. Before the paper was even published, the Netherlands government invited Matheny to discuss his idea at a meeting of the country's agricultural officials. Matheny didn't know it, but the Dutch had received a proposal from a scientist who wanted to do lab research on in vitro meat. A few months after his visit, Matheny received the news—a scientist named Henk Haagsman had received 2 million euros and four years to develop his in vitro meat idea. "It was my happiest moment," Matheny recalled. "It was no longer theoretical. We actually had a chance to see if this could work."

WE WERE ALONE in the nearly empty Harmony Chinese restaurant, chosen by Matheny as an example of "old-school mock meat" (Chinese Buddhists have aspired to vegetarianism for thousands of years and have developed a whole mock meat culture and industry). A mock pork cutlet, one of the legacies of the Buddha's advice "to cultivate compassion for all living beings," was sitting half-eaten on our table. It was half-eaten, in part, because we were still full from earlier soy nuggets, but also because it was dreadful—a tough, sinewy thing that tasted like a tenderized piece of balsa wood.

Matheny had just explained the essentials of how culturing meat could be applied to the revival of extinct animals (Jurassic Park scenario). He had told me about some of his other interests—smallpox management and catastrophe aversion. He had recently done a cost-benefit analysis of asteroid deflection strategies in a paper titled "Reducing the Risk of Human Extinction."

I popped the question.

Have you tried it?

"No," he said. "But I'm looking forward to that first burger."

Has Henk ever tried it?

In one story, I dimly recalled Henk Haagsman had said something about sprinkling pork bits on a pizza.

"No, that was speculative," Matheny said, correcting me. "They can't eat it now." He then went on to explain that it would be illegal for Haagsman to eat in vitro meat, for exactly the same reasons you can't eat transgenic squash or transgenic tomatoes from the UC Davis Plant Transformation Facility. The European Union has an FDA equivalent with its own guidelines. In vitro meat is, right now, a forbidden food.

But then a smile cracked across Matheny's face and he added, "If you get them drunk, they might tell you."

It wasn't the first time Matheny had done this—he also told some *New York* magazine scribe the same thing. I could get them drunk, I said, and immediately imagined myself with a tottering Haagsman opening a freezer filled with burgers.

We laughed.

When I told Matheny that I hoped to visit Haagsman's lab in the next two months, he provided details on each of the three labs (Haagsman had collaborators at two other universities—one team was working on the bioreactor; another was working on the growth factor). He told me about the personalities involved ("Bernard is a great guy, a really dry sense of humor"), described campuses (Eindhoven is the MIT of the Netherlands), and the highlights (Klaas Hellingwerf is doing great on the growth factor). Matheny sent me contact information. And, sure enough, days after my "Jason referred me to you" email, I heard back, with favorable responses from all.

8.

Among the Meat Growers

THE WORLD'S FIRST SERIOUS EFFORT TO GROW test-tube meat is in the Netherlands. The world's most ambitious effort to raise insects, like grasshoppers and locusts, as an industrial-scale food source for insect-phobic Westerners, is in the Netherlands. The world's only 20,000-person plus barbecued-ant eating festival is in Wageningen, in the Netherlands. The first government to create a program specializing in funding research into "NPFs," novel protein foods—the Netherlands.

The interest in insect eating and in vitro meat is not simply because the Netherlands, land of legalized prostitution and legal pot smoking, is a progressive place. Or because the Dutch, due to their geographical predicament, largely below sea level, have developed a history of resourcefulness and engineering feats, building dams to stave off the sea, reclaiming miles of low land. And it's not even entirely because of their particular ingeniousness in pioneering food production methods. The Dutch, famous as the world's tulip breeders, are renowned among agricultural scientists for figuring out how to grow fruits and vegetables indoors, in winter, at industrial scale.

The Dutch have a meat problem. The country is small (the size of Maryland), densely populated (comparable to Florida), and highly carnivorous. They have the highest per-capita pork consumption in all of Europe. Because they don't have vast tracts of Texas panhandle for cattle grazing, or rural Iowa to spread out their pig farms, the Dutch have a more intimate experience with meat production. Large-scale hog containment facilities are located within twenty miles of all of the Netherlands' largest cities, Amsterdam, Rotterdam, and The Hague. So the unmistakably revolting smell of industrial pig farming is familiar to any Dutch person. Add to this the Netherlands' overall gestalt of big problem solving and it makes sense that the Dutch have been aggressive in dealing with meat. Way back in the 1970s, they created an organization called PROFETAS (Protein Foods, Environment, Technology and Society) that has supported what most consider far-out research into plant-based proteins, mycoproteins, and insects. Arnold van Huis, an entomophagist, is one of the world's leading advocates of using fried grasshoppers and mealworm quiche to end hunger.

The idea of in vitro meat is not new in the Netherlands, and although most English-language news accounts I'd read had credited Haagsman as the architect, the idea predated him by decades.

The key figure was actually an eccentric elderly physician named Willem van Eelen, who traced his interest in meat growing to a near-death experience almost fifty years ago in Indonesia. Van Eelen, a Dutch soldier during World War II, was captured by the Japanese and spent most of the war in POW camps. Notoriously brutal captors, the Japanese used prisoners for slave labor and fed them almost nothing. By the time American soldiers liberated his camp, van Eelen was so emaciated that his spine could be seen from the front of his body, and he barely had enough energy to say his name. The experience inspired in van Eelen a lifelong interest in nutrition and a commitment to end starvation.

While training to become a physician in the Netherlands, van Eelen had an epiphany reminiscent of Winston Churchill's. In a medical school class, a professor showed students how easily he could get a piece of muscle to grow in a petri dish. Van Eelen almost immediately saw in the tissue growth experiment a whole new application—protein-rich food could be, he thought, grown like a crop.

Van Eelen had a highly eclectic career—doctor, owner of art galleries and cafés, founder of an organization for troubled youths, manufacturer of dollhouses—but his lifelong obsession was the meat-growing idea. He talked about lab meat enthusiastically for decades, trying to persuade other scientists (biologists, engineers, physicians, anyone he thought could help). He filed a patent for industrial meat production in the late 1990s. But even in the libertine, progressive, novel-protein-food-friendly Netherlands, no one showed interest in van Eelen's meat growing patent. Many Dutch scientists laughed at him, thinking the idea was a prank.

Henk Haagsman wasn't drawn to in vitro meat growing for the same reasons as the former POW. Van Eelen saw it as a solution to world hunger. Haagsman saw it as a solution to his own dilemma in the meat sciences department at the University of Utrecht.

A biochemist by training, Haagsman had been working as a professor of meat sciences since 1998. The job of "professor of meat sciences" in the Netherlands is typically straightforward—you figure out ways to make the livestock industry safer and more productive. Your research is largely funded by the industry.

But Haagsman, a newcomer to the world of meat production with no farming experience, was troubled by some of the practices he saw. The Netherlands had the lowest use of antibiotics in the world for humans, but the highest use of antibiotics for animals. Haagsman felt the Dutch pig industry abused hormones and growth promoters. He was critical. As a tenured academic, he wasn't beholden to the industry. They couldn't fire him. But his work, aimed at improving quality and safety, was ignored. Frustrated ("I was persona non grata," he says), he developed a curiosity about meat alternatives. He began to research protein derivatives of dairy. When he first heard about van Eelen's idea, he, like most, thought it was preposterous. But at some point, as he explored novel protein ideas, he started warming to the thought. In 2003, he concluded that it was at least worth exploring, and along with van Eelen and several others, he approached the Dutch Ministry of Economic Affairs about a research project.

Amsterdam—the Broth

The "Vitro Meat Project," as it's called in the Netherlands, has three teams, based at different universities across the Maryland-sized country.

Before visiting Haagsman, I went to the University of Amsterdam to meet with a biochemist named M. Joost Teixeira de Mattos who is working on the "growth factor." Sometimes called "media culture," the growth factor is critical because it fosters cell growth—the cells that become the meat that become the burgers of the future.

The big challenge in the Amsterdam lab, Matheny had told me, was to develop a vegetarian growth factor. Animal growth factor strikes the average human as a level beyond gross—it has a nearly unbearable odor, worse than cat urine, and the worst possible name, fetal bovine serum. FBS, standard in hospital labs, would not work for the Dutch team for two reasons. One: as the name hints, it's taken from pregnant cows during slaughter, effectively contradicting the no-kill idealism of test-tube meat. Second, FBS is incredibly expensive. One liter of it is almost five hundred dollars. It's one thing if you're growing a heart valve or cartilage, but for industrial-scale meat production, which would require literally tons of growth factor, the price was too high.

Teixeira de Mattos, a tall, elegant man in his sixties who is an expert on biofuels, echoed Matheny's enthusiasm about the progress in developing more affordable growth factor. The lab's goal, Teixeira de Mattos said, was to create a broth of amino acids, salts, and sugars derived from yeast and plants, essentially using plants to mimic hormones. Figuring out what ingredients can be added, subtracted, increased, or decreased was a painstaking process of trial and error. "Glucose," said Teixeira de Mattos excitedly. "Too much makes cells sluggish. We've been able to reduce it. And then it makes them grow, faster and more efficiently. We're getting closer."

There was another far more exciting outgrowth of the growth factor visit. "It's only a short-term solution," said Teixeira de Mattos. "The real goal is to fix carbon dioxide." Instead of piecing together a complex plant hormone soup, meat farmers would merely rely on a solar-powered growth factor. Photosynthetic bacteria, he said, would become the fuel of meat factories. Like so many biotechnologists I'd heard, Teixeira de Mattos made it sound like an effortless process.

Using biotechnology, you could engineer (or "fix") bacteria so that they would, under sunlight, consume carbon dioxide. The bio-engineered bacterium (called cyanobacteria hydrolysate) will have a fermentative capacity, so that it will supply the growth factor. Even more important, this approach could solve one of the great problems with in vitro meat production. Many criticize the whole idea, Teixeira de Mattos said, because they believe it uses too much energy (electricity and water), that it would be too costly, and that it's not actually such an earth-friendly solution.

Teixeira de Mattos predicted that by 2035 this objection would be obsolete. He went to a chalkboard and drew a map of his fixing-CO_2 vision—what looked crudely like the sun, a factory, and then a lake on top of the factory. "The growth factors are harvested from here," he said, pointing to the roof. Then it's converted into what he likened to a bouillon cube, which functions as the source of the growth factor. He pointed to a crudely sketched bioreactor, where the cells are converted into texturized meat. "This will also be solar powered," he said, smiling.

Parting ways with Teixeira de Mattos, though, I got my first inkling that the other parts of the projects weren't progressing as well. They were not working with cow, chicken, or pig cells in Amsterdam yet, because, Teixeira de Mattos said, "that's Utrecht. They still need to get the right cells. Stem cell selection is a very complex process. I can't even begin to explain it. Henk Haagsman will tell you."

Utrecht—Unlocking the Pig Code

Utrecht, a picturesque Dutch town of a half million people, crisscrossed by canals and carpeted with tulips, is home to the Netherlands' largest university, one of Europe's grand cathedrals, and the largest in vitro meat-growing project in the world.

Curious to get a sense of whether this was a source of civic pride, intrigue, or horror, I asked the first Utrechter I met, my cabdriver, if he knew about the in vitro meat project. No. Henk Haagsman? No. When I arrived at the Utrecht University campus—the home of the meat-growing lab—a very un-Gallup-like poll (three girls standing in front of the cafeteria) all yielded looks of unrecognition.

The in vitro meat lab is in a three-story brick building, not far from Utrecht University's towering medical center in the veterinary sciences wing of the campus. There are labs devoted to bovine and porcine studies and to pet health. The ground floor of the building had a sign with instructions for visiting dog and cat owners. But on a Wednesday afternoon, there was no barking, no talking; it was completely empty.

I met Haagsman and Bernard Roelen, the chief microbiologist

of the project, in a quiet office on the building's second floor. In his photo, Haagsman had a bowl haircut, chubby face, and angular eyebrows and seemed brilliantly cast for the role of "test-tube meat inventor." In person, the professor of meat sciences looked quite mainstream—a sport jacket, a modern haircut. Roelen, the junior colleague, was in his thirties, thin, blond, wearing a polo shirt.

Haagsman had just come from a meat sciences departmental meeting when I arrived. As I waited for him to get settled, I surveyed the surroundings. Some molecular biology texts, a book about "birds of the Netherlands," an Iron Maiden coffee mug. The nearby lab had the ordinary mix of electron microscopes, labcoated techs, and petri dishes with colored agar. No visible signs of any bread-making-like appliances churning out in vitro pork.

I soon learned that the closest thing to an in vitro meat maker—the bioreactor—was not in Utrecht yet; it was still being developed in Eindhoven. Worse, I learned—little more than eleven minutes into the interview—some crushing news. In short, PETA is unlikely to have to give up $1 million for a "commercial lab-grown meat product that has a taste indistinguishable from chicken-meat flesh."

I learned this after explaining why I had come five thousand miles for a week of in vitro meat lab tours. I told them that much had been written about test-tube meat in the American media—much hope centered on Utrecht. I fessed up—admitting to being personally greatly excited about the project—especially after talking with Matheny. And then I asked the almighty question.

Matheny had predicted "within five years" and Haagsman had predicted, in 2005, "a commercial product would be ready in ten years."

How close are we?

Haagsman stuck out his hand as if to say "no more."

"We were a bit overly optimistic," he said.

The next two hours were spent learning the molecular biology of why the Vegan Rapture wasn't imminent.

The Dutch, from the outset, took a different approach from

that of the bioengineer Morris Benjaminson, who led a NASA-commissioned experiment. Benjaminson's method sounded elegantly simple. You drop a chunk of tissue in the right media and you feed it. It grows, much like a plant. It did work. It was ideal for, say, a single shuttle mission, a handful of astronauts repairing a satellite.

But Haagsman and Roelen—and Matheny and his collaborators—all believed that when thinking about industrial-scale commercialization, there was a better way. Regular cells eventually stop growing. But stem cells could grow forever. The media has focused on a particular class of stem cells called pre-embryonic stem cells as a source of potentially miraculous medical therapies. These stem cells can turn into different types of tissues (heart, cartilage, larynx), and they have the wondrous ability to renew themselves rapidly and endlessly. So instead of harvesting more cells, you could, the thinking went, feed the world on a single cell line. There was ample reason for optimism. Scientists had already cultured human stem cells and mouse stem cells. Haagsman planned to apply this human formula to the pig first, and then eventually to cows and chicken. It was in this frame of mind that Haagsman told *Beef* magazine, "We'll have a minced pork product in 2009."

It turned out that the recipe for culturing human stem cells didn't work for pigs. Not only did they struggle to get the pork cells to proliferate, but they also had trouble controlling the cells to create the right tissue—their cells tended to turn into brain tissue, not bacon-friendly muscle tissue. They tried the mouse cell culture protocol—that didn't work, either. There was no master key.

Pigs were somehow unique—and hence Haagsman and Roelen embarked on a quest to figure out the code to culture pig stem cells. They had some clues, some tips from the scientific literature on mouse and human cell-culturing techniques. They varied the level of proteins—because, Roelen said, they knew that this was crucial to culturing mouse stem cells. They experimented with pipetting the cells in different ways—even the seemingly simple act of transporting cells was critical in culturing human stem cells. The material used in the pipette had an impact. (The cells don't like polymer, Roelen said.) Maybe, he speculated, that causes the cells to die? Rat stem cells were successfully cultured in 2008 and that presented a whole new body of knowledge and whole new set of variables to test. Frustrated by their struggles with pig stem cells, the team started experimenting with another category of cells, called adult stem cells. The adult stem cells would at least eliminate the "brain, not bacon" problem—these cells have been preprogrammed. So one could be certain they'd turn into the desired muscle tissue. "They can't live indefinitely," Roelen noted, "but for several months, which could get us somewhere."

But here's the really depressing part for no-kill vegetarians looking forward to a cheeseburger. After understanding the daunting, almost needle-in-the-haystack-esque challenge of cell culture, I learned that the world's only in vitro meat lab had only two graduate students and slightly more than half of a professor on this case. Haagsman devoted only 25 percent of his time to in vitro meat. Roelen estimated his effort at 35 percent.

That seemed hardly sufficient, leading to my observation that in vitro meat had virtually no chance of hitting the supermarket anytime soon. Ten years seemed preposterous. Haagsman didn't disagree. But he saw a path. "To get an in vitro meat product in the marketplace in ten years, we'd need an Apollo project–like commitment." The Apollo Program, funded by the U.S. government, successfully achieved the goal of getting a human on the moon for $170 billion. Another comparison thrown out: the Manhattan Project. That was thirty universities, three countries, 120,000 people, $22 billion (in present value) for a nuclear bomb. As I absorbed the Apollo/Manhattan Project remark, Haagsman suggested that Paul McCartney had an interest in vitro meat.

Really?

"He's a very wealthy man," Haagsman added.

The Paul McCartney scenario?

The Dutch were making a radically different forecast than what Matheny had offered at Whole Foods in D.C. After the primer on pre-embryonic pig stem cells, it led inevitably to suspicious thoughts about another Matheny claim. He had told me that the Dutch have the technological know-how to produce petri-dish chicken nuggets or hamburgers *right now*. But then he told me they don't produce these burgers because it's so expensive. He also told this to *New York* magazine, quipping, "If there were a McDonald's for millionaires, it would probably already be on the menu."

I asked them about their burger-making capability.

Haagsman glanced at Roelen, then gave me a studious look.

"What is meat?" Haagsman asked, tipping his eyebrows.

I had planned for this trip for weeks, had thought about various aspects of in vitro meat, including the ethical aspects of stem cells, but it never occurred to me to think deeply about this one, the definition of meat. It's a pretty nebulous term—you think of meat as just muscle tissue from animals (porterhouse, pork chops, chicken breast), but it's also, more broadly, skin, brains, kidneys.

"When does a cell become a meat?" It was a rhetorical question. He shrugged.

We both turned to Roelen, who was busily sketching some calculations on paper.

"There's the surface area of a petri dish. You would have to make several, and then you would cut each layer. That's seventy-five cubic centimeters." It would be expensive—the vegetarian growth factor wasn't complete. It also wouldn't have texture—the bioreactor project isn't complete.

"But yes," Roelen said, "it is possible."

He estimated that it would take roughly a month to make a burger's worth of in vitro meat. Haagsman looked uncomfortable. "Cells," he said, to his colleague. "Cells."

But this was merely semantics.

There was mutual agreement—some agglomeration of lab-spawned pig or cow cells could be grown in a petri dish right now. It would be tofu-like in texture and not very appetizing, but it would be animal protein, and it could be layered, stacked one on top of another. It would be edible and, hence, a burger. So Matheny was right—technically. One time Matheny had urged them to make a burger, just one. His point? Although costly and premature, it would be worth it, because it would generate worldwide attention and help advance the mission.

Matheny, it was becoming increasingly clear, understood how to work the reptilian-sized brains of journalists like me. I started thinking about his other seductive comment ("if you get them drunk . . ."). A few moments later, in a fumbling, apologetic way, with a mealymouthed I-know-it's-illegal preface, I asked point blank:

Have you ever tried it?

Haagsman didn't say anything, just a slight head shake, expressionless, negative. A barely discernible head shake from Roelen. It was an "of course not" no, the kind of no that seemed immune even to multiple shots of Jägermeister.

"Why would we?" Roelen asked me. Aside from being illegal, it's just not "a good laboratory practice," he said. "You're supposed to wash your hands, wear a lab coat, and," he added, dryly, "eating cells would just not be good." Haagsman then said "it's premature" and added that eating pork cells would be "like eating beer before it's fermented."

The Mouse Burger

The mouse burger came up after I had brought up the Jurassic Park scenario, which I had feared was a Matheny-engineered public relations stunt.

They both agreed the JPS was scientifically plausible.

You would simply need the DNA, Roelen said, and then you would begin culturing the cells, just like with human, cow, or pig cells.

The obvious issue with T. rex or wooly mammoth meat, Roelen pointed out, was consumer acceptance. Earlier, Roelen had told me a story about a talk he gave at an Amsterdam club. At one point the staff presented chicken nuggets to the hundred or so attendees, but they were told it was in vitro meat. Nearly everyone tried it. Roelen smiled broadly.

Even at this fetal juncture, both scientists expressed concern about how people will react to in vitro meat. "We don't want to make something people won't eat," Haagsman said. Consumer concerns have already played a role; another promising means of culturing pig cells used biotechnology to create what are known as pluripotent cells; they elected not to pursue this route because it relied on genetic engineering, and so many European consumers fiercely oppose GMOs.

I asked them to forget about consumers.

Haagsman and Roelen then said that extinct or endangered species could be just as plausible an in vitro meat product as pig. In fact, Roelen said, a flash of mirth crossing his face, it could actually be *easier* to culture woolly mammoth than pig. Haagsman added that it probably wouldn't taste different, either. The professor of meat sciences said there's a meat taste that's fundamentally similar, crossing all mammalian species. A minced mouse meat product would taste very similar to minced pork or minced beef. It would have iron, zinc, and vitamin B_{12} and you could modify taste, adding fats and salts and varying amounts of protein, pretty easily. "We could culture mice cells right now," Roelen added, and exchanged a glance with Haagsman. "But people don't like to eat mice."

Before I left Utrecht, Roelen walked me through his lab. It was a short tour—there's not much to see. He gazed over the facilities—

two lab assistants listening to music, peering into microscopes. "Someday it will happen, and we'll think it was so obvious. Why did we treat animals like that? Why did we use so much land?" He smiled. "And this is where it all started."

I asked him for a prediction. Roelen shook his head and laughed. "Winston Churchill said we would be growing meat in fifty years. He said that in 1933. And we don't. He's a far smarter man than I."

Eindhoven—The Mouthfeel of Lab Meat

It was a rainy day in Eindhoven, but inside room 412, the Tissue Engineering Lab, it was warm and bright, filled with young women in white lab coats, shuffling between what looked like small refrigerators filled with beakers of Kool-Aid. Marloes Langelaan, a graduate student in bioengineering, guided me toward the place where she kept her mouse cells. Langelaan was designing a tool that had the enormously important assignment of simulating the experience of a cow or pig's physical movement.

As we headed toward her cells, we passed more of these mini-refrigerators, which are incubators, used to grow cells for cartilage growth and heart regeneration. The lab's primary work was for human medical needs. You might think that growing a heart or kidney—complex human organs—would be much more challenging than growing muscle tissue. Muscle tissue is relatively simple, after all. But the human organ engineers have one enormous advantage: the body's extraordinary potential to regenerate itself. If you implant tissue in a human, the human body intervenes, remodeling the tissue itself. It's still not fully understood why this happens, but it does, and it's something the meat growers lack.

Langelaan opened a door to one of the mini-refrigerators and pulled out a small tray that had six small dishes, each filled with a gelatinous substance. It looked, to the naked eye, like pink Kool-Aid resting in a Velcro dish. "You can't see them," she said, "but there are more than three million cells there." These cells, tiny brown specks under a scope, are then exercised; electrical stimulation, Langelaan explained, forces the cells to move at intervals, as if on a treadmill, a kind of personal trainer for lab meat. A few steps away, Langelaan opened up another incubator and pointed to a tiny device. This was the "scaffolding." You might imagine something called scaffolding to be an elaborate structure—imagine the outside of a building—but the in vitro meat version looked like little more than an earplug. She pointed out that the "scaffolding" was made of a biodegradable sugar polymer and is critical because it enables the lab meat to be grown in "3-D." You can grow layers of cells in a petri dish, but once they get thicker—more than a few layers—some of the cells die off. Essentially, the scaffolding would mimic what the bloodstream does. You have to feed all of the cells (top, bottom, interior) with nutrients to create a nice, big hunk of lab meat.

I had come to Eindhoven on the last day of my trip to the Netherlands to see the bioreactor.

It was the last piece of the meat-growing project, and it was supposedly the most tangible. I had expected to see a crude prototype of a toaster-sized machine, like the ones that I'd read about. But Langelaan's bioreactor, her PhD project, was still a collection of components to be assembled. As in Utrecht, everything in Eindhoven was at an early research stage—asked about her personal grand achievement after four years, Langelaan said it was getting a mouse tendon to flex. She excitedly offered to send me a video clip of the tendon's movement. This might strike some as a small achievement, but it was, she pointed out, one of the crucial baby steps toward meat farming.

Mark Post, the director of the Eindhoven group, compared the bioreactor work to that of mainframe computer makers in the early 1960s. Room-sized mainframes could do only simple computations. That's essentially what flexing a mouse tendon means to meat growers. Right now the Eindhoven bioreactor—using mechanical and electro-stimulation—could match 60 percent of the movement of an actual ruminant. The remaining 40 percent, Post said, was elusive. Right now, he said, they could create only "wasted muscle," which means mouse meat with the texture of tofu. The largest piece of meat Eindhoven had created was 8 millimeters long, 2 millimeters wide, and 400 microns thick—that's the thickness of a contact lens.

Post, a vascular biologist and medical doctor who has worked on cartilage and kidney regeneration in the United States at both Harvard and Dartmouth, was the most high-minded member of the team—"Nothing I've worked on has been even close to the potential societal impact of this," he told me—but he was also the most blunt. "This is a joke. Three universities, six graduate students. Please." The project was up for grant renewal, and if it got another grant, Post said wearily, "we'll publish papers, and follow clues, and do all that. But it won't have any societal impact. If you really want to develop this, you have to seriously change the commitment."

I asked him what it would take to bring in vitro meat to the market in ten years.

"We need at least a hundred million dollars to make this serious, to get this going."

An Apollo project–like investment?

"Yes."

FOOTBALL-FIELD-SIZED FACTORIES SUPPLYING chicken, beef, and pork to Chicago, New York, and New Delhi. A toaster-sized home appliance that makes meat making as simple as bread making. Jubilant vegans dancing naked in the streets, then gorging themselves on no-kill bratwurst and Italian sausage . . . Reduced fossil fuel emissions, the disappearance of hog lots, ranch land restored.

After a week in the Netherlands, it all seemed more remote than ever.

Crossing the puddle-filled campus of the Technical University of Eindhoven ("the Dutch MIT") with its modern architecture suddenly grim and creepy, I thought about "$100 million" and "Apollo project" and mouse burgers and began to think, not positively, about Matheny and all his pithy quotes and predictions, and, worst, that coy "if you get them drunk . . ." Was this the spirit of the Kumbaya co-op?

This frustration started to pass. I went to a Dutch coffee shop to see if marijuana is still legal in the Netherlands, and then I found an Indonesian restaurant and had a wonderful satay, and a dish called *dendeng belado* (beef served with a hot chile sauce) and a *rijstaffel* (an Indonesian dish, not readily available in Chicago), and, at last with a broader mind and full stomach, it occurred to me that $100 million was not so much.

The ConAgras, Krafts, General Mills, and Nestlés of the world routinely invest tens of millions on product development research for such things as instant coffee and microwavable buffalo wings. What's more, from Post's perspective as a physician, from a world where big pharmaceutical companies regularly spend tens of millions on drug development, raising $100 million was not an outrageous notion at all.

As for Matheny, it is easy to miss it on his busy CV, but he also has an MBA. At one point he suggested I speak with a friend of his at Kleiner Perkins, the legendary Silicon Valley venture capital firm that provided seed money for Google and Netscape and Silicon Graphics. For KP, $100 million was pocket change. The KP green tech investor told me the firm wasn't ready to invest now, but he expressed genuine enthusiasm. From the venture capitalist perspective, the Dutch in vitro meat project was merely a "proof of concept." Perhaps Matheny, in his irrepressibly optimistic, asteroid-deflecting-strategy worldview, was right—maybe meat factories were really achievable in ten years and the only thing missing was that one angel investor.

THE LAST TIME I checked in with Matheny, he had left Hopkins for Oxford, to study risk assessment and bioterrorism at a place called the Future of Humanity Institute. His specific interest: preventing smallpox.

He had some in vitro meat bad news to report: the Dutch multi-university grant had not been renewed. The quest for the embryonic stem cell in Utrecht, on hold.

But that was a speed bump; the news would get better for the movement.

A New Harvest–funded study showed that cultured meat was, as Matheny hoped, the green choice; lab-grown, vat-raised meat would reduce carbon dioxide emissions by 80 percent and land and water use by 90 percent. In 2011, private investors were finally on board; an Australian entrepreneur was consolidating patents, an American biotech company was planning to develop a lab-spawned shrimp product. A spate of articles had also appeared—*Scientific American*, a full-literature review in *Science*. A story in the *New Yorker* spurred more interest in meat growing. In a seeming endorsement of the idea, the *New Yorker* asked a few marketing gurus to deploy their talents to fight the "yuck factor" by "rebranding lab-meat." One ad guy's idea: stay positive, highlight the number of pastures reclaimed, and the freshwater saved.

And Matheny's own public relations idea—the one that Roelen and Haagsman had resisted, the one that would captivate the world—that was happening. In the summer of 2011, Mark Post told me that he had a funder. With $300,000, two full-time technicians, and three incubators, Post's team will spend a year growing 10 billion cells. At some point in 2012—if all goes as planned—these cells will be formed into a patty, spiced with some non-meat ingredients, and served as the world's first lab-grown hamburger.

PART
FOUR

FISH

9.

Where Is the Next Salmon?

THE FOLLOWING EXCHANGE OCCURRED 989 DAYS after Dan Benetti, the University of Miami scientist who started this whole journey, said, "It's not a ninety-nine percent chance that cobia will be sold in Costco in five years. It's more like ninety-nine-point-nine-nine-nine percent."

> JS: Do you have cobia?
>
> FISH GUY: What?
>
> JS: Cobia . . . Co-be-a. The fish?
>
> FISH GUY: No.
>
> JS: Have you ever had cobia?
>
> FISH GUY: No . . . What is it?

We were talking at the South Loop Whole Foods Market, but I could have been at any number of grocery stores in the Chicago area. And every time I got the "what is it" reply, I thought, It's not here yet.

Cobia was different from Treviso radicchio or in vitro meat burgers or genetically engineered Brandywine tomatoes or anything else I'd looked at, really. I'd seen the data. I'd read the experts (it wasn't just Benetti predicting cobia was the Next Big Fish). I'd tasted cobia. I believed.

My faith in the inevitability of McCobia burgers and Lean Cuisine Cobia Marsala was finally shaken when I got the news that Virginia Cobia Farms—one of the centerpieces of my research, and by far the largest cobia farming effort in the United States—wasn't going to the 2009 International Boston Seafood Show.

I HAD BEEN TRACKING the Virginia guys since the winter of 2007. A couple of months after leaving Miami, I received a call from Refik Orhun, who managed Benetti's cobia hatchery. Orhun basically reaffirmed the hype—cobia was exploding, he'd been traveling the world with Benetti (Brazil, Vietnam, Thailand, Mexico), production numbers were up. He even had developed a website to track cobia data. But then he mentioned something that shocked me: "People are giving up on the open-ocean aquaculture idea."

Just a few months earlier, Orhun and Benetti were touting aquapods and underwater ranchers as the Solution to the Great American Aquaculture Conundrum. Although no law specifically banned it, if you wanted to raise cobia off the coast of Florida, you'd have to get permits from at least ten government agencies—the Army Corps of Engineers, the Florida Department of Agriculture, the Florida Department of Fisheries, EPA, NOAA, etc.

Getting permission was functionally impossible. The Byzantine set of rules, permits, and prohibitions was erected in response to fear of "another salmon industry." Environmentalists, for good reason, have blamed salmon farmers for a litany of problems— from threatening wild salmon populations to infecting endangered species with sea lice to polluting coastal waters with fish excrement.

Benetti, who freely admitted that traditional aquaculture had "its dark ages" and had done great harm to the environment, had researched the underwater sea farming idea for more than a decade. The Miami professor argued passionately that ecologically sensitive, deeper-water aquaculture was The Answer—that it could sate America's appetite for seafood, *and* create an industry and jobs. Along with a small group of others, he had been aggressively lobbying lawmakers to support a bill—the National Offshore Aquaculture Act—that would open up 200 miles of federal waters for AquaPod-style fish farming in the United States.

And now Orhun was telling me that he was giving up?

The bill was going nowhere, Orhun explained. Benetti and others were tired of the fight. They're looking to try open-ocean aquaculture internationally. "They think it's hopeless here."

But there was another technology, Orhun said, a "closed system." It's indoors, on land, away from the ocean. Everything is recirculating. "The environmentalists will have nothing to complain about," said Orhun, laughing. He added that one of these indoor aquafarms was raising cobia.

I soon learned what Orhun was talking about. A group of investors, aided by the state of Virginia, had announced that they would invest $30 million in a massive football-field-sized indoor farm. The facility was on land, 300 miles from the ocean. They had circumvented all the usual permitting obstacles, securing the biggest marine fish farming permit in U.S. history. One investor said the farm would eventually produce 200 million pounds of fish a year.

The most intriguing thing about this farm was not just the proposed scale or even the location. The indoor farming idea was predicated on the claim that cobia could adapt to freshwater conditions. Fish farmers often manipulate the natural behavior of fish. When I visited Benetti and Orhun they were trying to figure out how to change cobia's biological clock so that they could trick the fish into believing it was mating season and thereby produce fish all year. The early pioneers of sea bass aquaculture had to manufacture an enzyme to spur the fish to spawn in captivity. But the Virginia team's claim was even harder to fathom. Cobia do not exist in freshwater in the wild.

I contacted Virginia Cobia Farms and made plans in the fall of 2009 to visit the farm and follow them to Boston. They had been to the Boston show and created buzz in the trade press; their cobia had even appeared on *Iron Chef* (Mario Batali versus Jamie Oliver).

One of the men behind the Virginia cobia venture, William "Bill" Martin, Jr., was an aquaculture veteran. His partner, H. William Harris, was a onetime pediatric kidney specialist, a former faculty member at Harvard Medical School. Here was a chance, I thought, to see the Next Salmon happen, to learn how to market an unknown fish to the world.

Then the discouraging news. In the months leading up to my Virginia trip, I learned from Tracy Mitchell, the farm's marketing manager, that plans had changed—Virginia Cobia Farms was not going to Boston this year.

But it wasn't just Virginia Cobia Farms that wasn't showing at Boston. Brian O'Hanlon, a protégé of Dan Benetti who farmed cobia off the coast of Puerto Rico, said he was going to Boston but wasn't showing. He wouldn't have fish for at least another six months. I tried to reach Owen Stevens, another cobia believer I knew from Florida, an idealistic Brit who had moved to Belize to work for Marine Farms, a Norwegian seafood giant expected to dominate the North American cobia market. No response from Stevens. And Marine Farms, the owner of the supposedly monstrous Belize farm, wasn't listed to show at Boston, either.

All of this—coupled with the fact that cobia was nonexistent in Chicago—got me wondering whether cobia was really such a sure thing after all.

10.

The Super Bowl of Seafood

ANYTHING THAT LIVES IN THE WATER (fish, cephalopod, crustacean, seaweed) that humans eat in any significant volume is here in a massive, unprecedented way.

There are 100 vendors selling shrimp; 120 selling tilapia; two dozen selling eels; more than 20 selling mullet and milkfish. Shrimp could mean either Asian, Central American, North American, warm water, cold water, tiger shrimp, sand shrimp, bamboo shrimp, Vannamei prawn. Crab—not simple. There's blue, brown, Dungeness, rock, snow, soft-shell, stone, and Jonah. There are 11 vendors competing for the frog leg business. Six people selling alligator, and five fighting for your langostino dollars.

And that's just the familiar stuff.

You can find specialists hawking southern-style pangasius,

lumpfish, ono, opah, horse mackerel, and hoki. To navigate the floor of the International Boston Seafood Show, you use a Fodor's-like two-hundred-page guidebook, and that omits, I learned, a lot of what's at the show.

It's not hard to see why each year about two thousand people with no connection to the industry pay $185 each for a floor pass. But Red Lobster customers are not the focus of the 140-year-old event, which has been held for years at the Boston Convention Center.

I was here because this was the place to see what was *coming* in the world of seafood. When I asked Dan Benetti in 2005 what would be the crucial next step for cobia, there was no pause—he said simply, "Boston." Boston is where the buyers, pundits, and chefs come to taste and shop and decide what will be in restaurants and on grocery store shelves. Boston is where new seafood ideas, fresh out of R&D, have their shot at the big time.

In the early 1990s, tilapia and the Lake Victoria giant perch debuted here. Tilapia is now the United States' fourth most popular seafood, produced in more than eighty countries. At the 2009 show you could barely walk twenty feet without seeing some vendor pitching cheaper tilapia, fresher tilapia, parmesan-crusted tilapia, or tilapia with smoky peach salsa. At the same show, only a single vendor was selling Lake Victoria perch.

Initially, my plan was to see the show behind the scenes, to see how Virginia Cobia Farms sold the world on a virtually unknown fish. Now my goal was to spend twenty-four hours in Boston seeing if cobia was happening, finding out what was going on with these once-giddy cobia promoters I had met five years ago.

The Black Salmon

A fish in booth 1313 looked awfully familiar.

It was labeled "Black Salmon." Packed in ice, about two feet long and displayed like a prize, it had a flat face, sort of like a cat-fish, tiny eyes, an ivory-white belly, two pectoral fins. And there was a dorsal fin—that unmistakable dorsal fin. Short spikes that looked like teeth, sawlike. I'm not a marine biologist or much of a fisherman but I was pretty sure I knew this fish. It wasn't salmon—any kind of salmon.

I eyed the vendors, Russian speakers in tight-fitting suits. They had a video playing, in which "black salmon" was being fed, some-where off the coast of Vietnam. A brochure featured three of the so-called black salmon frolicking in blue seas, like dolphins at Sea-World. In the happy fish brochure they had all the details a seafood buyer needs (cuts available—fillet skin on, fillet skinless, loin), dif-ferent preparations, farm location (Phu Yim province). Below one photo, a list in tiny type revealed that "black salmon" had other names: Black Knight, Crab Eater, Sergeant Fish, Cobia.

So it *was* cobia. The first booth I visited in the whole 17,000-person, 870-vendor show had cobia *that wasn't even being advertised as cobia*. Even more significant than the realization that off-the-guidebook cobia lurked on the show floor—cobia was clearly part of the seafood name game.

The most famous example of this name game is the Patago-nian toothfish. In the early 1970s, a Los Angeles fish merchant who felt that "toothfish" wasn't a savory name started pitching it as Chilean sea bass. The new name had a hint of exoticism, yet also a tinge of familiarity: "sea bass." Menus all over the world now carry Chilean sea bass. Imitators followed. A fish called "tra" in Asia has become popular in Europe under the moniker "pangas-ius." The American Catfish Association has even been trying to sell its farmed catfish as "delacata."

In the case of "black salmon," it turned out the Russians weren't making this up or pulling it out of a marketing focus group (like delacata). Like many fish, cobia is a fish of many names, with more than twenty different aliases. In Texas it's known as "ling";

in Brazil it's called "the prodigal son." But black salmon? Cobia is a white fish, while salmon is pink. Cobia is tropical, salmon is cold-water. They bear little resemblance. As ridiculous and counterintuitive as it sounds, there are places in the world, such as Belize, where people call it "black salmon."

I kept an eye out for black salmon, but never saw the name again. But at least five other booths were hawking cobia: one from Panama, two from Taiwan, one from Vietnam, one from China. There might have been even more cobia on the floor, but I would never find them all. There was the pesky name variability. The guidebook clearly didn't list many fish on display. You could come closer to inspect a booth, and find layers of offerings. Then there was the language issue. A significant part of the show had Chinese signage—with no English translation. China is a major cobia producer.

Still, one thing seemed clear after a floor walk. The show wasn't overflowing with cobia, black salmon, black king, or whatever you may call it. And given the fact that twenty vendors were selling milkfish, it certainly didn't seem like cobia was on the verge of becoming the Next Salmon.

There were plenty of other Next Great Seafood candidates out there, like sea bass and sea bream, stars of the Mediterranean aquaculture world. A group of Virginians were pushing Chesapeake Bay stingray strips to some skeptical passersby. One vendor was promoting a tilapia hot dog, claiming it was hugely popular in the Philippines.

One fish attracting plenty of buzz was barramundi. Native to Australia, unfamiliar to most Americans, staff for a company called Australis wore T-shirts that said "The Better Fish: Better Tasting, Better for the Environment," and handed out barramundi samples to a steady flow of curious visitors. I tried a piece—it was a softer, flakier white fish than the more steaklike cobia. Not bad.

I loaded up on the barramundi brochures. One sheet was a

reprint of a *Boston Globe* feature story about the Next Great Fish. It was eerily like my *Miami New Times* article about cobia—a pioneer, a hot species, an earth-saving ambition—except the up-and-coming species was barramundi and the pioneer was a man named Josh Goldman, who, like Benetti, had spent years searching for the perfect species. Shortly after glancing at the sheet, I spotted Goldman, the company's president. I told him about my focus on cobia. "I think cobia is overrated," he said almost immediately, before launching into a pitch for barramundi. "It's a whole category of fish that most of the world missed."

Barramundi are unusual, in part because they're *catadromous*. While fish such as Atlantic salmon and sea bass spawn in fresh water and live their adult lives in the ocean, barramundi do the exact opposite: born in the ocean, they mature in fresh water. During their commute between fresh and salt water, barramundi often get stuck in small lakes that the Aussies call billabongs. This internment in billabongs, extremely hot and low-oxygen water, partly explains why they're the perfect species for aquaculture, as Goldman sees it. Barramundi are used to being trapped in tough, cramped conditions; they're famously docile and compliant in captivity, and they're good breeders.

Goldman, who has a background as an ecologist, also pointed out that due to their stint in the billabong's low-oxygen water, the Aussie fish have developed huge gills that make them highly disease resistant. But above and beyond all this, Goldman was pitching barramundi as "the better fish" because of their diet. Goldman told me that, even though barramundi are carnivorous, they thrive on a diet that is about 80 percent plant-based—soy, wheat, corn, canola.

After getting a quick taste of barramundi hype, I learned that Goldman was an indoor fish farmer. His farm, in Turners Falls, Massachusetts, was trying to achieve the same thing as Virginia Cobia Farms. Goldman wanted to create the world's largest indoor recirculating system.

The Prodigy

"This fish tastes like shit," said Brian O'Hanlon, scowling as he finished a Dixie cup–sized sample of "black salmon" sashimi. I tried the cobia—seemed fine, good, really. O'Hanlon shook his head. "It tastes like a frozen piece of cobia," he said, "or a piece of cobia that was not extremely fresh."

He glanced over at a video of the "black salmon" farm in Vietnam. The water was murky, O'Hanlon observed. The cages were too small. And the feeding? "Look at that," O'Hanlon said with oh-my-God disgust as a Vietnamese man dumped what looked like a bucket of small fish into the water. "That's so inefficient. They're feeding them pure protein."

After critiquing the video, O'Hanlon turned to greet a Panama-based fish farmer. "Those guys aren't going to make it," he said to me afterward. "This is a tough business. There's a steep learning curve." When we passed another cobia vendor, O'Hanlon shook his head. "Why would they photograph a fish that looks like that." O'Hanlon pulled out his Open Blue Sea Farms business card with a photo. "That's what cobia is supposed to look like."

Brian O'Hanlon might strike some as an unlikely figure to be laying out such Simon Cowell–like criticism—he's youngish (in his late twenties), a college dropout, tall, lanky, boyish, and disarmingly friendly. One of his business partners calls him "Opie."

The reason why he's so cocksure—why his critique of such things as water quality in Vietnam is so know-it-all—is because, within the world of marine aquaculture, he's something of a legend. He's the United States' first commercial cobia farmer, and the first to try Benetti's underwater sea ranching idea. He has lectured the world's leading aquaculture researchers on eco-sensitive marine farming techniques. He's probably been the subject of more stories about aquaculture in general-interest magazines than any other fish farmer.

O'Hanlon has a great story. He's the third-generation son of a New York City seafood family. In sixth grade, prompted by a grade school project, he asked his father, a Fulton Fish Market fishmonger: What's the future of your business? "Fish farming," was the answer. O'Hanlon took his father's prediction seriously. He started growing fish as a teen in his family's Long Island home. At one point he set up a three-thousand-gallon tank stocked with red snapper in his basement. The tank used so much energy that the Greenlawn, New York, police investigated the O'Hanlon home, suspecting a possible marijuana-growing operation.

A few years later, O'Hanlon attended a seminar taught by Benetti. The then-eighteen-year-old was so inspired by the Miami professor's vision of zero-impact aquaculture that he decided to drop out of college and start his own fish farm. Meanwhile, Benetti was so impressed by the aquaculture-mad kid that he actually flew up to New York to see his basement experiment. In 2002, O'Hanlon, at the ripe old age of twenty-two, started Snapperfarm, an underwater sea ranch off the coast of Puerto Rico.

Battle scars earn respect among fish farmers, and in seven years in Puerto Rico, O'Hanlon has been the victim of all the requisite disasters (hurricanes, shark attacks, disease). I was interested in talking with O'Hanlon, by now a grizzled, well-respected veteran, to get his insight into why the show wasn't overflowing with cobia, as his mentor had predicted in 2005. I also wanted to know why O'Hanlon didn't have any cobia to show himself.

O'Hanlon told me he was fishless because "we're relocating." The first cobia farmer in the United States gave up on fish farming in the States for the same reason virtually no one tries to fish farm in U.S. waters anymore—bureaucracy. O'Hanlon had weathered the ocean farmer's natural adversity: he'd endured red tape from twenty agencies and had managed to net $500,000 in 2008. But the regulatory agencies limited him to producing fifty tons of cobia a year. That was it. You can't run a fish farm at that scale, let alone prove the viability of deep-sea, open-ocean aquaculture. The goal was always to prove both the environmental *and* economic sustainability of Aquaculture 2.0.

O'Hanlon was moving his cobia farm to a new location off the coast of Panama. Less bureaucracy, lower hurricane risk, and a permit to grow 10,000 tons of fish. Hearing O'Hanlon talk about the location—his description of the near-perfect conditions, the swift current, the pristine water, the pleasant climate, the logistical superiority of this spot over any other—was like déjà vu. Just like when we talked in 2005, during my reporting on Benetti, he was *on the verge.*

The issue was not cobia. The fish's potential was unimpeachable. It lived up to the 2005 hype (growth, consumer appeal), he said. The problem was money. "It's a capital-intensive business. We need five million dollars to get the 'fingerlings in the water.' Then we'll have fifteen employees by the end of the first year. One hundred in two years . . ."

The media was still hot for O'Hanlon. "We're going to be in *Fortune,*" he said, nonchalantly. "It's great to get the attention, but we need money."

The Eco-Seafood Elite

Walking the floor of the Boston show with O'Hanlon was exciting; he was appalled by things that I simply could not see. At one point we passed by the Taiwanese pavilion and spotted a billboard that said Cobia, Cobia, Cobia, with a massive cobia head. O'Hanlon scowled. To me it looked like an ordinary fish head shot. "That fish looks horrible. Sick. Look at the gill."

O'Hanlon's too-cool-for-show demeanor started making sense when we arrived at the CleanFish pavilion. It appeared to be a gathering of a younger, hipper species of fishmonger.

He brightened, spotted some acquaintances, and quickly got

rid of me—amiably, of course—saying simply, "I need to talk with some people."

We had left the world of conventional fish farming. CleanFish was a coalition of elite, ecologically sensitive seafood providers. The Benetti and O'Hanlon ideals—"guilt-free seafood," "zero environmental impact," "sustainable methods"—had coalesced into a business. CleanFish, which billed itself as "a company, an aspiration, a movement," functioned as an umbrella, vetting members, guaranteeing a certain set of standards. "We believe that by sourcing delicious seafood by people who care, we can spark a return to healthy and regenerative ecosystems," declared the CleanFish credo. It was the fish farming version of the organic movement, and it was headquartered in the heart of organic-dom, San Francisco.

There was proselytizing to do. With O'Hanlon drifting off to speak with another eco-minded fish farmer, I was now being chaperoned by Michael Albert, Open Blue's marketing director. Albert, a veteran ad man who had worked for casinos and horse tracks and consumer packaged goods companies before having an epiphany about the world's oceans while walking the beach in Santa Monica, escorted me to a table to speak with a Scottish salmon farmer. I had little interest in talking with a salmon farmer.

Waiting for the farmer to finish talking with another journalist, I leafed through a brochure of stunning images—Scottish lakes and moss-covered mountains against a deep blue sea.

Finally, Andy Bing sat down next to me and explained that his company, Loch Duart, was "a different type of salmon farm. We're not multinational, we're not aimed at profits. We're focused on sustainability first." He told me about Loch Duart's stocking density: 98.5 percent water to 1.5 percent fish, much lower than those of traditional farms. He mentioned his farm's version of crop rotation. "We let our sites go fallow for a year, so that it regenerates itself." Bing told me about Loch Duart's polyculture project growing seaweed alongside salmon. "It achieves a nutrient balance," he said. "It's how it's done in nature."

Bing said Loch Duart had no interest in expanding its sixty-employee operation; they're small and independent, and they want to stay small and independent. Bing struck me as eerily familiar—an aquatic microfarmer—a kind of Bob Cannard of the sea.

After Bing left, moving on to dazzle another trade show journalist, Albert explained why it was so important to meet Loch Duart Scottish Salmon. "They're our model. They have the same set of values. And they're targeting the same type of consumer we want. It's not people who want fish. It's people who want Loch Duart or Wild Nunavut salmon or Open Blue cobia.

"It'll be costlier, but our belief is that people will be willing to pay more for something they trust, something that's good for the earth. It's a model that's already working in the terrestrial world."

Albert then ticked off the examples—free-range chickens, grass-fed beef, organic produce. And now, artisanal fish farms. "The old model of seafood for thousands of years is pile 'em high, sell 'em cheap," said Albert. "In order for us to be successful, that's gotta change."

ASKED ABOUT THE Virginia Cobia Farms approach—raising cobia in a warehouse inland—O'Hanlon, perhaps not surprisingly, scoffed.

He thinks it's wasteful. "It's like taking a barge out to sea to grow corn." He said it was unnatural. "I just don't believe in the system of trying to raise cobia in fresh water." And it's inhumane. The indoor farm would have to raise fish at "mind-boggling" densities to succeed. "I just can't imagine what one hundred or two hundred kilograms of fish per cubic meter looks like. . . . We raise them at one tenth of that and our cages look pretty thick.

"Cobia are big fish," O'Hanlon said. "They evolved to live

in low-density situations with a lot of clean water and a lot of freedom."

O'Hanlon was so consistently critical of the fish on display and the practices of other farmers at the show that it was a surprise when he *wasn't* critical.

Interestingly, he wasn't appalled by Goldman and his indoor barramundi farming. "It's a different species," he said. "It's much more adaptable to higher density and low salinity. It's a good fish."

Before leaving the Boston show, I needed a second try of the fish that had earned O'Hanlon's respect. Barramundi (aka giant sea perch, Asian sea bass) has, on closer inspection, a faintly pinkish color. It was delicate and had a sweet, mild taste. It reminded me of red snapper. I had another sample.

The Next Salmon vs. the Better Fish: Mano-a-Mano

Jacky's is a small, upscale, European-style bistro that is about a ninety-second walk from my house.

After four years of searching futilely for cobia in Chicago, my wife and I visited Jacky's and, in a small-world moment that rivaled the discovery of a cache of Treviso radicchio 1.1 miles from my house, we looked at the menu to discover cobia *and* barramundi.

By some stroke of divine intervention from the food gods, Jonadab Silva, an adventurous chef, with an interest in lesser-known species of fish, opened a restaurant on my street in Evanston, Illinois. (Later, Silva told me about his particular interest in working with tautog, sea bream, and snakehead.)

Trying to conceal my excitement, I played ignorant. Our waiter gave a textbook description of the two fish, both mild and white (barra is delicate, sweeter; cobia is thicker, steakier), and then we asked him for a recommendation. "Well, people love barramundi," he said, "but they come back for cobia."

We ordered both.

The cobia was served with roasted fennel and topped with potato crème sauce. The barramundi had an almond, garlic, red pepper romesco sauce.

The barramundi preparation was sublime. The fish's soft, subtle sweetness paired beautifully with the romesco. Barramundi was, in my subjective view, better tasting than red snapper. And it really was, as advertised, "the better fish." It received the Monterey Bay Aquarium's highest ranking for sustainability. The food editor of *The Atlantic* has urged readers "Eat Barramundi! And Forget Salmon." Paul Greenberg, author of *Four Fish*, perhaps the best book about aquaculture and the state of fisheries, called barramundi a "fish that could fulfill Green Revolution promises of the early days of aquaculture."

Why such love for the Aussie fish? It has a staggering FCR. That's feed-conversion ratio—the miles-per-gallon of fish farming, a term you hear again and again among ecologically concerned fish farmers. FCR indicates the number of pounds of feed required to produce one pound of flesh. Atlantic salmon requires as much as three pounds of smaller fish, such as anchovies and sardines, to produce one pound of meat. Net protein loss: two pounds. Bad.

But barramundi, like tilapia, can get by on a mostly vegetarian diet. Even though it's carnivorous, you can almost get the barra's FCR close to one-to-one. That's the holy grail of aquaculture—or any form of protein production, for that matter. With a one-to-one FCR, you could, in theory, solve the world's protein deficit. Cobia, by contrast, was typically around a pound and a half of feed per pound of flesh.

Intellectually, rationally, environmental-consciously, barramundi made perfect sense as the Next Salmon. It has a wonderful, mild, non-fishy taste and it is the ultimate sustainable fish. However, it became clear to me on the ninety-second commute home from Jacky's that the data alone didn't tell the whole story. I was not neutral on the Next Great Fish matter. I had a weakness for thick, meaty, grillable fish. In short, I was happy about a future with more barramundi, but I was truly excited about a future with more cobia. I wanted cobia to be the Next Salmon.

11.

The Last Perfect Species: St. Peter's Fish

IF YOU'RE A DOUBTER—if you have trouble conceiving how cobia or barramundi or yellowtail or tautog or some other "new fish" could, within a few years, vault from obscurity to near ubiquity—consider the case of the Peace Corps' favorite fish, St. Peter's fish, aka tilapia.

In 2000, the average American didn't know what a tilapia was. Some thought it sounded like a venereal disease. By 2005, it was a fixture at Red Lobster and Costco. By 2010, it was the most popular farmed fish in the country.

Tilapia didn't come out of nowhere. A native of the Nile basin, it's been a staple in Egypt and throughout the Middle East for thousands of years. It's mentioned in the Bible. (Jesus fed five thousand people with five loaves of bread and two fish—that's tilapia. When the apostle Peter caught a fish with a coin in its mouth—tilapia.) It's not necessarily new to non–Bible reading Americans, either. Peace Corps volunteers have taught tilapia aquaculture since the 1960s. The fish is a great source of protein, easy and cheap to grow.

But it was still a nonfactor in the American seafood section. Tilapia had a flaw that fish people call "off flavor."

One of the virtues of tilapia is that they are filter feeders— they can live off human waste, algae, and other microscopic plankton. That's what made it so appealing to the Peace Corps. A poor farmer with just a patch of stagnant water could grow tilapia, thereby adding protein to his diet. The problem is that the wild tilapia develop the harmless, earthy flavor that people describe as "muddy." Fine as a protein source for the Third World, not appealing to most First World consumers.

But in the 1980s, aquaculturists started raising tilapia in clean water, feeding them a steady diet of corn and soy. By controlling their inputs, fish farmers found that they could change the flavor of the fish. Instead of tasting like mud, tilapia tasted like, really, nothing. And a flaky, soft white fish that tastes like nothing is what many American consumers want. Americans, by and large, don't like fishy.

As soon as the new, flavorless tilapia started appearing in the American market, it became an immediate hit. Hailed as the "New Orange Roughy," tilapia began appearing on the menus of fine restaurants, with adventurous diners seeking to try the new fish.

But with its fast growth, its relatively low production costs, and its bland flavor (a *New York Times* reporter called it the "Meryl Streep of fish, capable of playing any role"), tilapia was just too good to be merely an elite fish. Called the perfect factory fish, tilapia spurred an aquaculture version of the dot-com boom. Beginning in the late 1990s it exploded on the American food scene. Last year Americans ate 475 million pounds of tilapia—that's one and a half pounds per person—and still growing. Tilapia sales are expected to grow by another 10 percent in 2012.

As in any rush, the tilapia boom gave birth to an industry, and early visionaries became what you might call tilapia millionaires. One of the people who rode the meteoric rise of St. Peter's fish was William Martin Jr. What made Martin so unusual among the tilapia pioneers? His farm was based in the United States (more than 95 percent of tilapia is imported) and his American farm is indoors (more than 99 percent of tilapia is raised outside).

12.

The Tilapia Tycoon with
Cobia Dreams

THE HEADQUARTERS OF BILL MARTIN'S SEAFOOD EMPIRE is in Martinsville, Virginia, a town of fifteen thousand in the foothills of the
Blue Ridge Mountains.

To get to Martin's flagship farm, head south of the town center
on Highway 58, and look for signs that say "race fans stop here."
You'll pass the "NASCAR Shell" and then you'll see the hulking
Martinsville Speedway, a kind of Yankee Stadium of stock car
racing. Make a right just before "Speedway Road," enter an industrial park, and there, adjacent to a box-making factory, is the
world's largest indoor fish farm.

Aside from a water tank and a sign declaring "World's Largest Sustainable Fish Farm," nothing suggests that Blue Ridge Aquaculture is ground zero for the indoor fish farming revolution. The retrofitted warehouse, which produces 4 million pounds of fish a year, blends into the surrounding industrial park.

The first clue to the Trump-like ambition of the place was the fireplace in the CEO's office. I'd heard and read some colorful stories about Martin—one of which included a fish farming epiphany while "riding an elephant in a jungle in Thailand"—so was not terribly shocked to be escorted into an office that felt like a hunting lodge.

In addition to a fireplace, Martin's office had other man cave treats—a mounted deer head, a replica of a Yankee schooner, a statue of a mastadon-like thing, a leather-bound collection of *Gray's Sporting Journals*, and dozens of pictures of hunting dogs.

While most of the Blue Ridge staff were dressed in business casual—this was, after all, an industrial park next to a motor speedway—Martin was ready for lunch at Jean Georges. He had a pressed blue shirt, dress pants, tie. He's a robust-looking man in his early sixties, tallish, with a thick head of salt-and-pepper hair and a square jaw.

It became quickly apparent that Martin, who has a thick, syrupy Virginia accent that makes one instantly think of a Confederate general in a Civil War reenactment, is an evangelist. His agenda involved cobia but he made it aggressively clear that it was bigger than cobia.

"I have no interest in any kind of aquaculture that is not land based," Martin said. "Period. I think traditional aquaculture is backwardsassed." He likened himself to the "Elmer Gantry of indoor aquaculture." He also called himself a "bloodhound" and "a bull in a china shop" in regard to indoor aquaculture. If you had to boil down Martin's philosophy, it's binary: Traditional aquaculture is very bad and indoor aquaculture is good. Very, very good.

THE ELMER GANTRY of indoor aquaculture does not come from a long line of fish people. And although his bearing, his name, and his fireplace-equipped office raised suspicions, he is not part of the royal family of Martinsville.

Martin was born and raised in Martinsville. He is related to the town's namesake, Revolutionary War general Joseph Martin, but he downplays the link. The oldest son of a newspaperman—his dad was former publisher of the *Martinsville Bulletin*—Martin had an eclectic career before his fish farming epiphany.

He was in commercial real estate, traded commodities in New York City, and then worked as publisher of small newspapers in places like Golden, Colorado, and Sanford, Florida. One of his papers was in West Memphis, Arkansas, which is in the heart of the catfish farming industry, an area that's sometimes called the Catfish Belt.

It was in Arkansas, during the early 1980s, a time when the industry was booming, that Martin read an article in the trade *Delta Farm Press* about a Purdue University professor who had developed a different system for raising fish.

Martin had no experience in fish farming, but the idea of raising fish indoors immediately appealed to him. Martin came to believe that the traditional method of catfish farming in ponds was "hugely inept. There are too many uncontrollable variables. Runoff from farms, bad weather. It was such an inefficient industry."

A few weeks after reading the article, Martin looked at two water tanks on an island in the Mississippi River, and had a flash of inspiration: "We'll run the water into the tanks, grow the fish, then scoop them out with a mesh thing." A few days later, the obvious caveat cut in. "No one will want to eat fish raised in Mississippi River water."

But Bill Martin had fish farming on the brain. By 1989 he had opened Blue Ridge Fisheries in Martinsville. It was indoors. "Of course it was indoors. I never ever thought about ponds," Martin said.

Blue Ridge Fisheries was a financial disaster. In 1989 they raised their first fish. By 1991, they'd lost over $5 million. The farm had hoped to raise 2 million catfish a year, but the fish were dying. When the problem was finally fixed—it wasn't disease, Martin said, it was a design flaw that was remedied by adding two centrifugal pumps—it was too late.

It was during the final days of Blue Ridge Fisheries, when they struggled to solve the mysterious catfish ills, that Martin and his team made a crucial discovery. They had been experimenting with other species as an alternative to catfish—striped bass, largemouth bass, tropical fish, and a little-known fish from the Nile basin. "Tilapia were amazing," Martin recalls. "We gave them a catfish diet and they still grew like gangbusters."

Blue Ridge Fisheries was broke and shuttered, but Martin was so encouraged by the improvements—the design flaw remedy and the success of this new species—that he rallied investors and bought back the farm for another try. Blue Ridge Fisheries reopened as Blue Ridge Aquaculture. It was a tilapia farm at a time, Martin said, "when a lot of people thought tilapia sounded like a venereal disease."

But there were more problems. Even with the superspecies and the structural change, the farm kept getting hit by disease. Once the farm's stock was infected by a live-haul truck. Another time it was strep-infected fingerlings. Finally, after two years of struggling to stay afloat, Martin had a revelatory conversation with his uncle, a doctor, about antibiotic resistance. He learned that by treating his strep-infected fish with amoxicillin, he could be contributing to antibiotic resistance in humans. Martin decided "at that very moment" to start from scratch. "We killed all our fish that day."

"No other fish will come on this lot," he declared. Instead of buying fingerlings from a hatchery, Blue Ridge Aquaculture would raise its own. It would become a cradle-to-market operation. The whole endeavor cost millions—it delayed production for a year. But it has worked. It's pretty much the cornerstone of Martin's stump speech.

"Disease-free since 1994. The most successful breeding program in the world. . . . You must have your own brood stock program. You cannot allow yourself to buy fingerlings," he says, pausing. "If you do buy fingerlings, you are buying every problem they have."

A new system, a new fish in place, and then Martin found his niche market. He couldn't compete price-wise with tilapia from overseas. But what he could do—that no one else could—is deliver live tilapia to major cities on the East Coast. "We can get you fish not in days, but in hours."

Martin didn't go into elaborate detail on how this all transpired, but at some point in the early 1990s he got a toehold in the live fish business—a business that caters mostly to Asians. By the late 1990s, William Martin, Jr., dominated the Asian live market in New York and Washington. By 2004 he was also king of the Asian live market in Boston and Toronto. "One hundred percent of my business is Asian. One hundred percent."

"The secret to success," Martin went on, "is loyalty. They have to trust you. One of my clients and I are so close. We don't call each other business associates. We are family.

"This trust doesn't come easy. You've got to be careful. There are so many thieves out there. I'm telling you. And the aquashysters."

Aquashysters

Thieves, crooks, and aquashysters—more often aquashysters. Martin does not have a high opinion of his peers in the seafood industry. In fact, he uses the word *aquashysters* so regularly that it was not at all surprising when his description of his typical day began with "looking for new ideas, fighting off the aquashysters."

Rampant aquashysterism is a part of why Martin expects that 80 percent of all seafood consumed in the United States by 2035 will be raised indoors.

Martin acknowledges that it is hard for most folks to conceive of an inland, indoor fish farming economy. Most people, after all, still expect their fish to come from an ocean, a lake, or a river.

But the way Martin sees it, there's a soaring need for seafood, and a growing disgust with seafood-as-usual. There's product fraud, "people selling tilapia as grouper." A 2010 study found that nearly 20 to 25 percent of seafood is falsely labeled. There are products coming from unknown sources. And that's just the entry-level shysterism. There's also the abuse of antibiotics, and high levels of PCBs and mercury, which pose a health menace to consumers.

It's hard to properly describe the experience of Martin talking about land-based aquaculture. He throws a lot at you—earnest recitation of facts, gloom and doom, metaphors (lots of metaphors), promises of a happy paradise, then just head-turning, uncategorizable stuff. "I don't even have to tell one lie," Martin said at one point, boasting about the virtues of indoor fish farming. "How many businesses do you know where you don't even have to lie?"

But if you unpack it all, there are three main components to Martin's support for a land-based system.

First, there's food safety. Martin claims there's no way to ensure safety in traditional aquaculture—there are too many uncontrollable variables, among them water quality, contaminants, and fish diseases. Indoor is, in his telling, the only way you can guarantee healthy, disease-free, contaminant-free, traceable fish. In fact, Martin argues that his indoor fish are far safer than wild-caught fish because of the variables that affect fisheries in nature, such as the BP oil spill in the Gulf of Mexico in 2010.

The second part of Martin's argument is a variation of the Benetti-O'Hanlon-CleanFish environmental message. Move fish farming indoors and you eliminate all of the problems created by aquaculture. No fish escape, no effluent pollutes the water, no unsightly farm mucks up the beach view. "This isn't Norway," he says. "We don't have hundreds of miles of uninhabited fjords. We have people living here."

Although Martin's message at times sounds like it was pulled from Dan Benetti's talking points, he does not think highly of the aquaculture professor. "Nice man. But I take what he says with a grain of salt the size of Utah." Martin's attack, which you hear time and time again in fish farmer to fish farmer pissing matches, is the ad hominem: "He's never run a fish farm."

The third argument is the one that Martin delivers with chest-thumping vigor. He points out, ad nauseam really, that a staggering 90 percent of the seafood in the United States is imported. (This isn't news. Go into any grocery store these days and you'll be hard-pressed to find domestic seafood. I'd experienced the absurdity of being in a grocery store in Key West, Florida, the home of the namesake Key West pink shrimp, and learning that you couldn't get Key West shrimp, but could get Indian shrimp.) But Martin's argument is that it's more than just an economic trade deficit issue. "This is about national security," he says, with mounting ire. "Many of the countries that supply the U.S. with seafood are not exactly friendly with us. I believe that outsourcing seafood is the same as outsourcing bullets. It's just plain stupid."

The only solution, in Martin's view, is homeland-produced seafood. And, in Martin's logic, the only option is indoor, inland aquaculture, because fisheries are collapsing and "Americans simply don't want coastal aquaculture." If you move it indoors, you can have your American aquaculture industry. "You could do this anywhere," he says of indoor fish farming. "Put it in downtown New York City."

It occurred to me at some point during one of his riffs that if you closed your eyes, blocked out the duck decoys, and tuned out some of the good-old-boyisms, and just concentrated on the words, Martin's pitch isn't wildly dissimilar from what activists at environmental organizations like Greenpeace or the World Wildlife Fund talk about.

He speaks highly of environmental organizations (Greenpeace, Friends of the Earth). He praises muckraking journalists (the Pollans and Schlossers of the world) for raising consciousness about the ills of food production. He talks passionately about the looming water crisis, fumes with outrage about the dangers of antibiotic abuse, argues for more government inspections, complains about "vulture capitalists" (venture capitalists) who don't have patience for green tech innovations. He talks about vermiculture and wastewater recycling and saving the oceans. He gets into a full-blown foam when the word *sustainability* is raised. "No one is truly sustainable until we give back what we take."

But then, just as you get ready to invite Martin to your Earth Day drum circle, he'll say something like "I'm not a tree-hugger, I'm a capitalist." Martin's oft-said line is "I'm an environmentalist, because it's good business." He predicts that the future of fish farming "ain't gonna be for little guys. I know environmentalists freak out when I say this, but it's gotta be like the chicken industry. Not their practices, but their scale. If you're gonna feed the world, that's what you're gonna have to do."

The Protein Factory

About two hours into the fireside chat, a man wearing a Virginia Tech T-shirt, jeans, and a Jesus fish belt entered Martin's office. This was Darin Prillaman, operations manager of tilapia. Prillaman gave me some blue booties (de rigueur in bio-cautious fish farms), asked about my fish history (no, I hadn't been in recent intimate contact with trout), and then we headed out.

I had requested a tour of Blue Ridge because, more than anything, I wanted to see what a warehouse packed with one and a half million fish looked like—not only to see the possible future of seafood, but also to see if I cared, to see if I would have a visceral reaction to the sight of industrial fish farming.

Prillaman, manager of tilapia for more than a decade, talks in a straightforward, flat manner that reminds one of a police officer testifying in court. He was a Virginia Tech student in the early 1990s when he caught the fish farming bug. After a summer job at Blue Ridge, he switched his major from communications to aquaculture, came home to Martinsville, and has been a tilapia farmer ever since.

Part of the reason tilapia is such a wonder-fish for aquaculture is because they're mouth breeders. Female tilapia hold thousands of eggs in their mouths until they're strong enough to survive. Every Thursday, Blue Ridge's "egg crew" (a group of staffers) pulls the eggs—nearly 500,000 of them—by hand, from the brood stock females. Day-old tilapia, called "swim-up fry," then go into a series of incubators. After three weeks in the nursery, they graduate, get a new name, fingerlings, and advance to an intermediary stint in a greenhouse. Looking into one of the incubators, I asked the manager of tilapia what percentage survive. "Sixty-six percent," he said without hesitation. "It's sixty-six percent."

As we walked through the stages of a tilapia life cycle, Prillaman revealed that although "Blue Ridge's tilapia are the tastiest fish you'll ever have . . . you kind of get tired of it after a while." He hasn't had a Blue Ridge tilapia in years.

The end of the road, the last stop before Cantonese dinners, is hot and humid and dark. Prillaman called it the "big room," and it felt like a miserable Miami night in July without air-conditioning. The nearly 100,000-square-foot warehouse is kept in this constant state of darkness because, Prillaman explained matter-of-factly, "keeping it dark limits the algae growth on our biofilter."

It was hard to fully appreciate the contents of the big room because of the darkness. But Prillaman ticked off data: forty-two tanks, holding 31,500 gallons of water each, producing between 45,000 to 50,000 pounds. (What is 50,000 pounds of fish? A typical Whole Foods buys about 1,200 pounds a week.)

Feeding one and a half million fish is a round-the-clock operation, in part because tilapia grow best with small, regular snacks. Feeding occurs once an hour, at six minutes after the hour. It's an entirely mechanized process. Behind the big room, a silo holds a mix of tilapia food. That mix flows through a cable bay system, which then drizzles on the tanks, not unlike the drip irrigation you might find in the Salinas Valley. The feeding is all centrally operated, controlled by Prillaman. The human factor is minimal; Prillaman monitors growth, checks water quality, varies inputs, tries to optimize water usage.

"Water," Prillaman said, waving toward a mammoth fan-like thing somewhere in the dark shadows of the warehouse, "is huge." Prillaman likened something called the "RBC"—the rotating biological contactor—to an algae-covered rock in a mountain stream. Like algae, the RBC uses microorganisms to filter and purify water. Blue Ridge recycles more than 80 percent of its water, Prillaman said, and is aiming for "more than 90." Because water is such a huge input cost, indoor farms have a tremendous incentive to recycle a higher and higher percentage of it.

The eeriest thing about the tilapia farm is the utter stillness.

Peek into any one of the tanks and you'll see a wall of fish—literally, a wall—every single visible space is occupied with fish. "There's a pound and three quarters of fish per gallon of water," Prillaman explained. Imagine taking a gallon milk jug and stuffing two nearly two-pound fish into it. That's dense.

There was no noise emanating from the mob.

"Why aren't they splashing?" I asked.

Prillaman grinned and said nothing. Thirty seconds went by; there were two splashes.

Blue Ridge's tilapia are not like the wild tilapia of the Nile or the Everglades. They're shorter and stockier, and temperamentally different. Ten years ago, when he harvested a tank, fish would jump out and spill all over the floor. Now, Prillaman said, only one or two get out. It's part Darwin—the fish evolve to adapt to their environment—but it's mostly genetic selection. He uses a rigorous process of choosing tilapia with the right attributes for industrial farming. The stillness in the big room is fifteen generations' worth of breeding. "We've selected a calmer fish for our brood stock."

Nearing the end of the tour, I peered into a tank holding larger fish, mere days away from harvest. I marveled at the docility of the mob—nary a splash. Getting closer to the tank, I reflexively moved my hand to touch the water. The ordinarily mellow Prillaman thrust his hand out and said, "Don't do that"—it was a disease risk.

Standing quietly in front of thousands of tilapia in a tank in a warehouse, I couldn't help but think about O'Hanlon and his underwater ranch in Panama. Would I rather have a fish that lived in its native waters, and experienced day and night, and, as O'Hanlon likes to say, "never sees the same water twice"? Hell yes. On the other hand, I was not repelled by a concrete tank stuffed with tilapia; it certainly didn't tweak me like the sight of thousands of cows on a feed lot.

Why Cobia Is Even More Perfect than Tilapia

Bill Martin is always looking for the Next Fish. He has tried raising trout in an abandoned coal mine in West Virginia (failed), he's tried striped bass (failed), Pacific white shrimp (still pending), tropical fish for home aquariums (it worked, sort of). And when I talked with him, he said that catfish—even catfish—is rattling around in the back of his head.

But the fish that he says was always "the Next Big Fish" was cobia. Martin's thoughts about cobia go back about fifteen years. He learned about ling—one of cobia's aliases—while sport fishing in Texas. He believed that the only reason cobia wasn't monstrously popular was that it wasn't a "schooling fish."

Unlike cod or salmon, cobia are loners. Beloved by sport fishermen because they grow to over one hundred pounds and are ferocious fighters that can take hours to reel in, cobia never became a popular food fish because they don't travel en masse. Hence they're hard to target and don't lend themselves to industrial-scale fishing. "If he had traveled in packs," said Martin, who often refers to cobia in the masculine gender, "he'd probably be gone by now."

Like many others, Martin saw cobia as having a potential to achieve a future quite different from tilapia. Tilapia was a white, flaky, tasteless fish, a brilliantly successful alternative to cod and flounder.

But cobia had a chance to enter a whole new category. With its thick, meaty flesh and higher fat content, it is more reminiscent of tuna or halibut than of cod. Cobia is even more versatile than tilapia. You can grill cobia. It's a great sushi fish. Martin foresaw the possibility that cobia could rival more expensive marine fish such as Chilean sea bass among white-tablecloth consumers.

And yet what made Martin believe that cobia could become not only a high-end fish but also a mass-market fish like tilapia were the freakish numbers. In the early 2000s, marine scientists in Asia had started to release data on their early work with cobia. At the 2002 World Aquaculture Society Conference in San Diego, a Taiwanese professor, I Chiu Liao, released findings that stunned many in the aquaculture world.

Cobia were growing six times as fast as salmon. Growing a thick-fleshed marine finfish in less than two years was unprecedented.

Early research also suggested that cobia, unlike other marine finfish such as mahi-mahi, had an unusual adaptability to captivity.

While mahi-mahi males were so averse to captivity that they would ram the sides of their cage, sometimes killing themselves, cobia seemed bizarrely comfortable in a tank. One researcher said of cobia, "It's almost like they like being in captivity."

After Martin heard about cobia's aquaculture potential—"This guy grows ten or twelve pounds a year"—he concluded, "this is my next fish, period."

But given Martin's beliefs—indoor/inland or nothing—there was the obvious problem: it's a saltwater fish. "I didn't know how to handle it." He was so tempted by cobia that he even considered a breach of his fidelity to indoor farming. Martin looked at Hawaii—the one place in the United States where the regulatory environment made it realistically possible to farm at sea. Another idea, piping salt water into a facility closer to the coast in Virginia, wasn't seriously considered because of cost. So he put the cobia idea on the back burner.

The "game changer"—the moment that Martin describes with the lushness of revelation—came in 2006. A man whom he'd never seen or heard of before came into his office one afternoon. Martin hears pitches from vendors all the time and is not easily impressed. "They come here saying they can double your profits. I say, 'If your idea is so good, why don't you do it yourself?'

"So Dr. Bill Harris comes in here, and he lays out his story, and he says he has all these patents on growing fish in low salinity and I listened as patiently as I was able. And then, about halfway through his story, I interrupted him, and said, 'Do you take drugs of any kind?' He said, 'No.' 'Because what you're telling me sounds absolutely ludicrous,'" Martin recalls saying. "'Growing marine fish in low salinity? Come on.'"

Then Martin told Harris, "'If in fact what you're telling me is true, you are the answer to my prayers. Because if I can grow this guy in seven-eighths-parts salt, then I can come inland with it. I don't have to be near the ocean.'"

It was, Martin concludes, like "manna from heaven."

They talked; Harris wanted to license the technology to Martin. Wary of aquashysters, Martin said no. "I told him if you really believe in this technology, you need to be a full partner."

Within months, they'd ironed out a partnership, found a site for the farm, and held a press conference—in which both Bills stood together beaming with Virginia dignitaries, declaring a $30 million investment. Bill Martin told the world that cobia would be the "chicken of the sea," the world's premier white fish, and that the farm would eventually produce 200 million pounds of cobia a year, and that Saltville, Virginia, would thrive, and have more than sixty jobs, and would become known as Fish City, USA.

Fish City, USA

Four years after that 2006 press conference, Fish City had fewer than ten full-time employees, and had produced less than 1 percent of projections.

"Mortality rate," Martin said, shrugging. "The juveniles are dying. It's not just us. It's everybody."

There was a flaw in the Perfect Species. I knew that marine fish were, in general, more difficult to spawn because their eggs were a fraction of the size of salmon and tilapia eggs. But cobia were supposed to be unique—one fish larvae expert told me cobia had among the largest eggs in the marine fish universe. I had also heard that cobia had a problem with cannibalism in the juvenile stage, but that, too, was dismissed as surmountable.

"Ninety-eight percent of the fish die," Martin said. "With tilapia, we kill twenty percent of our eggs. I'm not worried about growing cobia. I'm worried about having cobia to grow."

Martin, in a turn from his usual sunny, let's-go-get-'em optimism, admitted that he was "very, very worried last year. It's just been blind alley after blind alley. I always thought we'd figure it out—but we were running out of money."

But what about their appearance at the Boston show? A seeming sign that they were on the verge?

"Big mistake," Martin said. "We did that to generate buzz about the fish and the idea. But we didn't have fish to sell. People were angry. They're not interested in ideas; they're there with their checkbooks out. We learned a lesson."

Virginia Cobia Farms will not go to Boston this year, he said.

"We'll go there when we're ready to put fish on the table," he said. "I can finally see the light at the end of the tunnel, and it isn't a train."

13.

The Nephrologist

SALTVILLE, VIRGINIA, MIGHT SEEM LIKE A PUZZLING location for Fish City, USA. It's three hundred miles from the nearest ocean. It's in the extreme southwestern part of the state—six hours from Washington, D.C. The closest airport is in a place called the Tri-Cities of Tennessee. The town has 1,500 people, four restaurants (two drive-ins, Bud's and Al's), a motel, lots of antique stores, the Museum of the Middle Appalachians, and a statue of a woolly mammoth. It was pretty hard to envision a Harvard faculty member settling in these parts.

But it turns out Saltville may be the perfect spot in America for an indoor cobia farm. As the name suggests, the town has plentiful salt deposits, which are key for the farm's needs. Saltville also has abundant clean water and some of the cheapest electricity in the United States, because it's close to the hydroelectric power of the Tennessee River Valley. Although it appears to be isolated, by the standards of aquaculture (fish caught in Alaska, processed in China, then sent to the States), Saltville is pretty much Grand Central Station. It's a fifteen-minute drive to I-81, one of the major truck arteries on the East Coast.

The cobia farm is in a yellow corrugated metal warehouse at the edge of town, next to the volunteer fire station and across the street from Bud's Drive-In.

My visit did not start well.

It wasn't because of Tracy Mitchell, the director of business development. Mitchell was enthusiastic and interesting. She told me about her background in husbandry (she worked internationally in agricultural development), and about the town's roller-coaster history—Saltville was featured in *Life* magazine, subtitle "Death of an American Town," after it lost its big employer, a chemical plant, in the 1960s.

She also shared some interesting insights about fish market-ing strategy—such as why the cobia farm was planning to pro-duce fillets of four pounds rather than six. "Chefs want that size because of the flavor profile. If it's too big, it loses flavor." She told me that cobia will be harder to market in California (name recogni-tion is much higher in the Gulf states), and she anticipated that the first major chain to feature cobia will be McCormick & Schmick's because of a cobia-loving corporate chef in Detroit.

The worrisome part of the visit came when Dr. H. William "Bill" Harris entered.

Harris didn't have the usual smiley glad-handedness that was typical of the food pioneer species. He is bald and beefy, with a large, square head and a mustache. He was wearing a pullover with a Virginia Cobia Farms logo emblazoned on it, and could easily have been mistaken for a maintenance man.

Harris sat down across from me and oriented himself so that he was not looking directly at me, but toward Mitchell. Harris came prepared. He had a stack of papers that, he said, explained his work. One was "Extracellular Calcium Sensing and Signaling." Another one was "Apical Extracellular Calcium Polyvalent Cation Sensing Receptor Regulates Vasopressin Elicited Water Permeability in Rat Kidney Inner Medullary Collecting Duct."

I looked at him, trying to feign sentience as he explained his papers.

His first response, to a general background question, was about as revealing as "Apical Extracellular."

"I'm a person who became interested in medical research through biology, and various aspects of human physiology and biology." He elaborated, using more abstract words that sounded like a biology course syllabus.

When asked where he was from, Harris answered, tersely, "Lots of places."

Sitting in the farm's nearly barren conference room, with "Apical Extracellular" staring at me, I realized that "lots of places" was just not enough.

"Where did you go to high school?"

"I lived in a lot of places," he grumbled. "I was born in La Crosse, Wisconsin."

I offered that I was from Kenosha, also in Wisconsin.

Harris said nothing.

Mitchell, overhearing this, interjected that she once lived in a town in Wisconsin called Lodi.

"I have family in Lodi," said Harris, eyebrows rising.

Mitchell revealed that she worked for a bovine production company called American Breeders Service.

"Aha," he said. "This is a real aha moment."

Steve Johnson, the bull inseminator, Harris added, is his wife's cousin.

"We worked together for how long and we didn't know that?" Harris said.

A pause.

"Suzy the Duck," Mitchell said.

"Suzy the Duck," Harris said, almost smiling.

Suzy the Duck, I later learned, is a reference to an annual Lodi contest in which a lucky duck is named Suzy.

That was, apparently, the icebreaker. Harris warmed and started generously explaining how he went from a prestigious faculty position at Harvard Medical School to a start-up fish farm.

From Harvard Medical School to Fish Farming

The whole audacious-sounding idea—to grow a saltwater fish in a warehouse in Appalachia—ultimately goes back to a medical breakthrough in Boston in 1992.

Harris, then a doctor at Children's Hospital Boston and a professor at Harvard Medical School, and two colleagues, Ed Brown and Steve Hebert, discovered the calcium receptor. Harris went into great detail on this but the simple upshot is this: the receptor is a protein in the human body that functions like a calcium thermostat. It senses and regulates the body's calcium levels.

This is important, Harris said, "because if your plasma calcium level in your parathyroid gland varies more than one percent you'll wind up dead on the floor."

Not long after Harris and colleagues discovered the calcium receptor, they made a series of other puzzling finds. Harris found the receptor in the kidney. Then Hebert found it in the heart. It turned out that the calcium receptor was widely distributed throughout the human body.

The discovery of the calcium receptor was a major breakthrough in the medical world, and it has led to a wide range of drug therapies, for treating hyperthyroidism, osteoporosis, and a host of endocrine problems.

But Harris and colleagues immediately saw that the calcium receptor had a whole other universe of applications. Harris told administrators at Children's Hospital Boston about his idea. "Fish?" he said, recalling their bemused reaction when he suggested they apply for a patent. "Are you kidding?"

It's not uncommon for physicians to study animals—medical school labs are filled with rats, mice, and fish. But the purpose was almost always to apply this research to human health needs. Not surprisingly, Children's Hospital had no interest in pursuing Harris' patent application.

THE IDEA OF a physician being interested in fish farming is less surprising if you consider Harris' specialty, nephrology. For decades, nephrologists have used fish as model systems for understanding the kidney. "The kidney is essentially a giant membrane, the human body's biggest salt and water exchanger," said Harris, who also likes to say, "humans are just modified bags of seawater walking on land." Early in his medical career, Harris spent a summer at Woods Hole Marine Laboratory, where he became fascinated with similarities between fish and human physiology. "The parathyroid gland," he told me, "is basically the gill structure of a fish."

In 1996, two nephrologists, Harris and Hebert, along with Brown, an endocrinologist, started MariCal, a company based on the seemingly upside-down idea that human medical research could be applied to fish. They rented a tiny lab space at Mount Desert Island Biological Laboratory in Maine, and for two years studied how the calcium receptor worked in marine organisms; they tried shark, flounder, salmon, cobia, cod, halibut, and others.

(When I asked Harris how he was able to manage the logistics of the commute—Mount Desert Island is in far Down East Maine, a six-hour drive from Boston—he scoffed. "I work two hundred hours a week. I only sleep for four hours a night.")

During one of those 200-hour workweeks (note: this is clearly an exaggeration; there are only 168 hours in a week) Harris and the other doctors made a breakthrough. "Most people think that seawater is sodium chloride. But it's actually sodium chloride and magnesium and other kinds of ions," said Harris, as he began a short seawater chemistry lesson. The water off the coast of New Jersey has one hundred times more calcium than the fresh water in Lake Michigan.

Through dozens of experiments with various fish, particularly flounder, the doctors found that the receptor didn't simply measure sodium chloride levels, or calcium levels. Rather, it measured the *ratio* of the mixture of compounds. Seawater, Harris explained, has a particular calcium-to–sodium chloride ratio. If they kept the ratios consistent in the right mix of compounds—the precise parts of sodium chloride and calcium to magnesium—they could activate the receptor.

That was the "master switch." Using a mixture of naturally occurring compounds, in a dilute form, they could make saltwater fish, such as cobia or flounder, perfectly happy in an environment with far less salt than seawater. San Pellegrino (the bottled water), Harris later said, actually has calcium concentrations not far from what activates the receptor. The discovery of the "switch," the doctors realized, had a revolutionary implication. "You don't need the ocean anymore."

From Fjord-Raised Salmon to Warehouse-Raised Cobia

One of aquaculture's greatest breakthroughs came from a man with no background in fish farming. A Norwegian sheep biologist revolutionized salmon breeding by applying the genetic selection practices used in sheep breeding to farming Atlantic salmon. In just fourteen years, the sheep expert nearly doubled the growth rate of salmon.

Still, most fish farmers, unfamiliar with the Trgve Gjederem story, met the three doctors with suspicion. Fish farmers, like their terrestrial brothers, are a naturally conservative lot, notoriously distrustful of vendors with newfangled ideas, not to mention a couple of Ivy League doctors with no fish farming experience.

"We were making a claim—'we can smoltify fish on demand'— that struck many fish farmers as impossible," Harris acknowledged.

Smoltification is a natural process in the salmon life cycle. In the wild, salmon have their famously romantic means of reproduction: they swim upriver, lay their eggs, and die. Salmon larvae hatch in fresh water, mature to juvenile stage, then reverse their parents' trip. As they're heading downriver, salmon enter progressively saltier water and physiologically prepare themselves for adult life in salt water.

That gradual process in the salmon life cycle has always been a trouble spot for the farmed salmon industry. Salmon larvae are hatched in inland freshwater labs, but then they're placed in tanks and shipped to "grow out" at salmon farms in the ocean. The process takes days and it's stressful. Some fish die, or get sick. The survivors, stunned by the abrupt transition in salinity, are more vulnerable to disease.

But Harris and his MariCal colleagues had figured out how to "smoltify" Atlantic salmon. Treated with the MariCal process, salmon juveniles arrived, preacclimated, as ready for seawater as wild salmon who had finished their migration.

After two years of pitching skeptics, some of the world's largest aquaculture companies started adopting MariCal's product, dubbed SuperSmolt. By 2005, Marical had offices in many of the world's leading salmon sites—Norway, Chile, and Canada. In 2010, Harris estimates that more than 15 percent of the world's farmed salmon industry uses SuperSmolt.

I wondered how Harris could leave one of the more prestigious posts in medicine, and God's work (saving children), for fish.

"Food is medicine," Harris told me at one point, gesturing to the barren Virginia Cobia Farms conference room. Harris had come to believe that he could do more for human health through aquaculture than doctoring. "It's frustrating to see a kid in a bed with a rare form of osteoarthritis, and you can't give him things that could make a huge difference," said Harris, expressing frustration with the health-care system. "I can help lower your risk of cardiovascular disease by giving you a salmon fillet. And I don't have to ask your health-care provider."

But what sparked Harris' interest in cobia, and what drove him to contact the indoor tilapia farmer Bill Martin, Jr., was the unhealthiness of fish farming.

During the rise of SuperSmolt, Harris had toured the salmon farming universe, visiting most of the major farms in Norway, eastern and western Canada, Alaska, and Scotland. "Seafood can do a lot of good for people," he said, "but we're growing it in an environment that is not very healthy."

Harris had been persuaded, in his own research, that the future of fish farming had to be indoors and inland.

Cracking the Cobia Code

All the disappointing trips to fish markets, all the puzzled looks to the "you have cobia?" question started to make sense when Harris opened a laptop and showed me a two-minute video clip.

First impression: It's dozens of fish circling around a tank. They're orderly, in a kind of formation. "It took us three years of work to get here," he said as the clip played. "It's like they're queueing for the London Underground.

"You see that fish cross the pinwheel?"

Harris pointed to the screen as a single fish broke from the group and crossed a post in the center of the tank.

"Now watch this," he said.

The mob of fish converged at the center in a violent frenzy.

"They're being fed," Harris explained.

Within a few seconds, as soon as the feeding ends, the frenzy dissipates. The cobia start circling the tank en masse, resuming their London Underground behavior. Every five seconds or so, a single fish breaks free from the pack, and crosses the pinwheel. "The fish that cross the pinwheel? They are the dominant fish." Harris turned to me. "Cobia are hierarchical.

"These are happy fish." Harris said. "They will eat and grow fast."

But if you change a variable, Harris explained, put that pinwheel in a different location, if the water quality is different, if there are too many fish in the tank, the circles will get tighter and the fish will stop eating regularly. Under some conditions, the fish might even develop cannibalistic tendencies. It's called the Labrador syndrome: they won't eat what another one doesn't want.

As he watched the cobia circle the pinwheel, I asked Harris why it's taken so long to achieve this "happy state." He said it was because, back in 2005, when they proclaimed Saltville to be Fish City, USA, "we thought we had the template." Harris thought lessons from salmon farming could be applied to cobia, just as Bill Martin assumed his tilapia farming knowledge would work with cobia.

"Feeding cobia a modified salmon diet didn't work; giving cobia a salmon vaccine for a disease didn't work," Harris said. Failure after failure led the team to the costly realization that they had a far more daunting challenge. "We couldn't just make adaptations from tilapia or salmon. This was a very different fish," Harris said. "We had to start from scratch."

"Imagine yourself trying to grow chicken for the first time. What's the ideal stocking density? Do they like pens or fields? That's basically where we had to go. We had to set up schemes to figure out what variables are important."

AQUACULTURISTS ALWAYS STRUGGLE with new species. It took twenty years of trial and error to perfect salmon-rearing techniques. Efforts to domesticate cod, flounder, and halibut have been under way for years and are still sputtering.

But raising fish in a "closed-loop" system, which farmers have tried for thirty years, poses an even greater challenge. Many things that the ocean takes care of, such as water temperature, oxygen content, and pH levels, the indoor fish farmer must figure out and control.

Furthering the challenge, indoor fish farmers must build a suitable physical environment: the size of the cage, the location of the piping, the lighting. A year before my visit, Harris had thought he had cracked the cobia code—he knew how to produce fingerlings, he knew what kind of tank they needed, the stocking density, the water and lighting conditions, and the cobia thrived in the grow-out.

But when they put the whole system together, they ran into a problem. The cobia juveniles looked perfectly fine when they were dropped in the tank, but 10 percent just didn't grow. "You simply can't lose ten percent of your fingerlings in fish farming," Harris said. "You'll fail."

Harris refused to elaborate on how the problem was solved, saying only that the process was "not unlike being a doctor in an ICU—you look for critical information."

I asked him if this is something that O'Hanlon and the other net pen farmers would covet.

"Oh yeah," he said, looking over at Mitchell, who added, "Absolutely."

The Supersecret World of the Hatchery

Some things could not be discussed—that was understood—as Harris led me from the conference room, past his office, into the cavernous warehouse.

But about five minutes into the tour, Harris noticed my cellphone-sized camera. "Not here," he said, wagging a no-no finger. "There are some things here that I don't want the net pens guys to see. You can take photos anywhere else, just not here."

We were in the hatchery. I was looking at a tank filled with inky water, surrounded by a web of PVC, a bunch of whirring generators. The tank held thousands of five-day-old cobia larvae.

Poking my head closer, I tried to make out the cobia spawn, but that was silly. In the first few days of their life, cobia are microscopic. Surveying the dark water and the hatchery apparatus, I wondered what the "big find" was—what might Brian O'Hanlon see in this? The lighting? The design? The water temperature?

"We feed them rotifers and artemia before moving them to the pellets," said Harris, pointing to the tank filled with 20,000 larvae, and disabusing me of any notion that it was some exotic feed concoction. Rotifers are the standard feed in aquaculture. Fish, fresh out of their eggs, are extremely vulnerable, helpless creatures—they can't see, they can barely smell. Rotifers, tiny freshwater animals that look to the naked eye like pond scum, vibrate when they move, making them ideal prey for tiny fish.

After a few days, the cobia get too big to survive on rotifers, and they're shifted to artemia, a larger, more nutrient-rich food source. A genus of tiny shrimp found only in super-salty areas (Utah's Great Salt Lake is the world's largest source), artemia are commonly used as a transition before the fish are weaned to the industrial pellets that will be their life's meal. Artemia might be more familiar to non-aquaculturists by another name—sea monkeys. (Yes, one of the aquaculture industry's building blocks are the same creatures I played with in fourth grade.)

We left the no-photo zone of the hatchery and headed over to see the brood stock. Seeing the brood stock is the highlight—a kind of reverent moment—on any fish farm tour. The brood stock are, after all, the big fish in the room. They're the matriarchs and patriarchs. The lifeblood of the business.

We just stood quietly for a few minutes, admiring them: fourteen fish, ranging between fifty and a hundred pounds, majestic creatures. Cobia, with their flat catfish face and sharklike body, never fail to intrigue. Gazing at his breeders, Harris had the proud papa look. "They spawn one hundred thousand eggs every two weeks."

Next, we went to see the freakish trait that I'd waited almost five years to see: the sitting fish. "There's one," Harris said. At the bottom of a tank with twenty fish, a four-month-old cobia was motionless. "It's not dead," Harris chuckled.

"Cats sit, dogs sit, people sit, but fish aren't supposed to sit." That's how one fish biologist described his first encounter with this cobia quirk. Most fish have a swim bladder, an organ that inflates with gas to keep them neutrally buoyant in water. This is what prevents them from having to constantly swim to keep from sinking to the bottom. But cobia don't have a swim bladder. In the wild, they constantly swim. In captivity, in a tank, they do a lot of sitting. It looked like the fish was playing possum.

Harris dipped his hand into the tank, dangling his fingers. None of the fish scattered. Two fish actually came toward him. "They're curious fish. You can feed them out of your hand. If you tried this with trout or salmon," he said, his hand still in the water, "they'd be cowering at the other end of the tank." Another pregnant pause. "Cobia just eat and eat and get huge bellies." And, he said, "they nap."

We passed some more tanks and more PVC, and more generators, and then we came to a vacant area where you could see the full size of the warehouse. It was airplane-hangar size, and only a fraction of it was being used.

Scattered across the empty floor were stacks of white pipe and piles of lumber. They were spaced out neatly in grids.

"We have finished testing," said Harris. "This is the next phase."

In four months, he said, Virginia Cobia Farms would build tanks in the spaces marked by the PVC. Each twenty-by-forty-foot tank will house 50,000 fish. The first wave of Virginia Cobia Farms cobia would hit customers in the Washington, D.C., area. In fifteen months they'll ramp up production to serve food service customers. "We'll produce four million pounds from here."

Harris added, "We own the land next door and another forty-thousand-square-foot building will be built. We have the largest permit to grow fish in the United States. We could grow a hundred million cobia of any size."

The Fish Stick That Will Save Americans

Loathsome, battered, deep-fried, the source of so many miserable Friday school lunches. It just didn't seem to jive with the high-minded eco-friendly message of Dr. Bill Harris.

I had heard about Harris' fish stick plan from a competitor, a consultant for Marine Farms in Belize. I asked Harris in part to see if it was a put-down. Maybe it was some more aquaculture trash-talking?

His eyebrows raised, as if I had just mentioned Lodi, Wisconsin.

"The fish stick business? That's further down the road. But you bet we're interested. Absolutely."

I couldn't restrain a quizzical look, apparently. Harris had a feisty look, perhaps detecting a bias against fish sticks.

"Have you had a fish stick?" he asked, testily. "Have you had a McDonald's fish sandwich? You're the food guy?

"Well," he said, "it kind of tastes like metal." He paused and glanced over at Mitchell, who had an expression that suggested she was no fan of the McFish.

"Do you know how they're made?" he said, cringing. "They're made from scraps. It's mostly Alaska pollock. They fillet it, then capture the leftovers, the part associated with the bones. It's basically condensed down into a fish wad."

He shook his head. "Bringing a better fish stick to America. The day that happens will be a very satisfying moment for me."

What's interesting about Harris' fish stick ambition is not its mere existence—plenty of seafood people dream of cracking the billion-dollar processed fish niche—what was interesting was how Harris articulated his longing. He didn't mention market potential, or the fact that he would become insanely wealthy if he got even a slice of the McDonald's market.

No, it was Dr. Harris the pediatric nephrologist talking.

At the mention of fish sticks, the usually understated Harris grew animated, almost salesman-like. A Virginia Cobia Farms fish stick would be PCB-free, antibiotic-free, hormone-free. It would be raised in a precisely controlled environment—"moms wouldn't have to wonder what their children are getting." It would taste so much better than Alaska pollock.

"You've had cobia," he said. "Would you eat a McDonald's fish sandwich if it was cobia?"

I nodded, vigorously, at the thought of the McCobia.

The tasteful cobia sandwich would inspire more people to eat fish than the crappy Pollock wad. And the cobia stick—produced on the Harris-Martin industrial scale in massive regional farms—would be affordable. The implication: more people would eat fish, which would, Harris believes, help save lives and cut waste from the health care system.

Cut waste from the health care system? Yes. That's the implication.

It's not news that eating fish is good for you. A famous study that salmon-industry types love to hype makes the explicit claim that "eating fish will save lives." But the fish stick, the lowly breaded fish stick, could improve public health? Save lives?

"Cobia is very high in DHA and EPA," Harris explained, referring to the omega-3 fatty acids. "Reams and reams of articles show its benefits. There's no question it reduces the risk of diabetes and cardiovascular disease. It's good for late-stage brain development, asthma, vision. And cobia would be significantly more healthful than tilapia or catfish or pollock. A portion of tilapia has 135 milligrams of the omega-3 fatty acids; a portion of cobia has more than 2,000 milligrams, more than salmon.

In Harris' vision, someday physicians would prescribe his cobia. "It will be a real milestone when a health care provider, who is part of an HMO, says that instead of a prescription for an inhaler, 'what you really need to do is eat more fish. Here are some products that have consistently high quality.' The day that happens will be a very satisfying moment for me."

If I'd heard this from anyone else, it surely would have struck me as meaningless marketing bombast. I had heard so many claims about greens bursting with antioxidants and high-protein candy bars that any health claim was just noise.

But there, in Saltville, looking at this stone-faced nephrologist turned fish farmer, who was working out of this nearly empty office in a corrugated metal warehouse, and was preparing for a six o'clock larval run, I found it hard not to get excited, for a flash, about the McCobia future.

14.

The Seafood Revolution
Will Be Indoors

THEY SPEND THEIR LIVES IN A CORRUGATED metal warehouse. They have broader heads and shorter bodies and, due to their imprisonment, a different personality. While their cousins cruise thousands of miles across tropical seas, they live out their nine- to eighteen-month life in a crowded tank about the size of a two-car garage.

It might be painful to hear this if you've walked through a wharf on a clear morning and watched some sun-scarred fisherman unload a net dripping with the catch of the day. It might be painful to hear this if you've dreamed about the origins of your catch—be it the North Sea, the Grand Banks, the coast of Brazil, or Lake Erie.

When I told friends about O'Hanlon's approach—farming the open ocean, free-range fish in their natural habitat—they were almost always intrigued, even the die-hard anti-farmed-fish types. When I talked about my Virginia trip and the indoor fish farming process, they invariably cringed.

It's one thing to accept the need for aquaculture; it's another thing to accept aquaculture in a warehouse in an industrial park. Another layer of artificiality, another step away from natural.

Whether you like the sound of warehouse fish farming or not, evidence suggests that it's coming. Aquaculture is the world's fastest-growing source of food production, and land-based recirculating aquaculture—indoor is a subset—is the fastest-growing segment. While the majority of the growth is in Europe and China, indoor farms, raising everything from yellow perch to shrimp to Atlantic salmon, have sprouted in the United States in recent years.

Indoor fish farming isn't cheap—energy and water costs are still high. There's a formidable barrier to entry, a steep learning curve. But the move indoors seems to be driven by a this-is-the-best-solution-available spirit. Marianne Cufone of the enviro-org Food & Water Watch is unconvinced by the open-ocean approach of Benetti and O'Hanlon. "Some do it much better (such as O'Hanlon) than others," she says, "but operating in the open ocean has inherent environmental risks. With pollution concerns, escapement concerns, we think the path to take is to move inland, where there's no risk of escapes. No problems with impacting existing populations."

If a massive migration inland does occur—barring a resurgence in wild fisheries or some radical change in attitudes to open-ocean, off-shore aquaculture—it seems likely that at least four things would happen:

1. AMERICA WILL BE DOTTED WITH MEGA FISH WAREHOUSES

"This ain't gonna be for little people," is how Bill Martin puts it. Because the costs of entry are so high for indoor farms, there will be a strong incentive to scale up. Indoor fish farms will eventually be dominated by large corporations. Using a model that would likely resemble the chicken industry ("In size," says Martin, "but not practices!"), megafarms will be responsible for regional needs. A farm in Arkansas could supply the Midwest. A California farm could take care of the West Coast.

2. BILL HARRIS WILL BECOME BILL GATES-ISH

Dr. H. William Harris is one of the owners of a subsidiary of Mari-Cal called Low Salinity Inc. He and his fellow medical researchers have more than thirty patents on low-salinity technology. If you're an aspiring indoor fish farmer in the United States and you want to raise perch, tilapia, or catfish, there's no problem. But if you want to raise marine finfish, inland, and you don't have a steady supply of salt water, you will likely have to license low-salinity technology—and that means Harris, et al. In the event of an indoor fish farming revolution, Harris and MariCal will likely become enormously important players.

3. THE SEAFOOD SECTION WILL LOOK DIFFERENT

Could there be a different set of names in the seafood section? An indoor fish-farming economy would likely favor several species of currently obscure fish. All of the usual aquaculture species selection criteria apply (adaptability to captivity, ability to breed year-round) as they do outdoors. But there's an even greater emphasis on throughput—that's the term fish farmers use to describe the length of time it takes to go from birth to market. Because of the higher input costs of indoor fish farming, the faster-growing fish is even more desirable. That will mean indoor systems will favor tropical species over the slower-growing coldwater species, like cod and halibut. In addition to cobia, Harris expects that some lesser-known, fast-growing fish like pompano and yellowtail will become far more popular in an indoor seafood world.*

4. GREENHOUSE GAS EMISSIONS—LOWER

You might assume that the fatal flaw in this whole indoor, land-based idea is that it's not energy efficient. Think about the electricity and gas required to heat the warehouse. The carbon emissions? But the reason I came to completely surrender to the fish-in-warehouse idea, even if it turns into an oligarchic chicken industry model, is because of biogas.

Virginia Cobia Farms is already experimenting with capturing its carbon dioxide emissions. The farm's fish waste will be collected, then routed through an aerobic and anaerobic digester to produce biogas, which will take care of more than half of the farm's power needs. When producing a million pounds of fish, the cobia farm expects to produce 400,000 kilowatts of electricity and almost 3 million cubic feet of natural gas. Waste will also be turned into fertilizer, a nutrient-rich water, that will be used to grow algae to feed the fish. Harris predicts the farm will become carbon-neutral within a decade. Also, having a domestic seafood industry closer to consumers will reduce carbon emissions from transportation (air, shipping, trucking). "Someday," Harris said, "unsustainable seafood will be as strange as leaded gasoline."

---

*The X-factor here is the Frankenfish. As of 2011, the FDA continues to debate the fate of the genetically engineered AquaBounty AquaAdvantage salmon, which grows six times as fast as a normal farmed salmon. The fish grows faster than ordinary Atlantic salmon because it has a gene from the Chinook salmon. If the FDA approves the salmon, if consumers accept this salmon, it clearly would have an impact on the varieties we find in Safeway. For instance, slower-growing coldwater species such as halibut could become more viable in a land-based system.

FOOD AND WATER WATCH champions land-based recirculating aquaculture, but they don't like the chicken-industry model.

"We want something much, much smaller," Marianne Cufone told me, when asked about the Harris-Martin venture. She offered examples of smaller, community-based farms in the Virgin Islands, upstate New York, and Milwaukee. These farms have a smaller footprint, put people in touch with their food source, and keep money in the community.

Small, local fish farms sound wonderful. I want more of them. I want organic, artisanal fish farmers who experiment with new species, like tautog, who play with new feeds to tweak flavor. I want, someday, to know my fish farmer like I know Henry Brockman. I also want the National Offshore Aquaculture Act approved, and a regulatory system that *encourages* rather than discourages environmentally responsible marine fish farmers. Brian O'Hanlon is now producing 30,000 pounds of cobia a week, and employing fifty; he shouldn't have to do it from Panama.

But as much as I want craft fish farming, and responsible open-ocean farming, I want, more than anything, the Chicken Industry 2.0—massive, mono-fish factories in places like Schaumburg and Piscataway that produce tons of cheap, safe, sustainable seafood for Walmart shoppers. There are virtues to big: cost containment, efficiency, waste recycling. Artisanal, small, local, yes; but if we're going to feed millions of increasingly seafood-hungry, health-conscious, cost-conscious consumers, we also need industrial-scale fish factories.

PART
FIVE

ETHNIC

15.

The Deadhead and the
Next Pad Thai

IT WAS LESS THAN SIX WEEKS BEFORE Jerry would die. It was a sweltering summer day in Washington, D.C., in the parking lot of RFK Stadium, hours before a Grateful Dead show. A fiftyish man who looked bald but had long hair (think Michael Bolton) was holding court before a group of tie-dyed college students and early-twenties politicos.

The man had strong opinions on many things—the weather, the set list at Alpine Valley, the interstate highway system, tents, the parking lot at Hersheypark, and Thailand. He had been to

Bangkok and Phuket and he loved all things Thai. At one point, in describing the cheapness, wonderfulness, and beautifulness of Thailand, he said, "a good pad Thai is better than sex." It wasn't just pad Thai; everything Thai was better—Thai fried rice, Thai egg rolls, Thai noodles. He predicted that Thai food would be more popular than Chinese food because "it's just so much better."

You've probably heard this type of talk before—a friend gushing over a recently discovered "ethnic" food, then likening the experience to sex, skydiving, or another rapturous experience. It wasn't the first or last time I encountered ethnic food hyperbole.

I remembered that Thai-loving Deadhead from the summer of 1995 because he was basically right. Thai didn't become quite as big as Chinese, but you can now find Thai restaurants in Kenosha, and Fort Smith, Arkansas. You can get Thai-style peanut chicken at T.G.I. Friday's and Thai curry wings at Buffalo Wild Wings. You can find tom yum soup, Thai chicken pizza, three different brands of pad Thai at Safeway—in Biloxi. You can get hot dogs, beer, *and* pad Thai at Safeco Field in Seattle. If you just can't bear to be without it, you can bring pad Thai on your camping trip—*dried* pad Thai.

The Thai Decade

No. of New Product Introductions with Thai Ingredients

*Graph based on data from Datamonitor's Product Launch Analytics, which tracks new product introductions in U.S. grocery stores. The key Thai words are: Thai, coconut milk, lemon grass, lemongrass, and satay.

I bring up the long-haired bald man not just because of his marketing prescience but because I basically agree with him (and all of those hyperbolists) that ethnic food discovery does rank right up there with the peak human experiences. It's unforgettable, it's euphoric, it's mind-expanding.

The search for the ethnic cuisine of 2035 is, yes, personal. Finding the Next Pad Thai is not as important as finding a more efficient means of producing massive quantities of seafood or figuring out a climate-friendly alternative to conventional livestock production. My interests evolved over the course of this journey, but I couldn't stop thinking about the ethnic cuisines of the future. I longed for a reprisal of the great food moments of my past—first pad Thai (near Argyle Street in Chicago); first sushi (Bethesda, Maryland); first moo shu pork (Zion, Illinois), age six.

I was profoundly curious about a few basic questions: Will some world or regional cuisine vault into the mainstream? Is some heretofore-obscure ethnic dish poised to impact our lives like pad Thai did over the past fifteen years?

Without access to the prophetic Deadhead, I made probably the smartest decisions of my two years of food research: I consulted a food futurist.

16.

The Food Futurists

THEY DON'T USUALLY REFER TO THEMSELVES AS food futurists. Instead, they'll use titles like "food and flavor analyst," "food trendologist," "director of trend insights," "menu tracker," or "VP of innovation." But they are all, more or less, food futurists: active contributors to the Food Future Industrial Complex.

Food futurist habits include reading newspaper and magazine food sections in bulk, for quantitative patterns, spending hours examining newly opened grocery stores (the organization, the product choices, placement, language, color, font). Food futurists have an unusually detailed knowledge of what's happening in Japanese supermarkets. If you ask a food futurist why they must check out the local street food scene in Mexico City, Bangkok, or Springfield, Missouri, they will say something like "you just never know where you'll find the Next Buffalo Wing." A good food futurist can tell you instantly whether "acai" or "chipotle" is going up, leveling, or nose-diving. FFs are data hounds. The quarterly releases of the Mintel Menu Insights (which tracks changes in five hundred restaurants across the world) and the Technomic MenuMonitor are like the Nielsen ratings or the latest Gallup poll for FFs.

If you spend time on the food trade show circuit, you won't be able to miss the food futurists. They have observations, data, and predictions to share, often in the form of sound-bite-friendly "top ten trends" in panel discussions, with titles like "What Snack Consumers Will Want" or "Meat: Today and Beyond." If you miss hearing a futurist tell the snacks-and-sweets industry that "in the future, candy will be the new health food," don't worry.

The trades will almost certainly cover any clever list. And if *Sweets and Snacks Daily* misses the forecast, don't worry. Every decent food futurist has her own blog or newsletter. Mintel, the producer of the *Menu Insights*, and rival Technomic both have regular trend reports. Technomic's Foodservice Monitor comes via email every day. One food futurist aggregates top ten lists of other food futurists. You can get it all—120 lists of trend forecasts from around the world neatly synthesized—for just $2,900 a year.

Food futurism isn't a new endeavor. People have been speculating and prophesying on what we're going to eat for centuries, and, not surprisingly, they've been both stunningly prescient and spectacularly stupid. Highlights: the American who predicted in 1907 that Americans would love hamburgers. Lowlights: the Italian who portended the end of pasta, and two idealists who, in the 1940s, predicted that algae and plankton were the future of food.

But what's created the current madness—food futurist as a full-time gig, an industry within an industry—is the innovation-mad food industry. In the 1920s, American consumers could choose from a few hundred food products. In 1965, there were still only 865 new products a year. By 1995, that number had nearly doubled to 1,600. And these days the 1995 number is laughable. According to Mintel, food makers introduced more than 17,000 new products into American grocery stores in 2010.

In short, an innovation-hungry public plus innovation-mad industry = lots of need for forecasting = Food Future Industrial Complex.

The Food Trendologist

I met Kara Nielsen, my ethnic enlightener, and my first food future professional, in a quiet hallway in the George Moscone Center in San Francisco. She had come well recommended and had a history of precocity: having "called" the gluten-free trend, the quinoa boom, and the pie surge far before the masses.

Nielsen, whose official job title is trendologist, is a tallish, fortyish woman with reddish curly hair and a big smile. She was in the dream habitat for a trendologist—it was the Winter Fancy Food show—yet she seemed unmistakably weary. Not the type of giddy enthusiasm one expects from a person whose job entails searching for cool food in a place filled with 200,000 square feet of cool, and free, food.

Earlier in the day, Nielsen had made a two-hour presentation on the latest research on "How Generation Y Eats." Before that, she'd spent four hours floor-walking, scouring the Moscone Center's south and north halls for patterns and new ideas, and she wasn't, she said, sighing, nearly finished. "I'll have to come back tomorrow." The week before, she did more of this—a speech on food trends, and hours of floor-walking—at another food show in Portland, Oregon. Every year she goes to several shows—starting with the can't-miss ones (Fancy

Food East and West, Natural Products Expo, the International Association of Culinary Professionals, the Consumer Trends Forum) and the discretionary shows, and then there's the day-to-day restaurant and grocery store scouting, and her blog.

It was clear, given Nielsen's travel schedule, her access to the troves of data (focus group, menu analysis), and a few offhanded comments (I mentioned acai, a superfood, and she quickly said that it was part of a lineage of superfoods that begins with pomegranate and continues through blueberry and goji) that I was in the company of an encyclopedia of food knowledge. On the one hand, this was a source of confidence. I wasn't going to be approaching the sea of the Fancy Food Show floor solo; I wasn't going to be duped by fads (that's a big part of being a futurist) or a fast-talking entrepreneur conning me into, say, believing that Swiss chard was "the next great green." On the other hand, it was semi-intimidating to be exposed to someone who could talk about the history of superfoods in such analytical and historical detail.

WALKING THE FANCY FOOD SHOW FLOOR with the trendologist was mind-expanding, revelatory, a gold mine of insights, but not necessarily fun. You may want to reconsider putting "food futurist" on your list of top five dream jobs. There were almost 1,500 vendors selling 80,000 products out there on the Moscone Center floor. A run-of-the-mill foodie could blitz the floor, search for cheese, wine, and yuzu products, reach a 30,000-calorie threshold, and then call it a day. A buyer for a grocery store or restaurant with a specialization could scour the one hundred chocolatiers or the European specialty food vendors and then retire for tea and crumpets at the Radisson. When I got a taste of the trendologist at work, it was a mere demonstration of "floor-walking"; the real walk—the four-hour one—happened earlier. And she wasn't nearly finished. "It takes two solid days."

Part of the reason Nielsen's walk is so time-consuming is that she's a generalist—there are produce experts and breakfast experts and health experts, but Nieslen tracks pretty much everything. She is the trendologist for the Center for Culinary Development, a San Francisco–based food research and product development specialist. CCD has dozens of food industry clients, and her mission is both to help clients respond to the zeitgeist and to give them specific ideas from her trendspotting that can fuel the creative process. Because CCD has so many different kinds of clients, it produces an eclectic range of trend reports—Artisan Foods, Street Foods, Breakfast Trends, Confections and Desserts, Global Barbecue Trends, and Mealtime Trends, to name just a few. And because CCD has such diverse clients, virtually everything is of some potential interest to its trendologist. "Every vendor, every booth," Nielsen said, after we passed the umpteenth vendor selling sea-salt-speckled chocolate. "If you go up there and ask them, they will have something new."

Listening to Nielsen talk about food trends requires a basic fluency in trendspeak, specifically CCD's trademark argot. You might be passing an avocado oil or flavored balsamic vinegar vendor, and she could describe it as a Stage 1. Or Kara might tell you that empanadas are Stage 4 on the verge of Stage 5, and umami is Stage 3. This takes a little bit of getting used to—imagine the heavenly taste of a miso-encrusted ceviche with yuzu—and then hearing that it was Stage 1. It's really just a more analytical way of explaining the trickle-down theory of salad innovation. Food trends follow a cycle of diffusion. They start with the epicures and the urban hipsters and then slowly progress to the middle-of-the-roaders and then— years later—they could get embraced by people who still eat white bread (laggards). CCD developed the five stages as a way of explaining to its clients where trends first happen, and how to capitalize on them.

Stage 1: The ingredient, dish, and/or cooking technique appears at upscale dining establishments, ethnic and popular independent restaurants blessed with creative chefs and diners with adventurous palates.

Stage 2: The item is featured in specialty consumer-oriented food channels such as Bon Appétit and Food Network, and retail stores such as Sur la Table that target culinary professionals and serious home chefs.

Stage 3: The item begins to appear in mainstream chain restaurants—Applebee's or Chili's—as well as retail stores such as Williams-Sonoma that target recreational cooks.

Stage 4: The women's magazines and family-oriented publications—*Family Circle*, *Better Homes and Gardens*—pick up the buzz.

Stage 5: Finally, the trend makes its way to quick-service restaurant menus and is either starting to appear or is having an increased presence on grocery store shelves.

It must be noted that, although Nielsen can speak in trendologist terms and look at food with the detachment of a social scientist, this is food and she is a foodie (a former pastry chef, with a master's degree in gastronomy, she moved to the Bay Area because of the food culture). There are moments of irrepressible food lust—both high and low food. She loves Yakult, a yogurt, and yuzu, and pastry. Once, while floor-walking, we passed what looked like a pancake mix retailer; without explanation, she left me in the aisle, rushed toward the Golden Pancake booth, picked up a box of the stuff, stuffed it in her bag, then looked at me bashfully, as if she had just swiped some baseball cards from a dime store. "I love this stuff." We continued walking, as if nothing had happened, and resumed talking about Culinary Trend Mapping. The Mapping Report paradigm became especially useful in thinking about ethnic food trends, which is, in CCD-speak, "emerging regional and global cuisines."

Why Some People Get Gelato and Others Get "Italian Ice Cream"

Though the insane amount of fancy food (chocolate, cheese, white truffles) and health food (organic, vegan, gluten-free) and ethically sound food (green, fair-trade) and just uncategorizable stuff (baconaise, bacon salt, tilapia bratwurst) can make you lose focus and develop a kind of food-induced vertigo, the show is an amusement park for the ethnic novelty scout.

There were hundreds of international food vendors—from French to French Polynesian. All of these foods are presented in booths: some are in country pavilions (the French, Italian, and Japanese have massive World's Fair–like pavilions; the Uruguayans have a small one). Almost all of them have samples. It's like walking into the most diverse neighborhood in the United States—except instead of having recent immigrants behind the counter, the staff is populated by PR people, smooth Ricardo Montalban–like guys, beautiful women, all trying to nail big deals with buyers.

A pattern quickly emerged on the Moscone Center floor: I would get excited, say, when approaching an unfamiliar ethnic dish or ingredient or word, and then I would turn to the trendologist, who was always composed, pure grace in the presence of Goan cuisine. When I asked about Malaysian food as a possible breakthrough cuisine, Nielsen answered, "It is in the pipeline." A vendor had Indonesian food—which I'd never seen in the States—and my guide was nonplussed. There's an Indonesian restaurant in Berkeley. "It's further off, but it'll come." I kept seeing the word *Oaxacan.*

"Get ready for Sinaloan and Veracruzan and Yucatecan, too," she said. "Italian. It's gone regional. Tuscan, or Sicilian, or Ligurian."

What seemed to be more intellectually stimulating for Nielsen was not the "if" question, but the "how"—how would an ethnic dish or flavor get "translated," how would they use achiote or aji amarillo at Chili's. There was a lot of talk in those giddy Winter Fancy Food days about Peruvian food, flavors, and drinks. A place in San Francisco was getting heavy buzz among the food smart set. Nielsen had blogged about it. The show was awash in foods from Peru, Brazil, Chile, and Argentina.

It was the "Pan Latin" trend, part of a growing hunger to explore Latin America, to move beyond just Mexico. And as a trendspotter, Nielsen was looking to see how chefs were playing with certain Latin American dishes and flavors, and how marketers were labeling them.

Take aji amarillo, a Peruvian yellow chile, and a candidate, perhaps, for next chipotle. "Will aji amarillo be called Peruvian?" Nielsen asked. Colored potatoes—blue, tiny fingerlings, which were popping up all over farmers' markets and Whole Foods–like grocers, those are from Peru, but they're not getting called "Peruvian." You could call aji amarillo a "Peruvian chile," or you could call it "Latin." Or you could call it by its real name. Or it could have all three names.

A dish or flavor could get called "aji amarillo" at one point, at Stage 1—among the authenticity-happy foodies—but not as it moves further into the mainstream. "Like mole verde," she said, referring to the green Mexican sauce made with toasted pumpkin seeds and tomatillos. "It'll be called mole verde at ethnic restaurants and innovative restaurants, but further down the line they might call it something like pumpkin seed sauce." This happens all the time. Adventurers get authentic terms; laggards get some blanderized version. (Another futurist I spoke with, while browsing a grocery store ice cream section, speculated that even the word *gelato*—old news to any sentient yuppie—would be too exotic for the mass-market crowd, that marketers might call it "Italian ice cream.")

We'd passed by some of the country pavilions, some of the amusement park–like features of Fancy Food (an Australian company selling bottled Tasmanian rainwater, the celeb chef Ming Tsai doling out some noodle incarnation), and we were heading to the hot zone for the trendologist—the fringe of the floor.

Nielsen, clearly expert at food show narration, was continuing to weave in nuggets of insight into the future and the art of floor walking—more hybrids (Tex-Mex, Cal-Ital, just the beginning), more miso-based products, and a valuable tip: "Always walk along the fringes of food shows." Why? They're the budget booths. The lower cost means smaller, independent companies that are more innovative. It was while passing a low-budget-looking vendor that Kara revealed that her job will only get harder. Food trendspotters are like journalists: everyone wants to be first, everyone wants to be on the record. And trendspotters are all racing to cover an increasingly fast-paced realm; the pace of new product introductions gets faster and faster. Not only did Nielsen physically scour shows, but she had a pretty demanding media diet, too (the foodie mags, the *Bon Appetits*, *Saveurs*, newspaper dining sections, Food Network shows, bloggers, Twitterers). Food trend tracking, it increasingly struck me, was not wildly unlike covering any other hyperactive industry.

The Gateway Thai

"Pad Thai," Nielsen said, passing a Malaysian vendor, and referencing the sublime dish of stir-fried rice noodles with eggs, fish sauce, tamarind juice, red chili pepper, plus any variation of bean sprouts, shrimp, chicken, or tofu, garnished with crushed peanuts, coriander, and lime, which is the national dish of Thailand.

"Pad Thai was the gateway dish. People ate pad Thai, they got interested in Thai food, they explored further. Ten years ago, pad Thai was new. Now people are tired of pad thai. They want something new. Pho, the Vietnamese noodle soup, is growing in popularity. Pho could be the pad Thai of Vietnamese food. Then people will become tired of pho and they'll want something new. Malaysian is a next step for people who like Thai.

Foodmakers have long known about this progression—soft Thai leads to hard Thai, and then hard Thai leads to Vietnamese, etc. The first wave of ethnic foods to arrive in America obviously had their gateway dishes, too. You get hooked on spaghetti or pizza, and then you'll be eager for ravioli. Pork fried rice leads to kung pao chicken. In the 1970s, the food industry journal *Processed Foods*, hot on the ethnic trend, urged food companies to "flavor-mine"—to experiment with Portuguese, Swedish, Jamaican, etc., for novelty.

But the pace of ethnic change has sped up dramatically. In 1969, the Fancy Food show had twelve international exhibitors. In 2010, the show had thirty country pavilions (many with dozens of vendors) and thousands of foreign food products.

You don't need to be VP of Menu Insights at Mintel to understand what's happening. The Food Network specials on Chinese, Indian, and Thai; newspaper food sections; blog proliferation. Anthony Bourdain and Andrew Zimmern trotting all over the world for the Travel Channel in search of culinary exotica. The food delirium is turning what was once a minority of the eating population— the adventurer who journeys to Queens for life-changing lamb vindaloo—into an increasingly mainstream phenomenon.

Fresh from her morning talk on Generation Y, aka the Millennials, echo boomers, Generation Me, Kara foresaw only more: a continued growth of ethnic exploration. Generation Y had an even greater appetite for ethnic novelty than the baby boomers or Generation X. They've grown up on pad Thai and Tuscan penne chicken and sushi—culinary adventure is part of their DNA. When asked in surveys and focus groups, Gen Yers say they expect to taste even more diverse cuisines. And it's coming.

Brazilian, Peruvian, Argentine . . . Pan-Latin—achiote, ceviche, pisco sours, empanada, churrascos—that's coming. Less than ten years away. More Vietnamese, deeper into Thailand, Malaysian—under way. All of Southeast Asia. Ten years. Indonesian? Further off. And yes, the American stomach will inevitably get filled with some form of the Javanese signature dish, the *rijstaffel*. Fifteen years. Middle Eastern, Turkish, that's happening now. Five years. Korean? Absolutely. More regional Chinese, Indian, more Japanese.

Everything was seemingly on the trendologist radar screen. Cambodian? Yes. "Just an extension of the Southeast Asian trend."

Hearing Nielsen's projections of the impending global smorgasbord was bittersweet. It wasn't surprising—yet another manifestation of globalization, a flatter earth. More trade, more communications, more access to foodstuffs and information from cuisines around the globe.

I thought about a future with better access to bulgogi, Brazilian-style riodizio, the possibility of getting rendang kambing. Imagine wrapping up a long evening at the bowling alley in Kenosha with . . . a pisco sour. It was a rosy future for ethnic adventurers.

The problem was that this coming cornucopia of ethnic options also meant the Age of Exploration was threatened. It sounded like manifest destiny—the whole world was being strip-mined for ethnic novelty, no corner of the world was unexplored.

Was there anything left?

Any frontier, still unknown, that *wasn't* on its way?

Kara paused, pregnantly—at last, a challenging question.

Anything that *won't* get here till 2035?

"African," she said. Not North African, she qualified, not Tunisian, or Moroccan, or even Ethiopian. She meant sub-Saharan Africa, black Africa.

There was an Africa pavilion in 2008, but it didn't return in 2009.

Rooibos—the tea flavor—hails from South Africa. And there was, at one point, a South African restaurateur/entrepreneur named Nando who was marketing a kind of South African chili sauce.

But African, she said, is not in the pipeline.

She paused, as if absorbing this unusual thought.

"African," she said. "It's not on the radar screen at all."

The Food Industry's Ghostwriter

A twenty-five-minute drive south of the Fancy Food show, tucked away discreetly in a nondescript office park, is the headquarters of the largest independent food research and development company in the world. I had come here to meet the president of Mattson, Steve Gundrum, who has within food industry circles a reputation for guru-like knowledge of the food future.

Mattson's 20,000-square-foot food lab, not far from the world headquarters of Oracle, was easily the most Wonka-like environment I'd experienced to date.

A short tour of the lab, led by Wonka himself, revealed a series of sprawling restaurant-sized kitchens, each outfitted with a chem lab's worth of equipment. Pantries had not just your usual food ingredients, but also hundreds of brown and yellow jars, stuffed with food science essentials—fifty different kinds of flours, hundreds of starches, other ingredients like xanthan gum, ferrous sulfate, thiamine mononitrate, soy protein isolate and that essential, T. Hasegawa Natural Wok Oil Flavor No. 98900. Mattson has its own pilot plant—complete with a flash pasteurizer and colloid mill—for testing its concoctions at scale. Adding to the Wonka-vibe, more than anything, were the staff: real-life Oompa Loompas, food scientists and culinologists and research chefs, wearing white lab coats, invariably smiling, working away at their confections. As my tour of the facility ended, we passed the "trophy room." A conference room, its walls surrounded by literally hundreds of creations recognizable to any human who has been in an American grocery store. None of them mentionable without permission.

You won't find the name Mattson on the shelves of any grocery store or menu of any restaurant. The thirty-year-old lab has invented more than 1,000 new products, nearly 300 product lines, has done work for most of the world's largest food companies, has created some of the world's most iconic products for stores and restaurants. But as an independent R&D firm, Mattson basically functions as a food ghostwriter—clients don't necessarily want the world to know they've outsourced their creative work. (Rumors persist that Mattson created the Frappuccino; it was even reported in *Popular Mechanics*. But asked about the frap, Gundrum angrily refuses to acknowledge any involvement.)

Given this behind-the-scenes role, Mattson has generally kept out of the sight of the public and mainstream media, save for a moment in 2005, when news spread about the lab's aim to solve one of the Holy Grails of the food industry—a healthful and tasty cookie. Applying the groupthink method more typical of the software world, Mattson's "open-source cookie" project, dubbed Project Delta, caught the attention of not only industry trades like *Food Engineering* and *Food Processing*, but also Malcolm Gladwell, who wrote about the cookie quest in the *New Yorker*.

Gundrum, the mastermind of what was known as Project Delta, and the man who refuses to accept any credit for the Frappuccino, is short and roundish, with a mustache and bushy, Spock-like eyebrows that give him a perpetually mischievous look. He's casual, wears khakis and track shoes, loves skiing and gadgets (he showed off a Bond-like pen-recorder, humbling my ancient digital recorder). He would fit seamlessly into any one of the software companies in Silicon Valley.

Although Gundrum is secretive about his current client

work, he did admit that his early career accolades include figuring out how to use a mainframe computer to more efficiently process pickle orders (a huge cost saver) and helping to create Chef Boyardee's first dinosaur-shaped noodle soup, a monster hit in the kids' soup world. (The key, Gundrum said animatedly, was to make sure noodles really looked like dinos.) When asked about his hobbies outside the world of food research and development, Gundrum cited "making old-school pasta" and "latte art."

Not long after I met Gundrum for the first time, one of the lab-coat-wearing staffers entered his office. She presented him with a sample—what food R&D people call a "protocept." Gundrum picked up what looked like a pickle, almost unconsciously, chewed it for two seconds, then delivered his verdict. "Ninety percent there. Try a white balsamic—keep it as no turmeric, make it as crystal clear as possible."

He turned to me. I couldn't name the client, but I could, it was established, try this embryonic food idea. "This is the first time *anybody* has ever tried a balsamic vinaigrette pickle. You're at ground zero!" Gundrum said with childlike enthusiasm as I started chewing. It was pretty good. I didn't have a broad range of pickle experience, but it was unlike pickles I'd had.

That was the point. "Infused with balsamic," Gundrum explained. "When was the last time you tried a pickle that wasn't a variation of garlic and dill?" We're trying to get our client to try something different. The food scientist who concocted the pickle brine, described by Gundrum as "our salad dressing wizard," departed, smiling, with her charge. This was step one. They'd reformulate, try it again, they'd pitch the client, then, if it got green-lighted, it would go to consumer feedback and they'd test it at a larger scale. (Sometimes protocepts work well in the kitchen, but not at a larger scale. *That's why* they have an on-site flash pasteurizer and colloid mill.)

It's not easy getting a product on a grocery store shelf, Gundrum said. Odds are against that balsamic vinaigrette pickle—there's internal politics, risk aversion, competing ideas, bureaucracy. Only a fraction of the protocepts Gundrum tries each week make it to a grocery store shelf or restaurant menu. Intrigued by this, I asked if there was anything potentially revolutionary or mind-blowing that, because of bureaucracy, *didn't* make it to market. "Yes!" Gundrum said, and pointed to a file folder beneath his desk. He coyly described a product that would create a "new category," have "big news value" and have a huge health and wellness benefit for some people. "Someone pulled the plug on it." Gundrum shrugged. After a frown, he went on a brief food-industry-isn't-properly-respected riff. Some people think this (inventing low-calorie hot pockets and microwavable brownies) is easy, he explained, but there are so many different situations, so many different clients, so many variables to consider. "It's like being a great musician," he said. "You have to be able to play jazz guitar, do a little Sarah McLachlan, a little Dylan, some Dave Matthews."

Ethnic Forecast #1: More Curry

The ethnic-cuisine-of-the-future question didn't provoke nearly as much animation as the balsamic pickle protocept or the latte art, or a discussion of food industry bureaucracy. Gundrum fessed up. "I'm jaded. We see sooo much." Mattson's a mercenary. Gundrum is focused on solving client needs with his seventy-person staff. If Client X wants to reach a new demographic (say, baby boomer females or vegetarian men), they might look at ethnic options. If Client Z, a quick-service restaurant, wants to differentiate itself from a competitor in the "health and wellness sector," they might look at ethnic options. "Ethnic is just a means to an end. It's an arrow in our quiver," he said, shrugging. "It's just a strategy to add variety."

But I had come to this food lab to meet with this man purported to be a sort of Steve Jobs of big food to get some additional insight, some juice, on what could be the pad Thai or kung pao chicken of the future. Gundrum was renowned for his ability to spot monster hits. Malcolm Gladwell had reverently described Gundrum's skills, how he assesses a potato chip for its potential for "rhythmic munching"—the key to a successful snack product.

Was there some equivalent of rhythmic munching foreshadowing the next big ethnic cuisine?

Gundrum didn't budge. He couldn't get specific. He corroborated what Kara said regarding cuisine change: the general food delirium is making everything faster. Consumers want more. Foodmakers create more. "Speed to market" is becoming even more important in the food business.

If anything, Gundrum seemed focused on bragging about how Mattson was built for speed. Indeed, the techs in their white lab coats buzz around the industrial kitchens as if it were a newsroom. Techs can interrupt Gundrum or Barb Stuckey (another taste guru at Mattson) to get instant feedback, and the staff use "shout mail" because it's faster, Gundrum says. Mattson uses the Internet to speed up the consumer feedback piece—all major food companies demand extensive consumer testing. Let's say that the pickle protocept gets approved (green-lighted by clients, is deemed to have potential to own a new pickle category). Mattson could overnight the latest iteration to hundreds of testers (the Consumer Guidance Panel, or CGP), then get responses in a day or two (the testers are like Nielsen families), get back to the lab, and continue to go through a process of refinement.

The payoff for getting to market first is potentially huge. "Starbucks still owns coffee culture," Gundrum pointed out.

The downside of this emphasis on speed is that that it has created mass nearsightedness. Ten years ago, food R&D specialists might look at a five-year plan with their clients—maybe even peek ahead at ten years. Now, they're usually talking about eighteen months.

Gundrum, though unwilling to prophesy what the food court of 2035 will look like, or explain what the rhythmic munching of ethnic food is, did make a short-range pronouncement.

"Indian," he said, as if intimating an insider trading secret. "Indian food is poised to encroach itself on the U.S. diet. All of the fundamentals are in place." When I visited Mattson a few months later, Gundrum was even more definitive-sounding, as if something had happened. "Indian is gonna happen. It really is."

INDIAN IS "GOING TO HAPPEN"? Indian? Please. Depending on where you fit on the foodie spectrum, this prediction might strike you as about as bold as saying "the Yankees will be a contender in the next decade." There's palak paneer and chicken tikka masala and Punjab eggplant and frozen samosa and chapatti and four different kinds of naan at Trader Joe's and Whole Foods right now. There might be two Indian carryout places within screaming distance of your Upper West Side apartment. It's really important to understand that Whole Foods and Trader Joe's represent less than 2 percent of the American grocery market and that the deep blue urban foodie enclaves are not what he's talking about.

When Gundrum, whose clients have included ConAgra, PepsiCo, and White Castle, says "Indian is going to happen," he's talking about a whole different scale. It's what Kara might call Stage 4 or Stage 5. If you want a concrete idea of what his prediction means in a Gundrum way, go to Great Britain. Mulligatawny soup is right there next to pea soup on the shelves of grocery and convenience stores. Classic fish and chips shops almost always offer curry sauce with chips. Brits spend $2 billion on Indian carryout annually. It's as ubiquitous as Tex-Mex or Chinese is in the United States.

Gundrum and others project that within the next decade Indian cuisine will move toward becoming the next Chinese or Mexican, in the way that it's assimilated into American food culture. When Gundrum talks about all the signs being there, he means things like the efforts to establish an Indian quick-service restaurant. One example of the arrival of Indian would be the appearance of an Indian equivalent of P.F. Chang's. (P.F. Chang's is basically Chinese food presented and packaged like Chili's.) And in 2010 a Chicago entrepreneur announced plans to roll out a franchise called Chutney Joe's—an Indian QSR.

Another key fundamental has nothing to do with culinary arts or marketing—it's simple demographics. Chinese, Mexican, and Italian food have been driven, in part, by immigrant communities that helped disseminate awareness. Indian communities are becoming more visible in large urban areas. For instance, Gundrum predicts that Indian food will mainstream first in the Bay Area, which has a large Indian community.

We could have had a very interesting conversation about how this "Indianization" process will happen, about how vindaloo or korma will be translated, how foodmakers will deal with the spices, about the fate of turmeric or naan in the hands of the ConAgras of the world. We could have talked about how Indian dishes will be tested, and reformulated, and about the food science and processing challenges. This would have been a very interesting talk. A coda to the "ethnic search."

But much like the floor walk with Kara Nielsen and the discovery of the impending ethnic cornucopia, I wanted something else—something further out, something that wouldn't be present at the Chili's in the mall in ten years. Something for 2035.

"I've seen it," he said, "once."

He raised his eyebrows mischievously. It was the this-latte-art-is-very-cool look. I had posed the inevitable question, the Final Ethnic Frontier theory; that there is only one great mystery remaining, one ethnic unknown.

Gundrum had been on a food scouting mission—a common practice for food futurists, to get a sense of the consumer zeitgeist.

Specifically, he said, "I was looking at fresh food at retail stores. It was last January.

"They were using sweet potatoes and ancient grains and a pilaf thing. . . . It was called African or Kenyan or something like that. It was entrees and side dishes. A lot of sweet potatoes."

He looked at me. "They were using African as a descriptor."

Where was this avant garde of African food?

"It was Detroit." Gundrum said, "It wasn't just one store. I saw it a few times. I remember thinking to myself, 'This is very, very interesting.'"

17.

The Last Culinary Frontier

YOU WILL FIND THE FOODS AND SPICES of sub-Saharan Africa in your strip malls and your quick-service restaurants and your big-box grocery stores in 2035.

That's not Chris Wolf, or Kara, or Suzy Badaracco or Phil "Supermarket Guru" Lempert. That's my first foray into food forecasting.

I came to believe in this inevitability after several months of African food research that began, in the fall of 2010, with a visit to Detroit.

————

DETROIT IS NOT historically a rival to San Francisco or Tokyo or New York in food trend hatching. But if you think about it, the whole idea that African food would appear earlier in Detroit than other places seemed perfectly reasonable. Detroit is one of the country's most African-American cities, a place that has long embraced Afrocentricity. And Detroit is one of the foodie cities of the moment.

Yes, Motown, poster child of Rust Belt decay, has emerged as a mecca for food innovators. Detroit has turned a problem—massive depopulation (down 1.4 million since 1960)—into a virtue. Frustrated by the blight, the extreme food desert conditions (there's not a single Safeway, Jewel, or Whole Foods in the entire city), Detroiters started growing their own. There are more than one thousand gardens in Detroit. It's Detroit—not Santa Monica or Madison, Wisconsin—that has the country's largest farmers' market (40,000 people converge on Eastern Market on some summer Saturdays).

All of this, changing Motown into Growtown (as some have dubbed the movement), has turned Detroit into a hive of foodie activism and innovation. A school for pregnant girls produces its own fruits, vegetables, and goat's milk; the MGM Grand downtown added a $1 million rooftop garden; the mayor's office has received proposals from urban farmers who want to grow fish in abandoned warehouses, build high-rise farms in vacant old hotels, grow wheat where cars were once tested. An investment banker bought up forty acres of cheap land and pledged to invest $30 million to build the world's largest urban farm, a kind of lab for agricultural technologies, such as vermiculture, aquaponics, and aeroponics.

You can see signs of Growtown throughout the city's carefully tended tomato plants, neat rows of Swiss chard, lettuce, collards against a backdrop of burned-out buildings and trash-strewn lots. It is wildly unlike the lush Eden of Cannard's Sonoma Valley microfarm, or even the sweeping vista of the Salinas Valley. But the sight of the Earthworks farm—at Meldron and St. Paul streets, across the street from a soup kitchen, kitty-corner from an abandoned housing project—is a breathtaker. Its mere existence, emerging from among the ruins, the most improbable of spots, is a beautiful sight.

Going to Detroit was worth it, simply to see the urban farming movement, but it was not so great for African food. Some food scouting, a blitz of Detroit grocery stores, did not reveal any clear signs of African takeout or African influence. Detroit's lone Nigerian restaurant had closed, and there was a Senegalese place in suburban Mount Clemens; it sold food, but it was mostly a dance club. The closest I came to African food at the country's largest farmers' market was a vendor selling African scents and shea butter. Later, I called grocery stores in Detroit and the suburbs (maybe I had gone to Motown during off-season for African food?). After checking with numerous stores I did find one that matched Gundrum's description—the executive chef at Holiday Market in Royal Oak said the market occasionally offered a Kenyan coconut rice pilaf dish with peanuts and pork.

CHICAGO WAS FAR BETTER. Over the course of two weeks, it was possible to try several Senegalese, Ghanaian, and Nigerian restaurants. Chicago also has the beginnings of an informal Little Africa (two restaurants, two African markets, a bookstore) in the Uptown neighborhood.

Eating African food in Chicago, circa 2010, was what Kara Nielsen might call a pre–Stage 1 experience. It was still ethnic for the ethnics. Most African restaurants seemed to function as informal community centers—guys, almost always guys, often cabdrivers, sitting around, talking, watching television news from Dakar, listening to Afropop from Accra, sipping on coffee, palm wine, not eating.

Because this is pre–Stage 1, and the presence of white guys with REI polar fleece arriving via Subaru was relatively rare, it was still possible to get a surprised eye. It was also not uncommon to encounter incredibly friendly restaurant owners who were happy to explain what fufu (ground root starch) was or how to make kenkey (ground fermented corn) or to offer advice on whether to have shittu with yassa or egusi with kenkey. They also would, with little provocation, offer lavish details about the many uses of the baobab tree.

The turning point in the African Period came after a carryout meal from a three-table Ghanaian place in an Uptown mini-mall. Generally speaking, I wasn't, at that point, terribly fond of sub-Saharan African food. I really liked the lamb yassa (grilled lamb marinated in mustard powder, vinegar, and lemon juice) at Yassa, a South Side Senegalese place. I was fond of baobab juice, palm wine, a lot of the apps (grilled plantains, pineapple fritters), and I would never kick a good egusi (spicy Nigerian stew) or peppercorn soup out of bed. But it was getting progressively harder to get pumped up for African night. Some mystery-meat dishes (oxtail, goat) hadn't fared well. A few of the starchy staples, especially fufu, a large white ball that looks like cream of wheat and tastes like raw sourdough, were wearing me down. (Admittedly, at one point, after a mediocre mafe—a peanut butter stew—it crossed my mind that the reason why there aren't many sub-Saharan African restaurants around is that they're not very good.)

One day, after a typically King Arthur's feast–sized West African meal (they seem to be generous with portions) at Palace Gate, I offered my wife some of the leftovers, a massive mound of jollof rice. She cringed, a gag-me look. Jollof rice is a staple of West African food; this Ghanaian take was flecked with spinach, stir-fried in coconut oil.

Kristi likened the jollof rice to greasy fried rice from a really bad Chinese restaurant, and, after some interrogation, confessed that she didn't care for the West African food we'd tried. This was semi-surprising, since she's usually pretty charitable on ethnic food adventures. She added, as if to soften her critique, "But I didn't used to like Mexican, either."

It was then that she offered a thought. "Maybe there's an African Bayless?"

The implication: visiting every West African place in every mini-mall was not the best approach to seeing the African future.

The Bayless idea sounded strangely familiar.

Later that night, I checked my notes. At the 2009 Fancy Food Show, in the original conversation, in which Kara had established that African food was not on the radar screen "at all," she described the potential for a kind of X-factor that could change that. "You never know," she said. "There could be someone like Rick Bayless."

Why Rick Bayless Matters to African Food

Rick Bayless—yes. That's the Mexican restaurant owner, host of Mexican-themed television shows, all-around Mexican food guru and mensch. Bayless is relevant to the future of Ghanaian and Senegalese and Nigerian food because he's perhaps the best illustration of the cuisine consciousness changer.

When Bayless opened his first restaurant in Chicago in 1987, he upset some people. Frontera Grill was a Mexican restaurant, but it didn't have burritos, nachos, or refried beans on the menu. Frontera offered things like posoles (soup stews made with hominy) and moles (green pumpkin moles, red chile moles, black moles), mosa cakes, and a spice called chipotle. Some customers left, angrily, warning the then-twenty-six-year-old chef that he'd better change his menu, or he'd fail.

Bayless, a onetime PhD student in anthropology, had spent close to a decade traveling back and forth to Mexico, researching its regional cooking. He soon found a following. A few weeks after opening, the critics started gushing, and Bayless' ascendance to überchef status began. He published a cookbook on authentic Mexican cooking, hosted a PBS show on Mexican cooking, continued to travel to Mexico, collecting more recipes, opening more restaurants, showcasing more of Mexico's culinary riches.

Bayless was not by any means the only Mexican food evangelist, but thanks to the PBS show and a mass audience, no one has been more influential. Foods and sauces he introduced to adventurers in the mid-1980s—like chipotle—have trickled down to mass-market, regular-guy food. He's not only expanded awareness of Mexico's regional foods—from Oaxacan to Yucatecan to Sinaloan—he's also helped inspire interest in other Latin American cuisines.

But Bayless' impact was even more fundamental. Other culinary pioneers had introduced ethnic cuisines to Americans. But Bayless' region of interest was the New World; it was Mexico, a country widely perceived as poorer, lower on the gastronomic hierarchy.

When Kristi spoke ill of that jollof rice from Palace Gate, she remembered the miserable ketchup-like Ortega "salsas" of the 1970s. She couldn't condemn all of jollof rice, because in our fridge, at that moment, was a cousin of that miserable 1970s salsa—Guajillo chile salsa, a smoky, tangy, wonderful concoction that she loves. Maybe, Kristi thought, that palm-oiled, spinach-flecked jollof rice was just one of dozens of jollof rices—with wonderfully different flavors and textures. Maybe there was a difference between Ghanaian jollof rice and southern Nigerian rice? Maybe that jollof rice was just not in the right hands.

African food—that's sub-Saharan, non-Ethiopian African food—was not well represented in the foodie literature. And within the whole five-hundred-plus food book collection at my local library (five books on Tuscan food, ten books on barbecuing), there were only two books for the wannabe African cook.

The first African food book I found had on its cover a round loaf of bread, a decanter of what looked like salsa, all spread on some kind of animal hide—and no title. This puzzling tableau was the kickoff to *African Cooking*, part of a Time-Life series, Foods of the World, published in the 1970s. The author was a South African globe-trotter, writer, occasional British intelligence officer, turned London theater critic who claimed he'd likely walked around the African continent more than any other human.

Reading Laurens van der Post's *African Cooking* was like finding a dog-eared *National Geographic* in your uncle's basement: photos of Kalahari bushmen with arrows drawn, women carrying massive washboard tubs of eggplant on their heads, giant African snails—ten times the size of escargot—a family breakfast with what looked like six-egg omelets made from a single egg. The book did make, at the outset, a critical point about the term "African food." Africa contains one-fifth of the world's land, nearly a billion people, fifty-four countries. Cameroon alone has eighty different tribes and two hundred different languages. Van der Post said that a cookbook about Africa is as preposterous as a "Europe cookbook." The book, a modest impressionistic account that limited itself to five regions, was filled with interesting information—including a gripping narrative on the Boers' migration from the Cape of Good Hope—but it certainly wasn't a Bayless text. It didn't make you hungry.

It was the one other Africa food book available in the Wilmette Public Library that seemed to have revolutionary ambition.

The foreword wasn't from Trotter, Waters, Emeril, or some other member of the celebrity-chef industrial complex. *The Soul of a New Cuisine* was introduced by Bishop Desmond Tutu, and the Nobel Peace Prize winner wasn't talking about the fufu or yassa poulet recipes; he was touting the humanitarian importance of what was, ostensibly, a cookbook.

The author had a puzzling name for an African food evangelist, a name that brought to mind fjords and herring more than palm wine and cassava. But it turned out that Marcus Samuelsson was straight out of central casting for the role. Samuelsson is Ethiopian. Born during the famine, orphaned, he was adopted by a

Swedish family, given the Viking name, and raised in Göteborg. He nurtured a love of Swedish foods as a child, and began a culinary career in Stockholm.

It wasn't until he moved to New York City, to work as chef for the Swedish restaurant Aquavit, that he had his African awakening. In New York, Samuelsson met Cameroonian dishwashers, played soccer with Ghanaians, tried Ethiopian and Senegalese takeout. The Ethiopian-Swede in New York hungered to learn more about his African identity, and, as chef, he was especially interested in the foods of his native continent.

But Samuelsson ran into a problem. Beyond North Africa and Ethiopian, there was almost nothing written about African foods. So he did it himself, traveling back and forth to the continent, collecting recipes, learning as much as he could about African cuisine. This sounded awfully familiar.

Like Bayless' *Authentic Mexican* twenty years earlier, *The Soul of a New Cuisine* is a cookbook on a mission. Bayless' aim: change minds warped by Chi-Chi's and El Toritos. Samuelsson had a consciousness-changing agenda, too. "All the news about Africa is bad. War, famine, dictators, AIDS," he writes in his introduction. "And that stuff happens. But that is not the Africa I know."

It's nearly impossible to read *Soul* without at least rethinking the assumption that Africa is poor, messed up, and therefore doesn't have great food. It's also pretty much impossible to look at this book and not get hungry, and develop a raging curiosity for African food.

Two hundred recipes with gastro-porno photos of extreme lusciousness—barbecued snapper from West Africa, curried trout with coconut chili sauce from Kenya, apple squash fritter from South Africa, pineapple cakes with caramelized papayas, Zanzibari pizzas, berbere-crusted rack of lamb. Monstrous red papayas, glistening mango couscous, exotic markets teeming with produce and spices and seafood and vibrant colors. Samuelsson describes Africa, more or less, as paradisical; the world in HD (colors are brighter, the spices are hotter). He goes to the ancient markets of Dakar and Addis Ababa, to the beaches of Zanzibar. We meet the fishmongers of Accra, learn the origins of Cape Malay cuisine, visit Nelson Mandela's favorite restaurant in Soweto. If the recipes, vignettes, and photos don't get you, Samuelsson also points out that Africa is a foodie paradise. A place where the cooking is looser—there's more freedom to improvise—and the meals are longer, more languid. There's even a Zulu word that captures this slow-food utopia: *ubuntu*. "I am what I am because of what I am," Samuelsson writes. "It's a universal bond of sharing amongst people."

What seduced me was not the ubuntu, but a recipe on page 215 for "Lobster Skewers with Couscous Avocado Salad."

I thought of lobster as one of the most upscale foods around until I visited the market in Zanzibar, where fresh lobster skewers were sold for a few shillings alongside sugarcane drinks, Zanzibari pizzas, doughnuts, samosas, and French fries. Sitting at a picnic table with my friends, feasting on the ridiculously inexpensive lobster skewers, while a blur of street people, tourists, and Masai vendors swirled around us, was one of the most perfect meals in Africa.

A few days after dreaming of sugarcane drinks, Zanzibari pizzas, and Masai vendors, I headed down to Little Africa—specifically, the Old World grocery store on Broadway. It's a tiny store, flush with Caribbean and African specialty items—Senegalese-style mint teas, Mozambican piri piri sauce, cornmeal porridge from Niger, Liberian soups, all the ingredients to make Nigerian peppercorn stew (names like *ataniko, gbafilo, uyayafanu*). They also had plenty of cuts of goat—goat head, goat feet, goat tail.

Later that night, guided by Samuelsson, I made a spicy okra salad, grilled shrimp piri piri, and a steamed vanilla pudding. I paired this all with some Castles (South African beers), then presented my first African meal to Kristi. The next day, Zanzibari pizzas—chapatti stuffed with eggs, meat, and spices and served off the grill—and red rice (yes, this was the Ethiopian-Swede's take on jollof rice). It was well received. The recipes were deemed "Baylessy." I was overflowing with *ubuntu*.

BEFORE READING *SOUL*, I had never heard of Marcus Samuelsson or the New York restaurant Aquavit. I'm not a regular tracker of haute cuisine and am not up to speed on *Iron Chef* or *Top Chef* stars. I soon found out that, within foodie chef-worshipping circles, he's worshipped.

He'd won scads of awards, had a TV show on Discovery, and was named one of *People*'s "most eligible bachelors"—before he turned thirty. He's a friend of Quincy Jones, has hosted a state dinner at the White House, and has been the subject of fawning profiles in the *New York Times* and *O, the Oprah* magazine. In other words, he's not some lonely voice in the wilderness, crying out for attention for his book or African food. I also learned that in 2008, he opened a restaurant in New York called Merkato 55. It was a follow-up to *Soul*. Africa-themed, named after a market in Addis Ababa, it was intended to introduce African-inspired dishes.

I CALLED KARA Nielsen in December. I wanted to know whether this was it—whether *Soul of a New Cuisine* and Merkato were, in fact, the beginning of the Baylessization of Africa.

Kara obviously knew Samuelsson (she's a proud Dane; he's a superstar in the world of Scandinavian cuisine). But I wasn't sure if she'd heard of *Soul*. I rolled out my find, not mentioning his name "There's this cookbook that I think could be the one, the African Bayless. . . . It's called *Soul of a New Cuisine*."

"You mean the one by Marcus Samuelsson?" she said with such a tone of afterthought obviousness that it reinforced my belief that she knows everything.

Kara agreed that Samuelsson was a Bayless figure and that he had enormous influence and celebrity, and she validated my hunch. "If anybody is going to bring some of those African flavors, it would be someone like him, or him."

But she also raised some points suggesting Samuelsson was not the African Rick Bayless. "His interests are much broader." He had been on a restaurant-opening binge. He opened Red Rooster, an African-American bistro. In 2010, he opened another restaurant in Stockholm—it was Scandinavian. He also had a new chain called Marc Burger. Bayless, by contrast, had Frontera, Topolobampo, Xoco, and was set to open one in Los Angeles—they were all Mexican. It could be Yucatecan or Veracruzan or Oaxacan, but it was *always* Mexican. Bayless was monomaniacal. Samuelsson was cosmopolitan, all over the place.

Kara pointed out that after *Soul* came out a few years ago, after the initial wave of hype, he hadn't done much with African food. Merkato 55 wasn't a long-term project—Samuelsson parted ways with his partners after five months—and there haven't been any sequel restaurants or cookbooks.

Was it possible African food was merely a phase for Samuelsson?

An African P.F. Chang's: Why?

Regardless of whether Marcus Samuelsson devotes his life to the cause of African food, African food will be a part of the ethnic mix of 2035.

It's inevitable. It's not 99 percent; it's more like 99.999 percent.

How, one might ask, could someone who knows about the history of spectacular miscalculation in the food prognostication biz, and who has himself complained of charlatanism and hyperbole in the food futurist racket, and who has firsthand experience being seduced by a fabulous flop—"cobia by 2010"—dare go down this same path?

The African future is, I think, a special case for three reasons.

1. IT'S THE LAST CULINARY FRONTIER

Take a look at the following algorithm, which evaluates culinary resources in a shrinking world.

A = A growing appetite for ethnic novelty.

. B = A shrinking world of exotic food to introduce.

π = There is only one unexplored continent—and it isn't Antarctica.

A + B * π = Senegalese version of P.F. Chang's.

Samuelsson and Schonwald aren't the only ones who see this inevitability. Mimi Sheraton, the former *New York Times* food critic, also portended the African influence in 2008.

2. 50 COUNTRIES, 500 CULTURES, A BOTANICAL GARDEN OF EDEN

Don't get me wrong. Foreign food trendmaking is not like natural resources extraction—there is a meritocracy here. In fact, when I posed my "African inevitability" thesis to Kara, she balked and pointed out that "consumers won't accept novelty for the sake of novelty." In other words, it has to be delicious, and it has to have a health benefit. Food companies thrust newness into the marketplace at a furious pace, and consumers reject it at a furious pace. In the early days of ethnic exuberance in the 1970s, foodmakers tried novelty and they learned a lesson—not all ethnic foods play well with American consumers. In short, there's a reason why pad Thai and pizza and kung pao chicken have caught on, while Swedish meatballs and lumpia have languished in obscurity.

My exposure to the foods of sub-Saharan Africa was admittedly minuscule; they're hard to find. But I love Nigerian soups, and shrimp piri piri and Zanzibari pizza and baobab juice and lamb yassa and Samuelssonized African dishes, like trout pasta. It doesn't take a culinary sophisticate to see there's raw potential—flavors, seasonings, street foods, textures, dishes. And again, it bears repeating the lesson from the Time-Life cookbook: Africa is not a country; this is the world's second-largest continent, the mother continent of cucumbers, rice, watermelon, and coffee. There is no such thing as "African cuisine." There are fifty-some countries, more than 600 languages spoken.

3. THE X-FACTOR: ECONOMIC DEVELOPMENT

Poverty, famine, AIDS, blood diamonds, Mugabe, Hutu versus Tutsi, apartheid, Darfur. Those are the reasons why Western developed nations don't know about Africa's culinary potential. That's why American gastronomes aren't playing with baobab juice, touring the fish markets of Accra, eating traditional Congolese peasant food. More important, poverty and hunger and war and sickness are why Africans—from Cameroon to Mozambique to Namibia to Congo—have been unable to develop a baobab-infused vinaigrette. You can't afford the luxury of culinary adventure when you're struggling to feed yourself. To date, much of black Africa's culinary life has been based on survival—simple preparations that make the most of what's available.

But let's take the optimist's view. Let's assume that Africa's fortunes change—that it becomes more politically stable, more integrated into the world economy, with improved access to basic nutrition (genetically engineered, vitamin-enhanced cassava could help), a better infrastructure, and access to technology.

And please note that this optimist's view is not some Pollyannaish fantasy; in 2010, *The Economist* forecast that seven of the world's ten fastest-growing economies will be in sub-Saharan

Africa during the next decade. The Goldman Sachs economist Jim O'Neill—who coined the term *BRIC* (Brazil, Russia, India, China)—predicts that by 2050 the eleven largest African economies will reach $13 trillion, making them larger than Brazil or Russia.

If Africa becomes even incrementally more prosperous, African nations will develop something that's vanishingly rare right now—a middle class with disposable time and income. This economic change will have a profound impact on the food culture; you can already see the signs of this in Lagos, where economic development has accelerated, spawning a middle class. Samuelsson describes the excitement of meeting Nigerian chefs who are beginning to play with the wide range of flavors and dishes of their native continent—using traditional dishes as a launchpad for exploration because, at last, they have an audience.

What's more, prosperity and political stability could pave the way for other crucial ingredients of food revolution: travel and trade. As Samuelsson has pointed out, in order for the world to discover African foods and flavors, "people have to go there. It has to be travel-friendly."

Not only will more Samuelsson-like chefs discover the foodstuffs and possibilities of African cuisines (encouraging sign: season eight of Bourdain's *No Reservations* features Mozambique) but the non-foodie travelers, the Deadheads of the future, will experience the street foods and market delicacies of Accra and Maputo and Ouagadougou, bringing back rapturous stories of Zanzibari pizza that is better than sex.

And, hence, the trickle-down can begin.

PART
SIX

THE END OF FOOD

18.

Achieving Metabolic Dominance

WHEN I STARTED TELLING PEOPLE ABOUT THE food pill, I didn't get a positive reaction. A smirk, a bemused chuckle, a dismissive shrug. If anything was verbalized, it was "That's certainly not the future of food."

I expected these reactions. There's a Food Revolution unfolding right now and it's about the return to natural ingredients, the revival of heirlooms, the pleasures of eating and cooking. Even Walmart is boasting of its "natural, organic, locally sourced" produce. Nothing could be more at odds with the prevailing trends than the idea that food could be entirely eliminated, replaced by a man-made (or lab-made), synthetic concoction.

Not that the food pill idea isn't out there.

For decades, sci-fi views of the future included food pills. George Jetson had his breakfast food pill and his chili dog food pill and Willy Wonka had chewing gum that replaced the three-course meal. Aldous Huxley gushed, "Imagine receiving all your necessary nutrients in the form of a single pill." In the processed-food-friendly, Wonder Bread–eating, Cheez Whiz–marveling 1950s, it wasn't a question of *if* we would have a food pill, but *when*.

But today is anyone pursuing the vitamin-sized food pill— for that minority population that still believes that, in addition to the right to bear a ray gun, an inalienable part of the future must include the option of not having to cook or eat at all?

As is obvious from my enthusiasm for rip-open-and-eat bagged salad mixes, I have a weakness for speed food. Still, I hadn't given a serious thought to the food pill until I heard Chicago chef Homaro Cantu, a molecular gastronomist renowned for his culinary pyrotechnics and brash ideas, mention saving starving refugees in Darfur with an edible food-pill-like product from his Kodak printer.

HOPES FOR A REAL LIVE FOOD PILL dramatically improved several years ago, when news started leaking out about the "Metabolic Dominance" program. The progenitor of the idea was not some chef in a restaurant with a jerry-rigged printer. It was none other than Defense Advanced Research Projects Agency (DARPA), the super-secret arm of the Pentagon and home base of some of the world's most radical, freethinking scientists. Over the years, DARPA has been responsible for high-energy lasers, night-vision goggles, stealth fighter aircraft, and, most famously, ARPANET, the earliest version of the Internet.

In March 2004, at a gathering of warfare engineers and battle-field intellectuals in an Anaheim hotel, not far from Tomorrow-land, DARPA revealed it was exploring the possibility of "mini food packets" that could sustain soldiers for days or weeks. The project was called Metabolic Dominance because it would give American soldiers an edge over enemies, encumbered by food packs and the time required to eat. Officials said these food packets might be ready for consumption in less than ten years. And about two years after the Anaheim "statement of intent" to explore the food pill concept, another Pentagon report confirmed that food pill research had begun.

The idea that the U.S. military, or any military, would drive the food pill campaign is not surprising. Napoleon Bonaparte, famously conscious of the central role of food in world conquest—he said, "An army travels by its stomach"—offered a cash prize to anyone who could develop a reliable method of food preservation. Within fifteen years, Nicolas Alpert made one of the great breakthroughs in food history: canning. If you heat and seal food and keep out the air, it won't spoil. M&Ms were invented so that American soldiers in World War II could enjoy chocolate that didn't melt in the heat of the South Pacific. Velveeta cheese and Spam were first created as long-shelf-life rations. Freeze-dried coffee, soup mixes, chopped and re-formed meat (best known to civilians as chicken nuggets), and lightweight backpacker entrées were all first used by soldiers.

The epicenter of the Pentagon's food science efforts is about thirty miles west of Boston. Officially known as the U.S. Army Natick Soldier Systems Center but more commonly known as just Natick, this almost-2,000-employee facility looks like a sleepy col-lege campus, tucked away in the burbs, adjacent to a small lake.

Far from it. Natick is what some have called the U.S. military's "mad lab." The bucolic seventy-acre campus holds some unique departments, like "Future Warrior Concepts" and "Human Subject Monitoring." It has chambers that can simulate arctic conditions of seventy below, rooms that model the air pressure at 200,000 feet, drop towers to test package impact.

Over the years, Natick has hosted some of the Pentagon's most important and esoteric research projects. In the 1950s, in an effort to develop sunscreen, scientists at Natick slathered a hundred pigs with a lotion before blasting them with high doses of ultraviolet rays.

Natick's Combat Feeding Directorate is among the most influential food labs in the world. Here scientists developed some of the earliest ancestors of energy bars and Chicken McNuggets, and have made industry-changing breakthroughs in food processing, something called "high-pressure processing." Natick researchers have also created the world's most indestructible sandwich (with a shelf life of seven years) and they've pioneered compressed meals—a stew of chicken, rice, and beans condensed to the size of a half pint of milk and the weight of a candy bar.

I visited Natick to learn about the status of what was now known as the "Peak Soldier Performance" program ("Metabolic Dominance" having been scrapped after some senators complained that DARPA projects were too "sci-fi."). Before meeting with the Combat Feeding director, I went on a tour of the facilities that was so detailed that I felt like I was a member of the House Armed Services Committee.

The Natick kitchen doesn't look that different from Mattson's R&D lab. There are ovens, sinks, stainless steel tables, a retorter (to sterilize food) as well as equipment to make squeezable tube food, the paste-like substance that Air Force pilots eat during marathon U-2 flights.

What distinguishes Natick from any other food-making facility in the world is outside the kitchen, elsewhere on the campus. When a food scientist makes a chicken teriyaki sandwich here, he or she can put it in the climate chambers (arctic, desert, or rain forest) or head over to the drop tower and see how it handles a forty-five-foot parachute fall. There's also an on-site entomologist who can help test how the sandwiches fare in a box with hissing cockroaches.

As Corporal Jeremy Whitsitt led me through the Natick facilities, passing microbiologists and chemists, most of the talk focused on MREs. This focus is not simply because Meals Ready to Eat are the signature product of Combat Feeding. It's also because MREs are controversial, a subject of journalistic exposés, and people often hate them in colorful ways.

Ask a vet from the Persian Gulf War about MREs and they may tell you not about their official Pentagon name, but about their nickname, "Meals Rejected by the Enemy," and describe some memorable entrées, such as "Four Fingers of Death" (smoky franks) and "Chicken à la Death" (chicken à la king).

MREs like corned beef hash were not just viewed as tasteless, they were blamed for a serious problem. Soldiers weren't eating their MREs. During the Gulf War, concerns about the pernicious effects of bad food reached General Colin Powell's desk. In 1992, Powell, then chairman of the Joint Chiefs of Staff, called Gerry Darsch, the Combat Feeding director, to the Pentagon for a famously brief meeting. The two-minute meeting culminated with a two-word command: "Fix it."

One might reflexively think that the world's most formidable military—with its technological prowess and its nearly limitless budget—could figure out how to make an edible sandwich. But as I talked with my guide, the scope of the challenge became clear. It's not just feeding 1.2 million cranky soldiers with different tastes; it's also about creating foodstuff that's lightweight, provides 1,000 to 1,400 calories, can endure up to three years in a warehouse or in the hull of an aircraft carrier, and survive extreme temperature conditions (100-degree heat, or 32 below zero) or a drop from an airplane. After Powell's 1992 directive, Combat Feeding has tried to spice up the MREs and catch up with prevailing tastes. (Even before the end of the Gulf War, they made Tabasco sauce standard in all MREs.)

Before I got to try one of the latest indestructible sandwiches, Corporal Whitsitt led me into a room called the Warrior Cafe that was part military food museum, part Combat Feeding trophy room. We looked at some Civil War–era rations and World War II classics. One of the newer inventions, the Unitized Group Ration Express, looked like a suitcase. You open it, pull a lanyard, and thirty minutes later there's a hot meal ready for eighteen soldiers. No power, no water, no equipment needed. It was an ingenious technology; the heat source, generated from a saline solution, is flameless. But why not just give soldiers MREs or First Strike Rations (an even smaller, more calorie-intensive meal)? "We found out that it's important for warfighters to have their group meals together. It's good for morale," Whitsitt said.

At 1400 hours, after trying seven different MREs (the indestructible pepperoni pocket sandwich and chocolate cappuccino cake were the highlights), I was escorted through the corridors of Natick SSI-Building 237 to meet with one of the most enthusiastic proponents of the food pill idea.

Gerald Darsch has been the Combat Feeding director for more than twenty years. He's presided over the development of the flameless ration heater, the polymeric trays, the compressed meal. Most famously, after the short meeting with Powell, he led the modernization of the MREs. (No more mystery meat, now it's "Thai chicken.")

Though a civilian, the wiry Boston native has the speech and hyper can-do energy of a marine. "Warfighter recommended, warfighter tested, warfighter approved," is a Darsch slogan. Asked about his job, Darsch said, "It's wicked cool." Darsch has one of the most unique jobs in food R&D—a staff of one hundred plus scientists and technicians and the resources and the mandate to explore "high-risk, high-return projects" that might not bear fruit for twenty years. "We can look at ideas that nobody else in the world can explore." When I told him I'd visited the in vitro meat lab in the Netherlands, he immediately expressed interest in exploring it as a protein source for the Navy.

AFTER DISCUSSING THE exciting new lines of MREs (chipotle!) and ambitious plans to add probiotics to shelf-stable products, Darsch broke the troubling news about Metabolic Dominance. "It's on the back burner," he said solemnly.

The original idea, Darsch explained, didn't work. When Combat Feeding took the charge from DARPA, there was great excitement about osmotic technology, given the surging popularity of the nicotine patch.

Why not, they thought, have a patch that would deliver encapsulated nutrients through the skin? The hope was never to replace food, Darsch explained. The Transdermal Nutrient Patch (TNDP) would be used during high-intensity conflict for a day or two. It would help fight against fatigue. "It wouldn't replace a turkey dinner," Darsch said, "but it would get them back to have a turkey dinner."

The patch idea had a significant problem, though. Natick scientists looked at vitamins and minerals crossing the transdermal membrane—no problem. But proteins and fats and carbohydrate molecules are huge (comparatively). Soldiers need 3,600 to 4,000 calories a day. Drawing on dose-response studies on mice and rats, they realized that delivering enough calories through a patch was impossible. You'd need something more akin to a transdermal nutrient shirt, or bodysuit, Darsch noted. Or, he added, "You could have a vitamin-like pill, but you'd have to take a pill every two minutes for the entire day."

After scrapping the patch approach, the Natick took a look at another food pill idea, dubbed "grocery in a chip." A group of MIT bioengineers, led by Dr. Robert Langer, had developed a breakthrough way of delivering drugs: a microchip sensor that could be embedded in the body to release medicine in a controlled way.

Combat Feeding saw warfighter use; the chip, working with sensors, would determine a soldier's metabolic requirements, then it could open skin pores through microdialysis and pump nutrients directly into the capillaries. It would be embedded in the body, not unlike the microchip used to track lost dogs. Darsch saw nonmilitary applications as well—you could use the patch in relief efforts, or for workers in high-risk environments, like mining.

But once again, bad news: Darsch decided not to explore the grocery in a chip. The molecule size was a formidable issue, as was the size of the cavity in which to fit the molecules. Darsch, who says his budget "couldn't replace the wing flap on a B-52," had to make the call. "We can't invest in any hobby shopping, and we don't invest in science for science's sake. You have to know when to say when."

Fortunately, Darsch was not ready to give up on some variant of the food pill concept; it has too much of an upside. The most promising approach, he said, is "buccal delivery." (Gum, wafers, and sports gels—anything absorbed in the mouth—that's buccal.) The area between the mouth and the cheeks presents a much faster way of delivering nutrients into the bloodstream than the digestive tract. Research has shown that absorption is dramatically faster; you can absorb drugs in two to three minutes instead of hours. Buccal delivery is already being used in medicine; people with brain cancer get chemotherapy through a wafer. And Combat Feeding is already starting to apply these findings to their rations—especially with caffeine delivery. (I tried "Stay Alert" gum, part of the "First Strike Ration." It's true, you get a caffeine buzz much faster via gum than via latte.)

Darsch said Natick scientists aren't exploring buccal delivery for a food pill right now, but it might be an option down the road.

There was a fourth food replacement idea on the horizon that sounded especially appealing—like the Gatorade of the future. It did not require a patch, a pill, or wafer. You simply needed to "turbo-charge the mitochondria."

University of South Carolina nutritional scientist Mark Davis had given mice a nutrient called quercetin, a flavonoid found naturally in apple skins, berries, and red wine. Davis found that the quercetin stimulated the mitochondria, often called the cell's power source, to enter a state called "biogenesis." The mice performed 37 percent better in endurance tests on mouse-sized treadmills. The Pentagon funded Davis to conduct a test in humans—which showed more encouraging results on the benefits of quercetin.

Now, mitochondria stimulation might not exactly qualify as a "food pill," or a nutrient source, but it still has the effect of reducing dependence on conventional, pack-filling food. It could take the form of a fortified energy bar or super-craisin. "The more energy that these little buggers can pump out," said Darsch, referring to the mitochondria, "then the more energy for the body."

But it wasn't being actively explored yet, said Darsch. "It's resources," he said, shrugging. "We have less than three one-thousandths of one percent of the total military budget."

19.

The Nano Panacea

THERE WAS ONLY ONE OTHER PLACE TO GO in the search for a food pill: nanotechnology, or more popularly, just "nano."

The claims for nano are as extravagant as those for the introduction of any technology in human history. It's been called the next digital revolution and likened to the industrial revolution, and it's purportedly going to usher in the green revolution and the health revolution and another computer revolution. It's going to change medicine, electronics, manufacturing, agriculture, computers, fashion. Packages tailored to a person's taste. Plants engineered to absorb ingredients. Buildings made of kryptonite-like materials.

Talk about nanotech makes the biotech revolution sound puny. Already you can find nano applications popping up in the marketplace—you can buy nanosized B_{12} vitamins and nano-tea. You can get a Samsung nano-silver refrigerator that is self-cleaning, killing bacteria.

The food industry, like every other industry, has gone nano-mad. Foodmakers are giddy about nano because of the possibili-ties of creating real, literal molecular gastronomy. Flavor makers could pin down tastes and textures and colors to build new, better flavors from the ground up. Health-minded engineers can deliver foods to specific parts of your body. You can fortify foods through nano. With nano, you can do things that are supposed to happen in a parallel universe, like make water dissolve in oil. Nano is already happening in the food industry, circa 2011, largely in antibacterial food packaging.

But nano poses a unique challenge to food people. There's a big difference, of course, between selling consumers a nano-silver toaster and a nano-engineered Thai chicken sandwich. At the 2010 Institute of Food Technologists conference, the distinction was strikingly clear. Hundreds of food scientists gathered to hear about the latest-hottest nano food frontiers, like nano-filtration and nano-encapsulation. The next day, at a panel on "Nanoscience and Food," a young Indian food scientist took the microphone and asked if the benefits of nanotechnology R&D would outweigh the costs of regulatory approval. "Is it even worth it?" he asked.

The reaction to a rumored Kraft beverage that apparently would use nanoparticles to create personalized flavors provoked a swift and powerfully negative response from NGOs. Greenpeace and the Union of Concerned Scientists warn of the dangers of nano. Foodmakers have been reluctant to discuss their nano projects, for fear of consumer backlash. Regulators in Europe and the United States are still developing their policies. It's been described as the next "kitchen war."

But much like in the agricultural biotech world, the basic research continues. I learned that there was, in fact, a nano-based food pill idea out there.

THE NANO IDEA would achieve two of the central tenets of my food pill fantasy:

It would end human dependence on regular eating—freeing writers to work for days without eating. It would also eliminate the need for agriculture—no crops, no animal livestock farming taking up 10 percent of the earth's freshwater, no CAFOs (concentrated animal feeding operations).

But that's stock food pill fantasy talk, straight out of central casting.

What was peculiarly fascinating about this nano-version is that it eliminated the need for even the food pill. That's right. No once-a-day vitamin-sized pill. No transdermal nutrient patch. No quercetin-enhanced Tang.

The idea was featured in *The Futurist*, a magazine that specializes in long-view speculations. *The Futurist* does not offer the typical gloom-and-doom future views you often get from activists on the right or left; it's filled with technophile, rah-rah, Space Age anything-is-possibilism.

An end-of-year feature, "Solutions for a Better Future," examined the usual issues confronting humanity (energy and transportation needs, surging population, global warming, the impending food shortage).

Patrick Tucker, a *Futurist* editor, observed that one "fix" to the impending hunger epidemic was the food pill. Tucker clearly knew his stuff; he'd learned that the vitamin-sized food pill idea was an extremely complex feat. According to Tucker, the most viable food pill idea of the day was "a nano-robot food replacement system," which was described as being "somewhat pill-like."

The featured idea, attributed to Dr. Robert Freitas Jr., hinged on the eventual creation of nanorobots that are a billionth of a meter in size, or about 1/80,000 of the width of a human hair. Said nano-robots could enter the human body through a single pill.

The hard thing to swallow about Freitas' idea isn't the existence of millions of nano-sized computers in your body: It's the *radioactive* part.

According to Freitas, the only reason people eat is to replace energy they expend—walking around, breathing, living life, etc. To do this, we take energy stored in plant or animal matter. A radioactive isotope, gadolinium-148, would provide all the fuel the body needs, Freitas argued.

The notion of eating a radioactive chemical might sound terrifying and lethal, but Freitas has this figured out. The nanorobots would make sure that the person's body was absorbing the energy safely and consistently. In other words, they would make sure the lethal radioactive stuff doesn't kill you, but simply powers you. "Because gadolinium has a half-life of 75 years," Freitas concluded in *The Futurist* interview, "humans might be able to go a century or longer without a square meal."

DR. ROBERT FREITAS is a doctor—but not of nanotechnology. He has a juris doctorate. Freitas was the "winner of the prestigious Feynman prize" from the Foresight Institute, but the Foresight Institute also happened to be the sister organization of his employer, a place called the Institute for Molecular Manufacturing. Freitas had written five books on nanotechnology, and each of them is available for free on his homespun-looking website. Freitas' interests in fields such as diamondoid mechanosynthesis and kinematic self-replicating machines were hard to decipher—but one thing in the gobs of citations on his website was plain and clear: Tolkien studies. In addition to his scholarly work on Middle Earth, Freitas had written a paper on the legal rights of robots, and was a pioneer in the study of sex in space (one of his papers was published in the *Journal of Sexology*).

I had spent time on the food frontier, and had grown familiar with Next Big Thing visions and grandiose claims. I accepted that there's an often blurry borderland between genius and kook. And I gladly explored kooky ideas in the hope that they might be The One. But when I told a more scientifically knowledgeable friend the basics of Freitas' food pill/radioactive isotope idea, he said without hesitation, "That guy is insane."

Just as I was mentally relegating Robert Freitas, Esq., to the file for interesting *Star Trek* screenplay ideas, there was the Steve Jobs/Steve Wozniak analogy.

A passage from *Feed* magazine directly addressed the Freitas phenomenon. Mark Pesce, a writer and futurist who is probably best known as the creator of VRML (virtual reality markup language), was describing his visit to a nanotech convention in the late 1990s. Freitas' new book *Nanomedicine* was the hot item. Then Pesce noted that "Freitas is an amateur, uncredentialed in the field he describes." This would be an "unrecoverable fault" in more established fields. But the rules are different here. This is early nanotech, Pesce observes, which is like the early days of computing. "As in the Homebrew Computer Club in the 1970s"—where Steve Wozniak and Steve Jobs got a chance to sell Apple I—"there's still plenty of room for amateurs. In a sense everyone working in the field is an amateur."

Pesce described Freitas' employer—the Institute for Molecular Manufacturing—as having the feel of "hackers on the verge of another revolution."

Steve Jobs, Steve Wozniak, Bill Gates—none of them had a PhD in computer science. In a "Who's Who of Nanospace," *Nanotechnology Now* listed Nobel Prize winners like physicists Richard Smalley and Richard Feynman. The twenty-person list was littered with scientists and engineers with elite credentials—MIT, Stanford, and Harvard physicist—yet there Freitas was, in a photo that looked like it was from a 1970s college yearbook. The Hobbitologist was described by K. Eric Drexler as the "the most important person in nanomedicine." (Who is K. Eric Drexler? He coined the term *nanotechnology*, created the field, and will almost certainly be regarded as one of the most influential scientists of the twentieth and twenty-first centuries.) Another Freitas enthusiast is Ray Kurzweil. Who is Kurzweil? He's an uber-scientist/inventor/futurist who created optical character-recognition systems, and has been called "rightful heir to Thomas Edison" and "the ultimate thinking machine" by *Forbes*.

TO UNDERSTAND HOW a patent attorney, who edited the *Value Forecaster*, could become one of the world's leading authorities on nanomedicine *and* the progenitor of the idea of eliminating human dependence on food, it's important to know two fundamental things.

One: Freitas is obsessed with extraterrestrial life. Two: he wants to live for more than one thousand years.

When Freitas was in his twenties, not long after graduating from Harvey Mudd College, he wrote a 500,000-word treatise called *Xenology*. Freitas' first book (available on his website) is one of the longest books ever written on the "scientific study of extraterrestrial life, intelligence and civilization." Spanning xenobiology, alien bioenergetics, reproduction, extraterrestrial civilizations, and culture, as well as offering tips for "appropriate interaction protocols during first contact," it is both an early peek at the exhaustiveness that would become the Freitas mark and the start of his interest in the "small world."

In 1994, Freitas had his nano-epiphany: *Unbounding the Future,* by Drexler. In *Unbounding*, Drexler described a world where nano-machines performed all the miracles anticipated in science fiction. Freitas was spellbound. He went on to read Drexler's book *Nanosystems*, which translated wild nanotech speculations into the hard science of mechanics and atomic chemistry. It was the first nano how-to manual—with gears and rotors and technical arguments.

Freitas, lawyer and former editor of *Value Investor*, veteran of pragmatic endeavors, obviously saw that nanotechnology had scads of revolutionary applications. But more than anything, he saw that nanotech offered the opportunity to realize a dream. "A century of life is just not enough," Freitas wrote in an email. "It is axiomatic that if we are not alive, we cannot enjoy life."

In a speech, "Death Is An Outrage," Freitas posited that molecular manufacturing could eliminate 99 percent of the causes of death and could increase the human life span at least tenfold. And, to boot, humans could elect to live their thousand years with the "physiology of your late teens."

Freitas was certainly not the first person to enthuse over the potential of nanomedicine. More than forty years ago, Nobel Prize–winning physicist Richard Feynman, in his famous "There's Room at the Bottom" speech, imagined a future with a "molecular doctor that would be hundreds of times smaller than an individual cell."

Not long after reading *Nanosystems*, Freitas contacted the Foresight Institute, the foundation that Drexler had established to support research. He started asking for information, but there were no nanomedicine papers, no designs for nanomedical robots, no books in progress. "No one was doing research," Freitas recalled. "Nor was anyone planning to."

He wasn't a doctor, nor was he a molecular physicist (he has a bachelor's degree in physics and psychology), but Freitas concluded that "the task needed doing. I finally realized that if no one else was doing it, it was going to have to be me."

When Freitas began the project, he envisioned something relatively modest—a *Scientific American*–like article. To date, he has written three volumes of *Nanomedicine*, each hundreds of pages, with two more volumes in progress.

The Key to the Food Pill: Nanofactory

Any effort to learn about food replacement led to the nanofactory. Freitas made excuses because of the nanofactory: "I haven't finished writing my food ideas yet. I may not get to them for ten years because I've been distracted by the need to create the nanofactory." Ralph Merkle, renowned in techie circles as the creator of the field of public key cryptography, and Freitas' partner on the nanofactory, reportedly quit one of the most desirable Silicon Valley gigs, researcher at Xerox PARC, because it didn't give him enough time to work on the nanofactory.

Every food replacement idea, every life-extending application, every kryptonite-strength building—everything, really—depends on the nanofactory. It's the Holy Grail of nanotech.

The nanofactory is crucial because it will enable humans to arrange atoms precisely in almost any desired form. In a nanofactory, engineers would be able to "pluck" atoms from a "bin" and put them into position.

A theoretical prototype of the would-be Holy Grail, posted on Freitas' site, looks like an ordinary desktop computer.

To create the nanorobots that will remove cancerous tumors from our cells and will enable us to live off radioactive energy, we need what Freitas calls "positional assembly." Diamonds have unique properties (extreme hardness, strength, stiffness, high thermal conductivity) that make them the logical choice as the "tool tip" for "mechanosynthesis."

The diamondoid nanofactory should be ready in 2030. Merkle, his collaborator, agrees. (But he's hedging his bets by arranging to have his body frozen cryonically if he should die before the nano-life-extenders are ready.)

The first wave of nanomedical applications, and the first nutritional applications, such as the food pill, should appear after the creation of the nanofactory. But Freitas cautioned: "If sufficient resources (money and manpower) are not applied to the effort, then the arrival date could easily slip by one to three decades."

The Gray Goo Scenario (Why the Nano Food Pill May Not Happen)

You'll find the word *self-replicating* used over and over on Freitas' many websites, on his curriculum vitae, in his emails. It's all over Drexler's *Engines of Creations*. Self-replication is one of the desirable traits of nanotech, yet it's also what could lead to the demise of the nanofactory idea.

Getting a machine to copy itself is an idea as old as the earliest computers. Yet self-replication has never been achieved at macro-molecular scale. It's easier to create a new computer from scratch than to get a computer to copy itself. But nano proponents argue that the opposite is true in the twilight zone of nanospace, where it's easier to self-replicate than to make a new one. In other words, once you build one nanofactory, you're in—you can simply make copies. That's not necessarily a good thing.

In *Engines of Creation*, Drexler used a colorful term that he would live to regret. Mindful of the history of another world-changing technology, nuclear power, Drexler didn't want to be another Robert Oppenheimer, the Faust of the Nuclear Age. He wanted people to know about both the possibilities and the risks in nanotechnology. It was this spirit of disclosure that led Drexler to describe "the gray goo problem."

In brief, if intentionally or through accident, a nanofactory were released into the environment with only the instruction "be fruitful and multiply," the entire surface of the earth would be reduced to, in Drexler's words, "gray goo within seventy-two hours." It's an end-of-world scenario that makes a nuclear holocaust sound comparatively pleasant. Even in a nuclear holocaust, the cockroaches survive. In the gray goo scenario, not even bacteria deep within the Earth's core would survive.

No one has done more to combat fears of gray goo than Freitas. He has coined the term *ecophagy* ("death of an ecosystem by a nanofactory"). He has written an exhaustive analysis—"Global Ecophagy Biovorous Public Policy Recommendations." He has developed a campaign-esque graphic: "Only You Can Prevent Gray Goo—Never Release a Nanorobot Assembler without Replicator Limiting Code."

The sign comes across as an arcane piece of nerdy humor now, but it reveals a massive concern. Just as fears of dystopian scenarios have seriously limited the potential of agricultural biotechnology, so too could the gray goo scenario thwart nanotechnology. And for Freitas, this could thwart his dreams of extra centuries of life.

Nanotech is still overwhelmingly abstract, in its infancy, but consider the power of Greenpeace's campaign against genetic engineering; its withering image pairing a flounder gene and a tomato. Fears of gray goo, and other unintended consequences, make the future of nanotech highly uncertain. Freitas is well aware of the power of the "precautionary principle."

But what if the Freitas-Drexlerian view prevails? What if the net gain from nano food and medicine applications exceeds the risk? Nanofactories march forward, supported by industry and the government (the government spent more than $100 million on nano research). What if Freitas proves to be Einstein, not Asimov?

If Freitas Is Einstein . . .

In December 2010, Freitas, in an email of Homeric length, predicted that humanoids should have a food replacement system by 2035.

Radioactive gadolinium-148 was not, he explained, the most likely food pill source.

> Please note that 1 cubic inch block of Gd 148 would not actually be used in practice. Rather, to avoid overheating and for other reasons, the block would be finely subdivided into trillions of individual nanorobots distributed throughout the human body whose collective power output is 100 watts for 76 years. Of course, Gd 148 is currently very expensive and thus is not currently practical, but the price would come down if there was huge demand. The point of this example was simply to show that with 1 cubic inch of low-radioactivity material you could create enough power within the human body to power a human body at the basal rate for time periods on the order of a century.

Freitas pointed out that gadolinium-148 was basically an outlier. Most of his food pill ideas are not nuclear-powered—they're powered "either chemically using serum and available oxygen or acoustically using ultrasound energy." In fact, he said, oxyglucose is probably the preferred nano-nutrition energy source.

Freitas later said that we would still need to eat some food for nonenergy purposes "to obtain proteins for rebuilding lost muscle mass and to replace lost iron atoms." And then he added, "But all of this will be addressed when my chapter comes out"—probably by 2020.

Freitas had several other food pill ideas. He called one the "food editor," or "the nutribot." Unlike the nuke pill, the "food editor" was an actual food pill to be taken with each meal. "You could take a pill with a meal that would have millions of nanorobots, pre-programmed to selectively absorb and either sequester or metabolize any molecule in the food stream before those contents can be absorbed into your stomach or gut walls. If you wanted to eliminate fat, cholesterol, known carcinogens, drugs, ethanol, heavy metals, take the pill."

Freitas also described another variation of the nutribot called a "lipovore" (another term he invented), which would travel through the tissue to deliver drugs and/or remove fat, a process he likened to liposuction.

There were more ideas: Something called a "pharmacyte" would "edit alcohol" from the bloodstream and the nutribot would allow people to eat what were previously poisonous substances. "Once the nanofactory is ready," Freitas wrote, "you can eat whatever you want without fear of doing any nutritional damage to yourself."

IF YOU'RE NOT hell-bent on immortality, a transhumanist, a subscriber to *Life Extension* magazine, or an enthusiast of nanopunk (a subgenre, think cyberpunk), you're likely dismissing the Freitas nanorobots as a Trekkie fantasy. That would put you in the vast majority of humanoids. Even among most nano-savvy scientists and physicians, Freitas' ideas are too far off, too speculative to merit serious consideration.

At the same time, there are incremental signs that Freitas' theories might move beyond the world of the Drexlerians and nanopunks. Interest in nanomedicine is surging; researchers have already used nanoparticles to treat rats with type 1 diabetes, and the National Cancer Institute has invested $100 million in nano-research in 2010 to deliver cancer-killing treatment to tumors.

One of the scientists on the nanomedicine frontier is MIT's Robert Langer.

Langer, a pioneer of tissue engineering and organ regeneration and drug delivery methods, has the largest biomedical engineering lab in the world—hundreds of researchers, seven hundred–plus patents. He's won scads of awards, including the Millennium technology prize, the engineering equivalent of the Nobel Prize. Langer's work, you might recall, is also the inspiration for two Combat Feeding food pill ideas: both the transdermal nutrient patch *and* "pharmacy in a chip."

In short, he's probably the best person in the world to evaluate food pill ideas. Asked via email about Freitas' nanorobots, paired with radioactive gadolinium, Langer responded almost instantly. "Maybe someday." He thought twenty-five years was too soon. "A lot of details on how to make nanorobots aren't a given—it will take a lot of science." And then he added, "And I'm not sure how the FDA will react."

CONCLUSION: THE PERFECT MEAL

A FEW QUESTIONS INEVITABLY POP UP WHEN you write a book about the future of food.

First, people want predictions: "So tell me . . . what are the foods of the future?"

Second, other people will want to know about foods of the future that have miraculous properties for a variety of highly personal health needs.

And, third, some people will expect that because of your food wanderings, you might be able to advise on what to eat.

Well, after a couple of years on the food-future beat, I still can't give a definitive "thou shalt be eating" answer to the first two questions. But . . . I have developed some pretty strong feelings about question 3. One day I sat down for coffee and assembled the Perfect Sustainable Meal.

Seasonal, Local Salad Mix from Farmers' Market It doesn't matter if it's radicchio, if it's puntarelle, if it's iceberg, or even sorrel. It doesn't even matter, really, if it's a salad. What is important is that you go to your nearest farmers' market and buy something local and grown outdoors from a small farmer. This purchase symbolizes the continuation and importance of the local, seasonal trend, as we reconnect to our land, our farms, and our communities.

THE PERFECT SUSTAINABLE MEAL

Genetically Engineered Hawaiian Papaya Track down some Hawaiian papaya, but not any papaya. You must make sure that it is genetically modified. Eat this papaya raw or cooked, share it with your friends, use this experience to dispel fears and myths about genetic engineering. Talk about how genetically engineered crops could help feed malnourished people in Africa and Asia.

Recirculating Aquaculture System-Farmed Barramundi or Tilapia Go to a live fish market in New York, Toronto, Washington, or Boston. Buy a fish that is raised indoors in a recirculating aquaculture system. As you eat your barramundi or tilapia, talk about how your fish choice symbolizes your acceptance of two realities: wild-caught fish should be a privileged indulgence these days, and indoor farming is a safe and environmentally responsible way to raise a boatload of protein. Why not cobia? You're choosing barramundi or tilapia right now because of their lower feed conversion ratio (this is the perfect sustainable meal, after all).

If you do not have time to prepare this meal, you can simply recall this slogan:

Go to Farmers' Markets. Eat GMO Papayas. Buy Fish from Indoor Recirculating Systems.

THIS THIRTEEN-WORD SLOGAN is an homage to one of the most important people in the Food Universe, a person so important that he's spawned a book genre, "the post-Pollan book." He's a regular topic of discussion at food industry conferences, i.e., consumers in the Age of Pollan. An email from Henry's Farm once reported: "NEWS FLASH! The rumors are true, Michael Pollan dropped by Henry's stand at the Evanston Market last Saturday, and bought some sugar snap peas."

I long ago concluded that the world's reaction to and celebrification of Michael Pollan are not solely because he is a brilliant and uncommon species, part journalist, part philosopher. It's because, more than anything, of his timing.

This is the Age of Food TMI. We're bombarded with information on carbohydrates, sodium, vitamins, minerals, antioxidants, saturated fats, trans fats. New ethnic foods, new superfoods, a nearly continuous influx of new and often contradictory health findings. Is caffeine good these days?

Amid this chaos, Pollan emerges. His ideas are complex, drawing from natural history, economics, cultural studies, but he always boils things down to a simple, sensible, adoptable message.

"Eat Food. Not Too Much. Mostly Plants." "Don't Eat Packaged Food." "Don't Eat Anything With More than Five Ingredients." "Eat Real Food."

Ultimately, I came to believe that these sticky, easily adoptable, cult-following-creating expressions were about 75 percent good. There were some negative side effects to the Pollanisms—

particularly this one: "Don't Eat Anything Your Grandmother Wouldn't Recognize as Food."

As the techie-foodie Nathan Myhrvold has observed, the Pollan philosophy has a disturbing implication. "If everyone follows his rule about great-grandmothers recursively back into history, nobody would have tried anything new. . . . Somebody had to be the first European to eat a tomato."

I MET TWO types of food innovators during the past three years, which I came to think of as romantic heroes and unromantic heroes.

Bob Cannard, microfarmer in the drop-dead gorgeous Sonoma Valley, friend of Alice Waters, who cares about the "souls" of his Swiss chard and feeds his crops lavender tea, is a romantic hero. Jason Matheny, health economist, who wants us to eat meat spawned from stem cells raised in a factory in the outskirts of Chicago, is an unromantic hero.

The romantic heroes have revived traditional foods, expanded our culinary consciousness, and reconnected us with the land and the sea and the pleasures of growing and cooking and eating.

The romantic heroes are often famous. Most people in America today who read, watch TV, or have Internet access know this type. As I write this, I'm looking at a *New York Times Magazine* food issue, theme "Community and Cooking," which features Michael Pollan's thirty-six-hour dinner party. There is also an Annie Leibovitz–esque photo essay spotlighting twenty food pioneers—artisanal bakers and urban chicken farmers and food truck evangelists. The connecting thread: they're doing wonderful things for the world through the medium of food.

It's undeniably harder to wax poetic about the other type of food revolutionary. Growing fish in a warehouse isn't quite as stirring as pulling them out of a choppy Alaskan sea. A meat-spawning bioreactor doesn't have the same allure as a dew-covered Virginia pasture.

But I think we should set some space aside in the foodie pantheon for the unromantic heroes. Let's continue to celebrate our heirloom fava bean growers and our grass-fed goat herders. Let's carefully scrutinize the claims of nutritional science and keep a wary eye on new technologies, especially those with panacea-like claims from multinational corporations with monopolistic aims and a history of DDT and Agent Orange production. But let's not be so black-and-white; let's not be reflexively and categorically opposed to any and all technological solutions.

Savoring the slowest food and foraging for wild asparagus shouldn't be viewed as at odds with championing lab-engineered vitamin A–enhanced rice that could save children from blindness. Pairing a locally grown, seasonal mesclun mix from Henry's "All Organic, All the Time" Farm with cobia, a saltwater fish grown in a warehouse, is not an incompatible, ethically confused choice.

I make this point because of the rising tide of food-specific neo-Luddism in America. While entirely well intentioned and often beneficial in its impact, this foodie fundamentalism is unfortunately often associated with a dangerous antiscientism. If we're going to meet the enormous challenges of feeding the world's still-growing population, we are going to need all the ingenuity we can bring to bear. My modest hope: Let's keep an open mind. Let's consider even the fringy, sometimes yucky, maybe kooky ideas. Let's not miss opportunities to build a long-term sustainable future for our planet.

RECIPES

THE MOUTHFEEL OF THE FUTURE

KRISTI'S TREVISO RADICCHIO BISON BURGER

This was the preparation that warmed me to the possibilities of radicchio's potential beyond the salad bowl. Here is the "power application": grilled Treviso paired with a new classic, the bison burger. The Treviso gives a nice bitter note and bite to the bison, a leaner alternative to ground beef. Pairs beautifully with a hoppy ale. Serve during fall while watching the Green Bay Packers.

One pound ground free-range bison, made into burgers

One head of Treviso radicchio

Olive oil

Sliced jalapeños (optional)

Grill burgers to desired doneness. Separate radicchio leaves and spritz or brush olive oil onto leaves. Grill leaves for one minute each side. Serve grilled radicchio instead of lettuce on burgers. Add jalapeños for additional spiciness if desired.

HENRY'S MESCLUN MIX

Henry Brockman's mesclun mix makes all other mixes I had previously tried seem flavorless and limp. His mix varies—depending on what's seasonal. What follows is a sampling of his mix when the "Amazing Wall of Salad" (forty-five salad greens, Asian, Italian, French heirloom) is at full power.

This is the mix Henry favors during the spring or early fall, when cooler temperatures make central Illinois a veritable Salinas Valley. To make his mix, Henry draws from a variety of greens in three broad categories: spicy, lettuce base, and bitter. A typical cool-season mix usually includes at least twelve different kinds of lettuces. In composing his mix, Henry considers both flavor and aesthetics, and tries to get a mix of different colors and shapes.

SPICY	THE LETTUCE BASE	BITTER
Arugula	Lollo rossa	Endive
Mizuna	Baby green romaine	Escarole
Ruby streak	Red romaine	Radicchio—Treviso, Verona, or Chioggia del Prego
Golden frill	Red leaf	Mustards
Baby tatsoi	Green leaf	Baby bok choy
Green oak	Baby mei quing choy	
Heirloom, e.g, Forellenschluss	Rouge d'hiver	

Any mixture involving spicy Asian greens, bitter Italian chicories, and more traditional buttery leaves needs, in my opinion, little or no dressing. A tasty olive oil, a dash of salt, and freshly ground pepper are perfect complements.

LUCIO'S RADICCHIO RISOTTO

One of my favorite experiences during my book travels was dinner at Lucio Gomiero's in the hills outside Salinas. His radicchio risotto is simple and offers a taste of why Italy's Veneto region is radicchio-mad.

1 head radicchio, finely chopped

5 cups chicken broth

2 tablespoons unsalted butter

1 tablespoon extra-virgin olive oil

⅓ cup finely minced onion

1½ cups arborio rice

½ cup dry white wine

⅓ cup grated Parmesan cheese

Bring broth to simmer in a saucepan. Meanwhile, heat the butter and oil in a 4-quart casserole and sauté the onion for 1–2 minutes, until softened. Add the rice and stir for 1 minute. Add the wine and cook until it is all absorbed. Add the radicchio, and then start to add the simmering broth ½ cup at a time, letting each addition be completely absorbed before adding another ½ cup. Reserve ¼ cup broth to be added at the end. It takes approximately 18 minutes to reach al dente stage. Then add the last ¼ cup of broth and the Parmesan. Combine well and serve immediately.

PAMELA RONALD'S MUTANT RICE WITH GENETICALLY ENGINEERED PAPAYA

Pamela Ronald's book *Tomorrow's Table* introduced me to the humanitarian and environmental potential of genetically engineered crops, but it also introduced me to a pretty damn good recipe for sticky mutant rice with Hawaiian papaya, which uses one of the few FDA-approved, *publicly funded*, genetically engineered foods.

1 pound mutant rice (called "sticky", "mochi", or "glutinous" rice)

1 tablespoon salt

¾ cup sugar

2¼ cups coconut milk

3 peeled GE papayas

Cover mutant rice with cold water and rinse. Repeat until the water runs clear, about three times, and drain. Place rinsed rice in a bowl and fill with cool water so the water is approximately 2 to 3 inches above the rice. Let rice stand in the water for 6 to 8 hours. Drain the rice, place it in cheesecloth, wrap it up, and put the cheesecloth inside a vegetable steamer. Put 6 to 8 cups of water in steamer and bring to a boil. Cover and steam rice for 45 minutes (or until tender).

To make the sauce, dissolve salt and sugar in coconut milk, and heat—stirring to prevent lumps. When coconut milk mixture boils, stir on low heat until reduced to one third of original volume. Remove from heat and set ¾ cup aside. Immediately after the rice is finished cooking, place in a container with tightly fitting lid and pour in coconut milk mixture. Stir vigorously, cover, and let stand for 15 minutes.

Cut peeled mangoes or GE papaya into slices. Spoon the cooked sticky rice beside the GE papaya. Drizzle on the reserved coconut milk mixture. Serve and enjoy.

JONADAB'S COBIA

This is the dish that reminded me I was in love—with this fish. Jonadab Silva's recipe takes advantage of cobia's flavor and pairs it nicely with fennel and a creamy white sauce.

6 cobia loins, 5 oz each	3 medium Yukon gold potatoes
18 slices of roasted fennel	3 sprigs thyme
18 roasted asparagus spears	1 teaspoon ground caraway
Olive oil as needed	½ tablespoon salt
Salt and pepper to taste	2 tablespoons butter
Clarified butter as needed	1 cup heavy cream

For the vegetables, halve 2 fennel bulbs lengthwise, and then cut in 1"-thick pieces. Rub with olive oil. Roast for 30 minutes at 400 degrees or until the fennel begins to caramelize. Coat asparagus spears with olive oil and roast in a 400-degree oven for 5 minutes.

Clean and slice potatoes. Place in a pot with 2 cups of cold water, ½ tablespoon salt, thyme, and caraway. Bring to a boil and reduce to a gentle simmer until potatoes are fork tender. Remove the thyme and add butter. Blend with a handheld blender until smooth. Stir in the cream. Taste for seasoning.

Pat dry the cobia loins and season with salt and pepper. Heat a sauté pan. Add clarified butter and cook filets 2 or 3 at a time. Once the loins get a nice golden color, place in oven at 350 degrees for 10 minutes.

To assemble, on the center of a warm plate, place 2 tablespoons of potato cream, three asparagus, and three slices of roasted fennel. Place the cobia on top, golden side up. Serve immediately.

JONADAB'S BARRAMUNDI ROMESCO

The Other Fish. While I hope for the eventual triumph of cobia as the Next Salmon, I am also a great fan of barramundi. Here is a particularly wonderful preparation.

6 barramundi filets, skin on

Salt and pepper to taste

2 tablespoons olive oil

2 cups oyster mushrooms sautéed with olive oil, salt, and pepper

¼ cup pancetta, diced into small cubes

1 oz white wine

1 cup Romesco sauce

½ cup parsley leaves

24 hazelnuts, toasted and skinned

21 almonds, toasted and skinned

2 cloves garlic

2 slices bread

2 plum tomatoes

3 red bell peppers

2 tablespoons olive oil

2 sprigs flat-leaf parsley, chopped

2 tablespoons sherry vinegar

Pat filets dry and make cross-cuts on the skin about ¼ inch deep. Season with salt and pepper. Heat oil in a sauté pan. Place the filets skin down. Once the skin is crispy, turn the filets over and place them in a 400-degree oven for 10 minutes. Remove the filets. Hold them in a warm place. In the same sauté pan, cook mushrooms and pancetta. Season with salt and pepper and deglaze the pan with white wine.

For the Romesco sauce, roast hazelnuts, almonds, garlic, and bread until lightly browned. Grill tomatoes and red peppers, then remove skin. Transfer all cooled ingredients to a food processor, and purée with olive oil, parsley, and vinegar.

To assemble, place the mushroom mixture at the bottom of each plate and place the barramundi on top, skin side up. Garnish with Romesco sauce, about 1 ounce per fish, and parsley.

JOSH'S EMU CHILI

While we're still waiting for the lab-raised, guilt-free, in vitro beef, we must explore other alternatives. Why not give one of the RMAs (red meat alternatives) a try? Here's a recipe for emu chili.

1 pound ground emu

1 medium onion, chopped

1 bell pepper, chopped

1½ teaspoons salt

3 tablespoons chili powder

1½ tablespoons paprika

2 tablespoons sugar

1 large can tomato juice

2 cans chili beans

2 tablespoons cooking oil

Mix the spices and sugar in a bowl. In a deep skillet or Dutch oven, sauté the onion and bell pepper. Add the meat as the onion begins to clear. As you brown the meat, add spice mix. The meat should be lightly browned, even left a bit pink. Add the tomato juice and chili beans. Simmer for one hour.

MARCUS SAMUELSSON'S SHRIMP PIRI PIRI

It was Marcus Samuelsson, the Swedish-Ethiopian überchef, who got me excited about the dishes and flavors of African food. Here is just one of the many wonderful dishes from *The Soul of a New Cuisine.*

12 jumbo shrimp, peeled and deveined

½ cup plus 2 tablespoons piri piri, divided

2 tablespoons olive oil

½ teaspoon salt

1 lime, quartered

12 Bibb lettuce leaves

8 red bird's-eye chilies, seeds and ribs removed, chopped

½ cup fresh lemon juice

1 tablespoon chopped cilantro

1 tablespoon chopped parsley

2 garlic cloves

½ cup olive oil

Toss the shrimp with ½ cup of the piri piri in a large bowl. Refrigerate for 20 minutes. Heat the olive oil in a large sauté pan over medium heat. Add the shrimp and cook for 2 minutes on each side, or until opaque throughout. Transfer to a plate and sprinkle with the salt. Squeeze the lime quarters over the shrimp. Spread ½ teaspoon of the remaining piri piri sauce on each lettuce leaf. Place a shrimp on each leaf and fold over bottom and sides to form a wrap. Serve immediately.

For the piri piri, combine the chilies, lemon juice, cilantro, parsley, and garlic in a blender and puree until smooth. With the blender running add the oil in a slow, steady stream and blend until well combined.

JESSICA B. HARRIS'S SENEGALESE CHICKEN YASSA

No one has done more to introduce African food to Americans than the culinary historian Jessica B. Harris. Harris' *The Africa Cookbook* features more than two hundred traditional and contemporary recipes collected from home kitchens across Africa.

¼ cup freshly squeezed lemon juice

4 large onions, sliced

Salt and freshly ground black pepper, to taste

5 tablespoons peanut oil

1 habañero chili

1 frying chicken (2½ pounds)

½ cup water

Two hours before, prepare a marinade by mixing the lemon juice, onions, salt, pepper, and 4 tablespoons of the peanut oil in a deep bowl. Prick the chili with the tines of a fork and add it to the marinade as well. When the dish has reached the desired degree of hotness, remove the chili and reserve (it can be minced and served separately to the chili heads). Place the chicken pieces in the marinade, cover with plastic wrap, and refrigerate overnight. (If you're pressed for time, you can marinade just 2 hours, but the flavor will not be as intense.)

When ready to cook, preheat the broiler. Remove chicken pieces from the marinade, reserving the marinade and the onions. Place the pieces on the broiler rack and grill them briefly, until they are lightly braised on both sides. Set aside. Drain the onions from the marinade. Heat the remaining tablespoon of oil in a deep skillet and sauté the onions over medium heat until they are tender and translucent. Add the remaining marinade and cook until the liquid is heated through. Add the chicken pieces and the water and stir to mix well. Lower the heat and simmer, covered until the chicken pieces are cooked through, at least 30 minutes. Serve the yassa hot over white rice.

ACKNOWLEDGMENTS

FIRST, THANKS TO ALL THE PEOPLE WHOSE name appears in this book for giving me their time and for answering naive question after naive question. In addition to the people in the book, I'm especially grateful to the many, many other people who generously provided their time and guidance—among them, Chris Wolf, Linsey Herman, Ari Weinzweig, and Darrell Corti. (One of the most enjoyable reporting experiences of my life was the time I spent with Darrell in Sacramento.) I am also grateful to many other writers, as this book draws heavily from their work. Frederick Kaufman, Paul Greenberg, Michael Pollan, Noel Kingsbury, Dan Charles, David Kamp,

Michael Specter, Burkhard Bilger, and Warren Belasco are just a few of the writers to whom I am indebted.

Thanks to Chuck Strouse at *Miami New Times* for assigning a story about aquaculture (that ultimately led to this book), and to Ron Rosenbaum (whom I have long worshipped) for thinking my fish farming story might actually have potential for something much bigger. This book would never have happened without Ron's encouragement. Thanks to Julia Cheiffetz and Bob Miller, of the late, great HarperStudio, for taking a chance on a first-time author. And thanks to my editor at HarperCollins, Hollis Heimbouch, and her assistant, Colleen Lawrie, for enthusiastically adopting my book after Julia's departure.

Before I got into book authoring, I didn't really know what literary agents did. I did, however, read acknowledgments and long snickered at the over-the-top praise agents received. Well, I hate to be unoriginal, but I also have over-the-top praise. I am very lucky to be a client of David Halpern of The Robbins Office. He's wise, patient, calm (a great bedside manner during book-related psychotic episodes); has consistently incisive editorial judgment; and has, not insignificantly, great taste in bourbon. Many thanks also to Ian King, Mike Gillespie, Kathy Robbins, and all the others at the office who have helped me along the way.

Over the course of working on this book, I did learn two heartening things about myself.

First, I'm a good judge of young talent. I greatly benefitted from the periodic fact-checking and research assistance of two excellent reporters, Christopher Bentley and Susie Allen. I was also fortunate to have the aid of the multitalented Duan Duan Yang, who developed my website.

I also discovered that I have many good friends. Friends provided all kinds of help (hosting my visits, reading passages of the book, testing new foods, listening to my babbling). Some of the people to whom I owe big-time favors: Max Grinnell, Giancarlo

Potente, Edgar Villongco, Bruce Stone, Will Coviello, Tom Tricoci, Scott Powell, Chris Pfau, Keith Glantz, Bits, and Jerry Gould, who is both a wonderful uncle and, I learned, a brilliant copy editor.

Conversations with David Galenson have almost never been about fish farming or genetic engineering or radicchio. Yet they have had a fundamental influence on this book, my writing life, and my worldview in general (I'll explain this in my next book). Richard Bell's general knowledge of everything and sage editorial advice were both a sanity preserver and *Titanic* averter. (If you don't like this book, trust me, it would have been a lot worse without Dick's feedback.)

There are two friends to whom I owe special thanks—i.e., spare kidneys and/or rides to O'Hare during rush hour. This book benefitted immeasurably from the generosity of Tom Valeo and Rob Jordan. Tom is the editor you dream about—incisive, patient, empathetic, articulate, creative; Rob, a friend of mine for years, is on his way to becoming the next Tom.

In addition to Tom or Rob, I must also consider naming my next child the "University of Chicago." I never would have been able to write this book if not for a string of wonderful bosses at the University of Chicago News Office (Larry Arbeiter, Julie Peterson, Steve Kloehn). I also greatly benefitted from a terrific bunch of colleagues who never seemed disinterested in stories about crop scientists or fish farmers. Most important, though, this book is quite literally indebted to the U of C because of a unique program there.

Robert Vare, now an editor-at-large at *The Atlantic*, established a program that brought top nonfiction writers to his alma mater each year. I took every class I could—Alex Kotlowitz, David Hajdu, Edmund Morris, Darcy Frey, Jonathan Harr, Ron Rosenbaum. I also had the extra good fortune of becoming friends with Robert. One of the greatest pleasures, and most edifying aspects, of writing this book has been the opportunity to talk with Robert about my work. I cannot properly express my gratitude for all his time and support and invaluable suggestions. I am certain his insights will impact my work far beyond this book.

Finally, to the most key people of all . . . Thanks to my children (Kate, yes, we will go to Disney World), my parents, and to my wife. Kristi, thank you for reading radioactively bad first drafts, for letting me go to coffee shops during primo baby-care time, for trying suspicious foods, for listening (again and again and again), for health-insuring. I owe you years of indentured servitude, and the world's longest vacation. But first, let's eat some radicchio burgers, watch SportsCenter, and nap.

ABOUT THE AUTHOR

JOSH SCHONWALD has written for the *New York Times*, the *Washington Post*, and Salon. He lives in Evanston, Illinois, with his wife, children, and indoor aquaponic system. Visit him online at www.thetasteoftomorrow.com.